NEW YORK AMISH

Karen Johnson-Weiner

NEW YORK AMISH

Life in the Plain Communities
of the Empire State

Second Edition

Cornell University Press

Ithaca and London

First published 2017 by Cornell University Press
First printing, Cornell Paperbacks, 2017

Printed in the United States of America

Library of Congress Cataloging-in-Publication Data

Names: Johnson-Weiner, Karen, author.
Title: New York Amish : life in the plain communities of the Empire State / Karen Johnson-Weiner.
Description: Second edition. | Ithaca : Cornell University Press, 2017. | Includes bibliographical references and index.
Identifiers: LCCN 2016047311 (print) | LCCN 2016048250 (ebook) | ISBN 9781501707605 (pbk. : alk. paper) | ISBN 9781501708138 (epub/mobi) | ISBN 9781501708145 (pdf)
Subjects: LCSH: Amish—New York (State)
Classification: LCC F130.M45 J64 2017 (print) | LCC F130. M45 (ebook) | DDC 289.7092/2—dc23
LC record available at https://lccn.loc.gov/2016047311

Contents

Preface

Although the first Amish settlers came to New York State in the early nineteenth century, it took more than one hundred years for the next group of Amish to arrive, and twenty-five more years for a third settlement to begin. Yet by the second decade of the twenty-first century, New York claimed the fastest-growing Amish population in the United States. Indeed, the first edition of *New York Amish* was already out of date when it hit bookstores in 2010. In the short time between sending the manuscript off to Cornell University Press and getting it in print, ten new Amish settlements were started. There are now fifty-two Amish settlements in the state.

In addition, New York's Amish population is becoming much more diverse than it was when the first edition appeared. Now, in many parts of the state, different kinds of black buggies mix with brown buggies and gray ones. In Steuben County, a new settlement of Nebraska Amish has even added white buggies to the mix.

Buggies are only the tip of the iceberg. While different groups have moved to the state, others already here have fragmented, giving rise to new ways of being Amish in communities that were homogeneous only a few years ago. The twenty-first-century New York Amish world now embraces communities who may be as different from each other as any of them are from their non-Amish neighbors.

Quite frankly, it's hard to keep up with it all. In fact, even as this work goes to press, I am learning of plans for new settlement in the state.

In revising New York Amish, I have attempted to do two things. First, I have tried to bring each chapter up to date. My goal has been to show how the different communities have grown (or not), whether there has been new settlement to the region, and whether there have been events that have altered the status quo or have particularly challenged the

Amish and those who interact with them. In doing so, I have relied heavily on publications for and by the Amish: the *Budget*, *Die Botschaft*, and the *Diary*. The *Budget* and *Die Botschaft* are weekly newspapers, and offer their readers news from Old Order communities across North America (and even beyond) in the form of letters from community scribes. The *Diary* comes out monthly and offers, in addition to community news, updates about migrations, new settlements, births, deaths, and ordinations.

My second goal has been to help non-Amish New Yorkers better understand their Amish neighbors. For example, I am often asked whether the Amish are Christian. Others ask whether they are "some kind of cult" and whether they are related in some way to the Church of Jesus Christ of Latter-day Saints (the Mormon Church). Many see the Amish as quaint, without realizing the depth of their commitment to living their faith.

In this second edition, as it was in the first, my intention is to introduce the Amish to their non-Amish neighbors and to highlight the diversity of Amish settlement in New York State and the contribution of New York's Amish to the state's rich cultural heritage. So that readers can better understand where the Amish come from and their relationship to other Christian groups, the first chapter explores the origins of the Amish in the religious confrontation and political upheaval of the Protestant Reformation and discusses contemporary Amish lifestyle and practices. Chapter 2 begins the discussion of Amish settlement in New York by looking at the oldest surviving New York Amish community, the settlement in the Conewango Valley, which began in 1949. Each subsequent chapter explores the history of different Amish groups that have come to New York, looking to the past to help explain why they have chosen to settle in the Empire State. Although the need for farmland is a common denominator, each group provides a lens through which to explore issues that have helped shape the Amish world. The Lowville Amish, for example, are descendants of Lancaster County Amish who left Pennsylvania rather than submit to new state laws regarding education. The Ohio Amish who have settled in the Mohawk Valley have been shaped by internal struggles over the behavior of young people, while the Troyer Amish of the Conewango Valley evolved in response to internal disagreements over excommunication and shunning. My examination of each of these different settlement areas has been updated to acknowledge new communities and to demonstrate the impact of growth, schism, and migration on existing settlements.

In describing life in different Amish settlements, this book also illustrates the diversity of the Amish world. We tend to talk about the Old

Order Amish as if they were all the same when, in fact, there are many different kinds of Amish. Frolics (work parties), weddings, dress, and buggy styles vary from community to community. Even within New York State, one Amish group may know little about the others and be surprised at their practices. Each chapter provides a snapshot of life in particular Amish settlements.

I focus on different regions of Amish settlement across the state, beginning with the Amish churches in Chautauqua and Cattaraugus counties in the west, and then looking at the diverse settlements of the Mohawk Valley in the east and the St. Lawrence River Valley in the North Country. The different congregations in these regions range from the most conservative to the most progressive. In looking at the interaction of Amish communities in particular geographic settings, we can see how the different ways in which the Amish realize core values shape their adjustment in new environments. We can also see how these differences in Amish practice affect the interaction between Amish groups and between Amish settlements and their non-Amish neighbors.

Several Amish groups have established multiple settlements in different regions of New York. For example, chapter 2, which explores settlement in Cattaraugus and Chautauqua counties, introduces the Byler Amish, who, since first arriving in New York in 1976, have established settlements in the Mohawk Valley and in Franklin County. Chapter 3 looks at the Swartzentruber Amish, perhaps the most conservative of all Amish groups. Since the first Swartzentruber Amish arrived more than thirty years ago, they have established communities in several regions of the state. Even as this book goes to press, several Swartzentruber families are in the process of starting a new settlement in Westport, in Essex County. Chapter 6 explores New York's Swiss Amish, who are historically and culturally different from other Amish groups. There are now five related Swiss settlements, two of them new since the first edition of this work. As Amish settlers from one church group move into different regions, we can see the impact of place on religious practice.

Finally, I have expanded chapter 8, which treats external and internal challenges to Amish settlement, and chapter 9, which looks in-depth at the challenges Amish settlement poses to neighboring non-Amish communities. Chapter 10 is new and looks to the future of New York's Amish. In revising these three chapters, I have paid particular attention to the impact of expanding Amish populations, changing laws, and the growing divide between the Amish way of life and that of their "English," or non-Amish, neighbors.

Doing research within Old Order communities is not always easy. I have found that the Amish are suspicious of questionnaires and surveys and generally decline to take part. They favor personal interaction, but they generally do not permit themselves to be photographed, recorded, or videotaped because they believe that these technologies violate the commandment against the making of graven images.[1] While I took most of the photographs in this book, the pictures of Amish children or adults were taken by others who have a different relationship with the Amish than I do.

In writing this book, I drew on personal connections in Old Order Amish communities across New York and in other states, including Pennsylvania, Indiana, Ohio, Michigan, and Missouri. My approach to the study of Amish culture is called "participant observation," which means that I supplement my constant questioning by joining in diverse ordinary activities such as canning peaches, butchering, correcting spelling papers, and going to church. I have stayed in Old Order Amish homes, eaten meals with Old Order Amish families, and accompanied them on shopping trips. I learned much while drinking coffee and peeling vegetables. When I go into an Amish home, I take a notebook with me. I ask permission before I write down what people are saying and rephrase what they have said in follow-up conversations to ensure that I have understood what they have told me. Letters from Amish friends tell me much about community activities, providing a window through which to view daily life in Amish homes. Amish friends in different settlements have read and commented on these chapters, and I am grateful for all they have taught me.

In addition to participant observation, interviews, and correspondence, I did research for the first edition of *New York Amish* in the Heritage Historical Library in Aylmer, Ontario, and in the archives of the Association Française d'Histoire Anabaptiste Mennonite in Belfort, France. Both collections provided invaluable access to historical documents and correspondence. In making revisions for the second edition, I returned to the Heritage Historical Library. I also took advantage of the resources of the Young Center for Anabaptist and Pietist Studies at Elizabethtown College in Elizabethtown, Pennsylvania. Interviews with non-Amish members of the different settlement regions provided additional insight into the integration of Amish settlers in New York society.

New York has a rich Amish heritage. Tracing Amish settlement from the nineteenth century to the twenty-first, I hope to demonstrate the myriad ways in which, as fellow New Yorkers, the Old Order Amish contribute to the diversity and vitality of the Empire State.

NEW YORK AMISH

1

Who Are the Amish?

Meeting Our Plain Neighbors

One of the things taught in the Gospel is a separation from the world.
  —*1001 Questions and Answers on the Christian Life*

Mention "New York" and we think of the "Big Apple," the Hudson River, the St. Lawrence Seaway, and the Finger Lakes. Most of us do not think of the Amish. The Amish evoke images of horse-drawn buggies, barefoot children, barn raisings, and bonnets and straw hats. The Amish live peaceful lives on bucolic farms. As we know from talk show monologues and Hollywood movies, the Amish are country rubes, comically unaware of machines, the Internet, and X-rated films. They are hardly "New Yorkers"—the fast-talking, hard-driving, "in your face" type A personalities that an article in the British newspaper the *Telegraph* once called "the most neurotic and unfriendly people in America."[1]

Nevertheless, the Amish have been a part of the New York scene for nearly two hundred years. They are our neighbors. And they are one of the fastest-growing segments of the New York State population. Between 1990 and 2000, the population of New York grew from approximately 17,990,455 to 18,976,457, an increase of 5.5 percent.[2] From 2000 to 2010, New York's population grew to 19,378,102, an additional increase of 2.1 percent.[3] During roughly the same period, New York's Amish population grew over 293 percent, increasing from 4,050 church members in 1992 to approximately 15,930 in 2013. By 2015, the Amish population of New York State had risen to 17,280.[4]

The first Amish settlers to the Empire State came from the French province of Lorraine. Like many other French immigrants of the time, they left France from Le Havre and arrived in New York City. From there, they made their way up the Hudson River to Albany, and then by the Erie Canal to Utica. Recounting the story of her ancestors, the historian Arlene Yousey notes that

with belongings strapped upon their backs, they entered an almost impassable forest where few had set foot, save the Indians, surveyors, and the

Figure 1.1. The Amish Market in Manhattan. The Amish are New Yorkers! Although not owned or operated by Amish, the Amish Market in Manhattan demonstrates both that the Amish belong in New York—and that we are surprised to think of them here. Photo by author.

few immigrants who had preceded them. . . . Mighty trees of the forest laid low by storms or death, their straggly, barkless branches thrown upwards and trunks covered with slippery moss, presented barriers through which a trail must be cut before the venturesome invaders could proceed with their burdens.[5]

In 1831, Christian Hirschey arrived in Lewis County from France. A single man, he soon returned to Europe to marry and didn't return to settle until 1834.[6] The first Amish family to settle permanently in New York State was that of Michael Zehr, a minister who arrived with his wife, Anna Jantzi, and their children in 1833. The family made their home in Croghan in Lewis County and helped to establish the first New York Amish congregation.

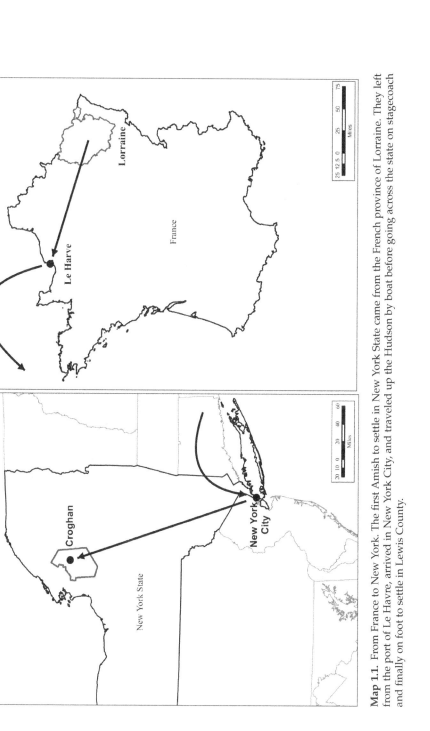

Map 1.1. From France to New York. The first Amish to settle in New York State came from the French province of Lorraine. They left from the port of Le Havre, arrived in New York City, and traveled up the Hudson by boat before going across the state on stagecoach and finally on foot to settle in Lewis County.

In several ways, these first Amish settlers set the pattern for Amish settlement in New York. First, they were fleeing troubles in their homeland. The military exploits of Napoléon I, emperor of France (1804–1815), had changed life for the French Amish. Napoléon needed soldiers, and so, under his reign, the pacifist French Amish had lost their military exemption.[7] Moreover, like many who have come since, the French Amish were attracted to New York by its cheap, available land. In upstate New York's "French Settlement," a 3,816,960-acre tract near Lake Ontario, land was selling at only $1.50 an acre. French Amish families were actively recruited by land agents to settle in the Empire State. James Donation Le Ray de Chaumont, director of a consortium of investors called the Compagnie de New York, sent his agent, Jacob Kiefer, to France to tell the Amish about the many advantages of settling in Lewis County. A native of Metz in Lorraine, Kiefer was alternately described as "Amish" or "a hook and eye Baptist";[8] he encouraged a number of families to come to upstate New York.[9]

Finally, and perhaps most importantly, in making New York State their home, these Amish settlers and their descendants demonstrated how a group's response to particular events, social developments, personalities, and faith uniquely shapes its practices and its interaction with the surrounding society. This first Amish community in Croghan, like every Amish congregation, was the product of an ongoing dialogue within the community and without.[10] In the mid-nineteenth century, for example, the visiting preacher Benedict Weyeneth persuaded nearly 80 percent of the Croghan Amish to leave the Amish community and form a new congregation, the Apostolic Christian Church.[11] The small group that remained Amish grew slowly, overcame adversity, and prospered. In 1910, the Croghan Amish church joined a number of other more traditionally minded congregations to form the Conservative Amish Mennonite Conference, which began to embrace Sunday Schools and evangelism. In 1954, only five years after a second Amish settlement had begun in Cattaraugus County, the descendants of the first New York Amish began to identify simply as "Mennonite."

As New York's first Amish settlement reveals, the Amish world is multifaceted and evolving. While we may see the Amish as a people trapped in a time warp—nineteenth-century pioneers somehow misplaced,[12] the Amish are, in fact, twenty-first-century people, daily confronting modernity, evaluating its impact on their lives, and making choices about how they will live in the world. Amish settlement in New York State reveals the diversity and evolution of the Amish world.

A Radical Beginning

The story of the Amish in New York begins in sixteenth-century Europe. The conservative Amish are descended from the Anabaptists, a radical faction of the reform movement that began at the end of October 1517, when Martin Luther (1483–1546) challenged Pope Leo X by nailing his "ninety-five theses on the sale of indulgences" to the door of the Wittenberg Cathedral, an act that ignited the Protestant Reformation.[13] In studying scripture, Luther had come to believe in salvation by faith alone. The Ninety-five Theses, or points of argument, radically challenged long-held notions about the nature of the church and the authority of the pope and priestly hierarchy.

Luther's intention was probably to start a discussion rather than a religious revolution. Nevertheless, his actions had immediate consequences for the Catholic Church. If, as Luther suggested, faith alone made one worthy of Paradise, then there was no reason to buy indulgences, or the good works of the saints, the sale of which had been authorized by the pope to raise money for church coffers. After Luther published the theses, sales of indulgences fell off dramatically. Further, when Pope Leo X ordered him to recant, Luther refused. Instead he wrote several additional pamphlets, including an "Address to the Christian Nobility of the German Nation" (1520), in which he challenged the authority of the pope by arguing in favor of a "Priesthood of Believers." "We are all one body," he asserted, adding that "this is because we have one baptism, one Gospel, one faith, and are all Christians alike; for baptism, Gospel, and faith, these alone make spiritual and Christian people."[14] In short, there should be no distinction between priest and lay believer.

Luther went on to argue that the Bible, not the church, is the final authority on doctrine, and that every Christian has the right to interpret the Bible. Consequently, in his opinion, the church needed reform. Luther trusted neither the Catholic hierarchy nor the general lay population to carry out the necessary changes. Instead, he called on secular government to take on this task.

Luther was not alone in his zeal to reform the church. Thanks to the invention of the printing press, many were reading the Bible in their own language for the first time. Numerous Bible study groups formed, and their adherents began to question a number of church practices for which there seemed no scriptural justification.

In Switzerland, the reform movement gained momentum when, in 1518, the city-state of Zurich elected Ulrich Zwingli (1484–1531), a former Catholic priest, to be its head pastor.[15] Zwingli was popular, and many hoped that he would move quickly to abolish the priesthood and forbid the use of holy images, such as statues, in the church. Nevertheless, like Luther, Zwingli felt that secular authority should guide reform, and he refused to proceed without the consent of the Zurich City Council, which had assumed full civil and ecclesiastical authority over the church. Zwingli's caution angered several of his young students, most particularly Conrad Grebel (ca. 1498–1526), the son of a prominent Zurich family; Felix Manz (ca. 1498–January 5, 1527), another well-educated Zurich native; and Georg Blaurock (ca. 1492–September 6, 1529), a former priest. For Grebel, Manz, and Blaurock, giving authority over church reform to the City Council meant subordinating the sacred to the secular.

The conflict between students and teacher ultimately came to a head over the issue of infant baptism, a practice that not only had religious significance but also helped to ensure that children were entered into state records. In other words, it served a secular purpose as well as a religious one, creating both church members and citizens of the state. Grebel, Manz, Blaurock, and their followers argued, however, that infant baptism was not mentioned in scripture and, therefore, had no place in the church. Instead, they asserted, baptism should be a sign of faith and one's commitment to the church, and the church should be a believers' church, a position that those in authority feared would bring anarchy.

Several meetings between Zwingli, his reform-minded students, and the City Council failed to resolve their disagreements. Finally, on January 17, 1525, concerned both for the unity of the church and, perhaps, for its own authority, the City Council enacted laws requiring that infants be baptized and authorizing fines for parents who refused to obey. Further, it outlawed any attempt to rebaptize those who had been baptized as infants. For Grebel, Manz, and Blaurock, this was the final straw. The three abandoned both their teacher and the state church, and, meeting secretly with some of their followers at the Zurich home of Felix Manz on January 21, 1525, rebaptized each other and launched the Anabaptist movement.[16]

Anabaptists and the Believers' Church

The new "church of believers" that Grebel, Manz, Blaurock, and their supporters established with that first, illegal adult "rebaptism" represented not only a complete break with the Catholic Church but also with the notion that church and state should be allied.[17] Although familiar now, a voluntary church of believers that neither sought to control the state, as the Catholic Church did, nor was controlled by it, as was the newly formed Lutheran church or the Zurich church under Zwingli, was profoundly threatening to officials in the 1520s. Zwingli denounced the "rebaptizers," or "Anabaptists," as they were called pejoratively, charging that they had brought division into the church, and those who joined the movement risked imprisonment, torture, exile, and death.[18] Conrad Grebel died in exile at the age of twenty-seven; Felix Manz was thrown bound and gagged into the Limmat River;[19] and Georg Blaurock, after helping to spread the movement to the east, was burned at the stake.

However, exile and martyrdom did not stop the spread of Anabaptist ideas. Small groups of Anabaptists, or Swiss Brethren as they called themselves, began meeting in secret, aided by a lay ministry that spread the evolving movement.[20] In February 1527, only ten years after the Anabaptist movement began, Michael Sättler (ca. 1495–May 21, 1527), a former priest from Freiburg, led a secret Anabaptist conference in the town of Schleitheim, north of Zurich. From this conference came the Schleitheim Confession, which was instrumental in defining the Anabaptist movement and remains a key statement of belief for today's Old Order Amish and other modern-day Anabaptist groups. The Schleitheim Confession put in writing for the first time the beliefs of the Swiss Brethren about how the church would function as a community within worldly society, but separate from it. It proposed that believers join the church voluntarily by choosing to be baptized, which ruled out infant baptism. It also rejected violence. The sword, the confession argued, "was ordained to be used by the worldly magistrates." Arguing that a Christian's weapons are spiritual, the confession reacted to the persecution church members faced by asserting that "the worldlings are armed with steel and iron, but the Christians are armed with the armor of God, with truth, righteousness, peace, faith, salvation and the Word of God."[21] Within the church, those who sinned were to be simply banned from fellowship. Further, the confession proposed a ministry chosen from among the church membership, and it called on pastors "to read, to admonish and teach, to warn, to discipline, to ban in the church . . . and in all things to see to the care of the body of Christ [i.e., the church]."[22]

The 1527 Schleitheim Confession redefined both Christianity and the church, outlining a belief system that continues to shape the lives of the Old Order Amish. It asserted that being Christian required obedience to Christ's teachings in everyday life and that this obedience would transform individual behavior. Faith was to be lived, and evidence of one's faithfulness was found in how one lived, with an emphasis on mundane activities. Moreover, the confession suggested that a true Christian could not participate in the existing social order because this order embodied neither Christ's teachings nor the practices of the early apostolic church. Only in the church, a community of believers, separate from worldly society, could Christians live life guided by divine principles.

Incorporating these notions of Christianity and the church, the Schleitheim Confession proclaimed a return to the apostolic church that many at the Schleitheim gathering felt had been lost over the centuries. It conceived of a church that was neither a building nor a set of rituals but rather a community, and it called on church members, as committed disciples, to be willing to take up the cross, to remain separate from worldly ways, and to be prepared to suffer persecution.

The confession built in a commitment to tradition and an ahistorical sense of Christian life, for it defined the church as sacred and sacred time as unchanging and eternal. Only the fallen world is changeable and temporary. Since God's truth does not change, the lives of those committed to God's truth should not be shaped by changes in popular style or secular notions of progress; church members should be distinguished from their worldly neighbors by their plain dress, unostentatious homes and furnishings, and rejection of technology. Further, acknowledging that individuals are too weak to follow scriptural guidelines without help, it urged those in the church to work as one. Together, the confession asserted, members could strive to keep the church pure and hope to achieve *Gelassenheit*, the complete surrender to God's authority and trust in God's will that would make them worthy of salvation. Even the most faithful church members could not be certain of salvation; redemption was the work of a lifetime.

Finally, the signers of the confession also agreed that "should it happen that through the cross [pastors] should be banished or led to the Lord (through martyrdom) another [was to] be ordained in his place in the same hour so that God's little flock and people [might] not be destroyed."[23] Building into the confession provision for the appointment of new pastors proved to be a fortuitous step, for most of the leaders present at the meeting in Schleitheim were martyred within a few years. Michael Sättler himself was burned at the stake only three months after the gathering, and his wife, Margaretha, a former nun, was executed by drowning two days after her husband died.

Persecution reinforced the Anabaptist belief in a sharp division between the church and secular society, a belief that continues to mark the lives of their Amish descendants. Anabaptists see the church as "a holy nation, a peculiar people . . . called out of the darkness" (1 Peter

Dirk Willemſz. 1569.

Figure 1.2. Dirk Willems rescuing his pursuer. This engraving by Jan Luykens is one of 104 that appear in the 1685 edition of Thieleman J. van Braght's *Martyrs' Mirror*. These pictures and the stories of Christian martyrs, especially Anabaptists, continue to reinforce the Amish notion of a church separate from the world. The story of Dirk Willems also teaches that one should follow Christ's example. In the engraving, Dirk Willems has stopped to rescue his pursuer, who will then arrest him. Following his capture by the river, Willems was burned at the stake in 1569. Mennonite Library and Archives, Bethel College, North Newton, Kansas.

2:9) and the world as a dark, sinful place, fallen away from God and Christ's teachings.[24] The Bible admonishes Christians not to love "the things of the world" (1 John 2:15), and calls any who would befriend the world "an enemy of God" (James 4:4). Further, the Bible admonishes true Christians not to conform to worldly ways (Romans 12:2). Today, in joining the church through baptism, the Amish, like their Anabaptist forebears, continue to commit to a life in which decision making is shaped by a desire to keep the church pure and by suspicion of society outside the boundaries of the church.

Persecution by the world also fostered the strong sense of group solidarity among the early Anabaptists that marks their Amish descendants today. It was plain to the Anabaptists that they were being persecuted by worldly society as the early Christian martyrs had been and that theirs was the church for which Christ died. This identification with the early apostolic church is clearly seen in *The Bloody Theater, or The Martyrs' Mirror of the Defenseless Christians*, which was published in 1660 in Dutch and subsequently translated into English and German. *The Martyrs' Mirror* contains the stories of those "baptized only upon confession of faith, and who suffered and died for the testimony of Jesus, their Savior, from the time of Christ to the year A.D. 1660."[25] Amish today still read *The Martyrs' Mirror* and find in it consolation for the difficulties they face in the non-Amish world as a result of unwillingness to conform to the dominant society.

From Anabaptist to Mennonite

In the sixteenth and seventeenth centuries, the Anabaptist movement threatened the European status quo. Many non-Anabaptist religious and secular leaders viewed the Anabaptist argument that all are equal in God's eyes as a challenge to hierarchical authority. Moreover, they considered seditious and dangerous the Anabaptist assertion of pacifism and nonresistance, which led adherents to refuse to take up arms in defense of civil and ecclesiastical authority. The Turkish army was threatening Vienna in 1529. The last thing those in authority needed or wanted was a religious movement that encouraged believers to turn the other cheek.

As a result, Anabaptists were persecuted by both Catholic and Protestant authorities. Nevertheless, despite all attempts by authorities to discourage the population from adopting Anabaptist beliefs, the movement continued to spread.[26] Anabaptist refugees helped to establish small congregations throughout the Palatinate region of Germany and into northern Europe. Others settled throughout the region of Alsace-Lorraine, in the mountains of the Vosges, where they held religious services in private homes or in remote outdoor locations to avoid the authorities.[27] The Anabaptists often chose to settle in remote rural regions, where, despite their religious beliefs, they earned the respect of their non-Anabaptist neighbors for their piety and willingness to work hard. In Alsace, for example, Anabaptist immigrants were not allowed to own property, but they rented farms, and as one modern-day descendant put it, "reared large families and excelled in animal husbandry."[28]

By the end of the sixteenth century, the Anabaptists were widely known as "Mennonites" after Menno Simons (1496–1561), a Dutch priest turned Anabaptist preacher whose teachings helped to shape Anabaptist views of the church, nonconformity, and discipline. For Simons, the church represented Christ on earth, and although church members were constrained to follow secular rules because God had set in place worldly governments to keep order, ultimately God's rule took precedence over worldly laws.

Further, asserting that the church was "in doctrine, life, and worship, a people separated from the world," Simons helped to reinforce the notion of the church as a fellowship of believers, who, through their commitment to following Christ's example, would maintain the purity of the

Figure 1.3. Menno Simons. A former priest turned Anabaptist minister, Menno Simons greatly influenced Anabaptist thought and practice. The movement he helped to shape became known as "Mennonite." This engraving by Christoffel van Sichem is the earliest known portrait of Menno Simons (circa 1607). It was first published nearly fifty years after Simons's death. Mennonite Library and Archives, Bethel College, North Newton, Kansas.

church by putting scripture into practice. "We do not believe nor teach that we are saved by our merits and works," he wrote, "but alone through grace by Christ Jesus." Nevertheless, he taught, the faithful practice of Christ's teachings would bring about a genuine change in one's life. In other words, he argued, true faith would lead to good works.

Simons also played a key role in shaping the church's notion of discipline. Emphasizing the need to reject sin in the church, he also argued that church members were obliged to excommunicate those who, through sin and lack of repentance, had removed themselves from fellowship, a practice called the *Bann*. Moreover, he asserted the need to practice *Meidung*, the social avoidance, or "shunning," of those the church had excommunicated. For Simons, the Meidung was to be *streng*, or strong, meaning that one could not eat, drink, do business with, or interact socially with any church member who had been put out of the fellowship. As he wrote, "a church without ban or separation is like a vineyard without an enclosure and trenches, or a city without walls; for the enemies have free ingress into it to sow and plant their pernicious tares unhindered."[29] Therefore, he argued, church members must "*shun* the apostates, lest they contaminate us with the impure, deceiving doctrine, and with their ungodly, carnal lives."[30] Even family members should be shunned if necessary, he asserted, for no one could contaminate a church member more quickly than a father, mother, husband, wife, or child. Simons noted the positive value of shunning, arguing that it could win back those who had sinned, but he urged church members to "take heed. If you see your brother sin, do not pass by him as one that is not concerned about his soul, . . . help him to arise immediately, by loving admonition and brotherly instruction, before you eat, drink, sleep or do anything else, . . . lest your poor erring brother be hardened in his sin, and perish."[31] Yet, for Simons, Bann and Meidung—excommunication and shunning—were the most effective means of guarding the purity of the church when "loving admonition" failed. In the end, he argued, "those whom we cannot raise up and admonish unto repentance . . . we should reluctantly separate from us . . . lest we also be deceived and led astray by such false doctrine which eats about itself like a canker, 2 Tim. 2."[32]

The practice of shunning those excommunicated from church fellowship was later upheld in the Dordrecht Confession of 1632, a statement issued by the leaders of a number of Mennonite factions who came together in the city of Dordrecht in Holland to iron out disagreements over church practice. The Dordrecht Confession affirmed social avoidance, but it also reaffirmed Simons's assertion of a dual role for Bann and shunning, noting that church members should have nothing to do with the sinner "so that we may not become defiled by his intercourse with him . . . but [also so] that he may be made ashamed . . . and thereby induced to amend his ways."

Far more detailed than the earlier Schleitheim Confession,[33] the Dordrecht Confession also further defined Anabaptist belief and ritual, outlining a Mennonite view of the church from Creation to Christ's return, and formalizing the practice of foot washing as part of the communion ritual.[34] Signed by ministers across northern Europe, it also circulated widely in southern Germany and Switzerland and became, along with the Schleitheim Confession, both a statement of faith for the Anabaptist movement and a guide to church practice.

The Amish and the Mennonites

Despite the influence of the Dordrecht Confession on the Anabaptist churches, not all ministers signed it, and not all who did sign it agreed with everything it said. Although ministers in Alsace had largely accepted the Dordrecht Confession and its assertion of the need for social shunning,[35] many of their Swiss brethren did not and were, in fact, unwilling to follow certain other aspects of the document; for example, many Swiss Mennonite congregations did not practice foot washing. Instead of the strict social avoidance of strong Meidung, a number of congregations preferred simply to exclude excommunicated members from communion.[36]

By the end of the seventeenth century, regional differences in Mennonite practice had developed, a result, at least in part, of the diverse social conditions in which Mennonites found themselves. For example, Mennonites in Switzerland were ruthlessly hunted and risked losing not only their possessions but also their families and their lives if they were found out. In contrast, Mennonites in Alsace lived comfortably with their neighbors. Following the Thirty Years War (1618–1648), Alsace came under French authority. The Alsatian population had been devastated by war and disease, and the French government offered land and financial incentives to attract new settlers. Mennonites who moved to the region could even pay a fee to be exempted from military service.

Comfortable in Alsace, the Mennonites in the region were increasingly integrated into Alsatian society. The danger they faced was not from persecution but from compromise.[37] As one German Mennonite put it, writing in 1702, "I fear that in the peaceful days we have been enjoying, undisturbed and untroubled by our persecutors, even some of us may have grown lukewarm, discouraged and physically fat and satisfied, and we may indeed have become carnally attached to the world."[38]

An Alsatian preacher, Jacob Ammann (1644–1730), confronted both the assimilation in Alsace and the failure of the Swiss churches to follow the Dordrecht Confession in its entirety, arguing that the Mennonites were becoming worldly. He lamented the apparent willingness of Mennonite church members to conform to fashions in dress and to interact with and even marry non-Mennonites, and he chastised congregations for their

Figure 1.4. Birthplace of the Amish movement. The village of Ste. Marie-aux-Mines in Alsace, France, where the Mennonite minister Jacob Ammann preached. The first Amish settlers to New York came from these mountains. Photo by author.

14

apparent willingness to do business with, dine with, and otherwise inter-act socially with expelled members whom they were supposed to shun.

Most of the Mennonite preachers and congregations in Switzerland and the Palatinate region rejected Ammann's call for greater separation from the world, and so, in 1693, Ammann excommunicated them.[39] Twenty of the twenty-three Alsatian ministers, along with one in the Palatinate and five in Germany, supported Ammann. They and their congregations became known as Amish Mennonites, or, simply, Amish. The groups were soon distinguishable by dress. For example, Ammann argued that men should not trim their beards and that church members should wear plain clothing. Locally, his followers became known as *Häftler* ("hook-and-eye people") because they often chose to use this simple means of fastening their clothing rather than buttons, which were considered more worldly. The Mennonites were called *Knöpfler* ("button people").

The Old Order Amish

Beginning in the early eighteenth century, Amish families began to leave Europe for North America. Although some Amish may have arrived with Swiss Mennonites, who bought land from William Penn in 1710, the first documented arrival of Amish immigrants was in 1737, when sev-eral families arrived in Philadelphia aboard the *Charming Nancy*. These new arrivals helped to launch the first wave of Amish immigration from Europe to North America, which lasted until about 1750 and drew from communities in the German Palatinate region and Switzerland. During this period, the Amish founded the well-known settlements in Lancaster and Lebanon counties in eastern Pennsylvania. By the time the second wave started in about 1817, Amish settlers had moved into Holmes and Tuscarawas counties in Ohio.

The second wave of Amish immigration, which lasted to 1861, brought settlers from the French territories of Alsace and Lorraine, as well as additional immigrants from Germany and Switzerland. These newcomers tended to settle in areas distant from Amish who had come earlier, establishing New York's first settlement in Lewis County and settlements further west in Ohio, Illinois, Iowa, and Ontario.[40] For the most part, the French Amish did not join with other Amish settlers in establishing new communities because they found them to be too con-servative. This resulted in Amish settlements that were culturally and ethnically diverse.

After 1860, Amish immigration from Europe ceased, but the Amish continued to move, and in seeking new areas in which to settle and establish new communities, they changed. Congregations were increasingly challenged by their non-Amish neighbors and by other Amish churches whose practices were different. Many of the Amish who had arrived in the second wave of Amish immigration, particularly those from Alsace and Lorraine, tended to be more innovative than those who had come earlier from Switzerland and the Palatinate.[41] As Old Order writer O. A. Graber put it, these later arrivals were "already of a different view in church matters than the former immigrants of about a hundred years before," and he noted that some wore more stylish "worldly" dress, were willing to have their photograph taken, and even played musical instruments. Most important, the newer arrivals did not always see eye to eye with their long-settled counterparts on a number of issues, including how baptism was to be performed, whether there should be church buildings, whether one could have assurance of salvation, and whether Sunday School and revival and prayer meetings were acceptable.[42]

In the early part of the nineteenth century, there were a number of regional *Diener-Versammlungen*, or ministers' meetings, to help iron out differences. Nevertheless, by the middle of the nineteenth century church leaders recognized that tension between those more open to technological and social change and those who felt that practices should, as much as possible, continue unaltered was becoming increasingly widespread. Many agreed with Lancaster County bishop David Beiler, who worried that "the split appears to be becoming almost irreparable." In 1862, the first in a series of annual Diener-Versammlungen was held in the barn of N. W. Schrock in Wayne County, Ohio. Church leaders hoped that by meeting and discussing differences they could standardize religious practices and ensure unity in the church. The conferences were open to all church members. Although the majority of participants were from Ohio,[43] ministers came from a number of different states, including Pennsylvania and Illinois.

At first, the annual meeting seemed to bring about the unity everyone had hoped for. The ministers attending were united in their opposition to "joining a state militia, holding membership in secret societies such as the Masonic Lodge, or posing for photographs."[44] Nevertheless, there remained deep divisions. In retrospect, it seems clear that those who came together for the Diener-Versammlungen had very different expectations about what the meetings would accomplish, in part because they had evolved different notions of *Ordnung*, a code of conduct that evolves through the consensus of the congregation and is reaffirmed twice annually before communion. The more traditional-minded church leaders understood the Ordnung as a guide to living according to God's unchanging truth, a discipline that had been worked out within the church by church members who were more concerned with eternity than with events in the secular world. Representing churches today's Amish would call "low," these leaders wished to limit both their interaction with non-Amish society and their reliance on worldly ways and technologies. As a result, they saw little reason for their Ordnungs to change. Moreover, these leaders continued to ground authority in the individual congregation and its ministry and so did not see decisions made at the meetings as binding. These more conservative church leaders hoped instead that the meetings would help to provide a means of enforcing boundaries the Ordnung had already set in place.

More progressive church leaders, however, understood the Ordnung as a fluid set of guidelines that would evolve through ongoing meetings of the church leadership. Representing churches that Amish today would call "high" because of their willingness to engage the surrounding society in new ways, they saw the Diener-Versammlungen as an opportunity to meet regularly on issues that confronted church districts and, together, arrive at a means of keeping unity between the various groups. Rather than seeking fixed regulations, they envisioned an organic process that would effectively unite the congregations under a central governing body.[45]

The differences between the factions were, ultimately, irreconcilable, and although the meetings continued until 1878, the 1865 meeting was the last one that the more conservative leaders attended. After that, asserting a commitment to the ways of their forebears, they withdrew from fellowship with their more progressive counterparts.[46] By the time the Diener-Versammlungen ended, those who maintained a more traditional understanding of the Ordnung were becoming known as the *Alte Ordnung*, or Old Order Amish. The Old Order churches were marked by a desire to continue with as little change as possible the practices of daily life and religious observance. The majority of the more progressive communities eventually formed several regional conferences, each of which later merged with the Mennonite Church.[47]

Other schisms followed as the lifestyle of the tradition-minded Old Order Amish became increasingly different from that of their non-Amish neighbors, and Old Order congregations struggled to define their place in a changing world. Church members debated their response to members who left the Old Order church in which they had been baptized to join more progressive Amish Mennonite congregations, many arguing that anyone who did so had violated the baptismal vow and should be excommunicated and socially shunned in accordance with the Dordrecht Confession. The issue divided many Old Order churches. In Lancaster County, Pennsylvania, for example, Amish opposed to the strict shunning of excommunicated members withdrew from the Old Order in 1910 to establish an independent church. This group, which became known as Peachey Amish, soon accepted more mainstream Protestant practices, such as Sunday School.

The Peachey Amish also embraced many of the technological innovations that were beginning to challenge Old Order communities, including the telephone, which may have been a factor in the schism.[48] The automobile caused particular problems. In 1927, the Old Order community in Somerset County, Pennsylvania, divided when Bishop Moses Beachy rejected streng Meidung, and within a year, members of the Beachy Amish (not to be confused with the Peachey Amish) had adopted both automobiles and electricity. Also embracing technology but to a lesser extent than the Beachy Amish, was the New Order, formed in 1966 when different Amish congregations began to emphasize spiritual values and to articulate a more individualistic belief in the assurance of salvation. Perhaps more properly a subgroup of the Old Order, the New Order Amish, also called the Amish Brotherhood, have offered a middle way between Old Order and Beachy churches, allowing tractors in the field but forbidding automobile ownership.[49]

Schism has also resulted in the formation of far more conservative groups, including the Swartzentruber Amish, the Nebraska Amish, and the Troyer Amish. These Amish, often reacting to what they perceive as "drift," or assimilation to worldly ways, have drawn a sharp line between the church and the dominant society and have restricted the use of all but the most limited technology.

Amish Communities Today

In the twenty-first century, as Old Order Amish communities continue to draw on tradition and scripture to define themselves in a changing world, the church remains the one pervasive force in Amish existence. The

Standard German word for church is *Kirche*, which, like its English equivalent, refers to the building in which services are held or to the services themselves. However, the word for *church* in Pennsylvania German, the language spoken within Amish communities, is *Gmay*, from the German *Gemeinde*, meaning "community." For the Amish, the church is the community, the fellowship of those who have signaled by their baptism that they are dedicated to putting the teachings of Christ into practice.

Within each Gmay, life is guided by the Ordnung, which specifies for the community what is sinful and worldly and, therefore, not to be tolerated. Not everything set down in the Ordnung has a biblical basis. Nevertheless, the practices that can't be scripturally supported are justified by the feeling that to do otherwise would be worldly and disruptive.

As in the earliest Anabaptist churches, each Amish congregation has its own Ordnung, which has evolved over time as the group has responded to changing circumstances. Some changes in the Ordnung may contribute to the economic viability of a community, such as when a congregation decides to accept the use of bulk milk tanks. Other changes are reactions to legislation and social changes in the dominant society, such as the decision to accept (or reject) the use of slow-moving vehicle signs on buggies or the decision to start private schools in the face of public school consolidation. Because no two communities have faced the same set of circumstances, no two Amish congregations have exactly the same Ordnung. Even when there is general agreement among communities, the results may be quite diverse. For example, all Old Order Amish forbid automobile ownership, but buggy styles vary from group to group, as do the rules governing when one can accept rides in cars from a non-Amish neighbor.

Although Ordnungs are normally not written, they are clarified, developed, modified, and reaffirmed twice each year, in the spring and in the fall, at *Ordnungsgmay*, or council church. At Ordnungsgmay, church leaders express their views on the Ordnung, comment on practices that are forbidden or discouraged, and remind church members of past decisions. After this, each member of the church is asked whether he or she is in agreement, a sort of "cleansing ritual," in which differences of opinion are ironed out and consensus reached.[50]

By creating norms with which all agree, the Ordnung ties the community together. It is a *Zaun*, a fence, against the outside world, and obedience to it is a symbol of love for the church.[51] In the end, if all church members are in agreement, the community can celebrate *Grossgmay*, or communion church, at its next worship service, two weeks later. On the other hand, if there are disagreements that divide church members, there will be no communion, and if differences cannot be resolved, the community will divide.

Regardless of the reason for disagreement, a split in a church district constitutes, at the most basic level, a question of how to define the church. It is about identity and how members of the group will be distinguished from nonmembers, a matter of utmost importance for a people whose religious beliefs call on them to remain separate from the world.

For a division within a community to be recognized as a schism, each side must have a minister or bishop. Those who openly disagree with church decision making and, without ministerial support, cease fellowshipping with the group, will be excommunicated and shunned. With ministers on both sides of the argument, however, the two factions recognize a sincere difference of opinion, a dispute beyond their ability to settle. In the weeks immediately following the schism, while each of the factions is regrouping, church members may move freely from one group to another, an open window to personal change that closes only when each group holds its first worship service as a separate entity. Because one party to the schism does not shun the other, a split provides relief for tensions that may have been building over a long period and allows smaller, more unified groups to emerge.

Schism within a church district divides families and ruptures work and social ties. During one split, for example, one Amish woman compared the emotional turmoil to that suffered by a divorcing couple. Nevertheless, a schism may be a healthy application of Anabaptist principles in the face of pressure, both from the dominant, non-Amish society and from forces within the group. Schism helps to shape patterns of interaction in the Amish world. A congregation may *dien*, or "fellowship," with others whose Ordnungs are similar, meaning that ministers from one group are able to preach in church services held by the others and that a member of one congregation might marry a member of one of the others. But, even within such affiliations, the congregation must ultimately find its own path.[52]

Defining the Boundaries

Everything about the Amish—dress, language, education, and transportation—reaffirms the Ordnung and emphasizes the lines drawn to keep the world out of the community. The Amish interpret literally biblical injunctions such as Romans 12:2 ("and be not conformed to this world"). Another passage, 2 Corinthians 6:14, says, "Be ye not unequally yoked together with unbelievers: for what fellowship hath righteousness with unrighteousness [and] what communion hath light with darkness?" Also interpreted literally, the passage forbids not only marriage with outsiders but also connecting to the electrical grid or to the telephone system.

Like the first Anabaptists, the Old Order Amish today not only refuse to perform military service, but they also refuse to fight to defend themselves. Every Amish child learns about the Hochstetler massacre; although under Indian attack, Jacob Hochstetler refused to allow his sons to fight back, and the family perished. Nowadays, when threatened, the Amish tend to suffer or move.

As in the earliest Anabaptist gatherings, one joins this fellowship of believers when one makes the decision to become baptized. The Amish believe that baptism is making a covenant with God, a vow of total obedience to Christ's church, which is the church district, and to its Ordnung, which is the community's attempt to put scripture into practice. Baptism is a ritual for adults, who are urged to think carefully before taking this important step. The Amish do not believe, as some Christians do, that baptism brings salvation. To assert that one is saved is the ultimate in *Hochmut*, or pride, for this is something only God can know. The Amish put their faith in God, strive to obey His word, which is equated with the rule of the Gmay, and hope for the best.

Church members who violate baptismal vows, fall into sin, fail to follow the Ordnung, or refuse to heed the counsel of the fellowship are believed to threaten the community and, as stipulated in the Schleitheim Confession, are subject to Bann, or excommunication. Moreover, as mandated by the Dordrecht Confession, they are subject to Meidung, or shunning.

Bann and Meidung remain, perhaps, the most difficult aspects of Amish life for the non-Amish to understand. Today's Amish do not believe that excommunication denies the wrongdoer hope of salvation, for only God has the power to do that. Instead, following the teachings of Menno Simons, the Amish will excommunicate someone who goes against the Ordnung as a last attempt to convince the erring member to return to the church. If the individual does not repent, then, as the Bann declares, that individual has by his own actions taken himself outside the fellowship. Meidung requires all others who have been baptized in the church to cease social and business relationships with the shunned person. Most Amish believe that the Bann and the Meidung contribute in a positive way to the unity and purity of the church by minimizing the threat posed by the offending individual and helping the Gmay to remain distinct and socially intact. Following the church service at which the Bann is imposed, even those closest to the excommunicated congregant will cut their ties. "I'd rather not see her dressed English," said one mother about her daughter, who had left the church.

The spiritual fence of the Ordnung is reinforced in a variety of ways. Although fewer and fewer Amish communities are agriculturally based, the Amish view the earth as a sacred trust.[53] The Amish believe that God created the world and enjoyed it and then created human beings whom he commanded to harness and cultivate the earth. The Amish don't worship nature, but rather they find it easier to be Christian close to nature. As one Amish text put it, "Farming allows us to be part of the cycle of life, death, and renewal that God planned in his wisdom. In our daily contact with creation, we cannot help but stand in awe and wonder of God."[54] The desire to maintain an agricultural lifestyle has brought many Amish families to areas of New York State where land is more affordable.[55]

The physical structure of the Amish community also reinforces church teachings. Amish settlements, collections of Amish homes in proximity to each other, are organized socially and geographically into congregations or church districts—that is, a certain number of families who will meet together for worship. The size of the church district is limited by the distance that can be easily traveled with horse and buggy and by the number of families. Like the early Anabaptists, who worshipped secretly in private homes to avoid arrest, most Amish groups do not have separate meeting houses; church services are held in family homes or, when warm enough, in barns, so the congregation cannot be too large. Church services are held every two weeks. On an off-week Sunday, people will visit friends or perhaps attend church in a neighboring district. There is no Sunday School, which many Old Order Amish believe undermines the role of the family in the children's religious upbringing.[56] The father will lead the family in morning and evening devotions and in silent prayer before and after meals. Preaching is for the ministers.

The church district is the primary unit of Amish authority and governance. Even if it has affiliated with others, the church district is autonomous, and decisions made within the congregation are binding for all its members, and only for them. A three-part ministry whose officials are chosen in a process that combines democracy and faith guides the church district. There is a deacon (called in German *Armen-Diener*, or "minister to the poor"), who assists in marriage arrangements and sees to it that the material needs of everyone in the community are met. Two to three preachers (*Diener zum Buch*, or "minister of the book") are responsible for preaching and counseling. Finally, there is a bishop (*Voelliger-Diener*, or "minister with full powers"),[57] who performs marriages, baptisms, excommunications, and funerals. When a new preacher (or deacon or bishop) is needed, all members of the church are consulted. Each is asked to nominate a baptized male who is married and settled enough to be a stable leader. Those receiving two or more nominations (depending on the size of the congregation) take part in a lottery. While the candidates withdraw into another room, church members set out on a church bench as many hymnbooks as there are candidates, placing in one of the hymnals a piece of paper on which is written a Bible verse. When the candidates come out, in order of their age, each chooses a hymnal, and the one choosing the hymnal containing the Bible verse rises to church office. Using the "Lot" to choose church leaders guarantees each member of the church a say in church government and the spiritual stability of the community. But God, not luck, is thought to have the final word in the selection.

Having been chosen by God, the ministry has considerable authority, and appointments, while unpaid, are generally for life. Nevertheless, an ordained deacon, preacher, or bishop may be silenced if the members of the congregation feel that he has transgressed or violated the Ordnung. Further, decision making within the congregation is subject to the *Rat der Gemein*, a vote of all church members, male and female. For example, all those baptized in a particular church district have a say in the decision to excommunicate or reinstate an errant member of that district.

The integrity of the community is reinforced by the continued rejection of the telephone, electricity, the automobile, and other technological innovations that would disrupt the daily face-to-face, local interaction that reinforces personal ties. Pennsylvania German, or *Deitsch*, also called Pennsylvania Dutch, is used for communication within the group. One uses English to talk to outsiders. Young children, who often do not begin to learn English until they enter school, are bashful in front of outsiders who communicate in a strange tongue. Plain dress further distinguishes members of the Gmay from outsiders, identifying the community of believers and giving the wearer a sense of belonging.[58]

The symbols of dress, transportation, behavior, and language unite members of each Old Order Amish community. They are of little meaning to the outside world, but then, the symbols of the outside world mean little to the Amish.

Amish children learn the symbols of their people and the values they represent through active participation in the life events of the community rather than in school. In their eight years of formal education, children learn English, arithmetic, German, and maybe geography and health. The important lessons—how to manage a farm and a household, how to raise children, how to be responsible and hardworking—are learned at home, where children participate in work, play, and ceremony to the extent of their abilities.

Social Life in the Church District

The family is the key social unit in the Amish community. Amish children are considered minors until they are twenty-one, and up until then they owe their labor and their earnings to their parents, who, in turn, are responsible for their room, board, medical care, and upbringing. The father's duty is to provide materially and spiritually for the well-being of his wife and children; the mother's duty is to help her husband and be "keeper at home." Both parents take seriously the need to teach their children the values and discipline they will need to be contributing members of their church.[59] As a writer to the Amish teachers' magazine the *Blackboard Bulletin* noted, "It is a serious matter that our youth be shown the right way, so that after they leave school, bad companions and the world's many temptations do not take the upper hand."[60]

Thus from birth an Amish child is treated as a future church member. Young children take on chores within the home as soon as they are able, and through doing, they learn to respect their parents, family, and church. Ultimately parents hope that children will do their best, trust in God, and accept what comes. As the Amish say, they want their children to "give up," because to be resigned, to submit to God's will as expressed in the Bible, is to achieve Gelassenheit, which incorporates the personal attributes of yielding and powerlessness.[61] In an Amish children's story, for example, a little girl complains about not being able to make pictures as pretty as those made by some of the other children. Her mother leads her, through gentle questioning, to the lesson of the story: "If we do our best with the talents God gave us, He will be satisfied."

In the Amish world, as children get older, the peer group becomes increasingly important. When Old Order Amish children turn seventeen, they join "young folk," or "youngie," who meet to socialize until they marry. This is *Rumspringa*, or the "running around period," when young people have a social life with each other distinct from family activities. In very conservative groups, the young folk gather in the evenings on a church Sunday to have supper together and sing hymns. In more progressive Amish communities, young folks may dress in non-Amish clothes and buy forbidden objects such as cameras, radios, or even cars and store them at the homes of non-Amish neighbors.

Because the Rumspringa period gives young people more freedom, it is a time of concern for their parents, who, like parents everywhere, find it difficult to watch their children make decisions that go against parental values and beliefs. One of the reasons the Amish often give for their decision to found a new community is that the young folk were becoming "too wild" in the old one. "We're trying . . . to keep kids away from the temptations," one grandmother commented. Yet, having seen one of her own children make the decision to leave the church, she knows too well that parents are not always successful. "It's hard," her husband agreed. "Harder than having a son who didn't live."

In his study of Amish teenagers, the psychologist Richard Stevick distinguished "adult-centered communities," which are marked by "the continuity of behavior from the teen years to adulthood," from "peer-centered communities," in which the behavior of young people is likely to be at odds with their parents' expectations. In more "peer centered" Amish communities, young folk may have greater access to and interaction with the non-Amish world. Consequently, it is more difficult to monitor and control the behavior of young folks to ensure that they act according to adult (and church) standards. One Amish mother, a member of a more progressive New York settlement, expressed concern about her teenage daughter, who was only a couple of years away from joining the young folk. "Misbehaving youth give the Amish a bad name," she asserted, saying that unwed pregnancy "happens more and more in the Amish than it used to." Her church has attempted to keep the young folk from straying by instituting guidelines that reinforce church teachings about drinking, dating, and personal appearance, and a guideline meeting is held every summer. However, attendance at the meeting is not mandatory, and the daughter insists that she will not bother to go when she joins the young folk. "It's too long," she insisted. Nevertheless, her mother approves of the guideline approach. "There are lots of children out there that choose to go to these meetings," she answered her daughter. "One girl moved here [to go to them]. She was with a wilder group and felt peer pressure to party. She wants to do what's right." The church further encourages the young folk to engage in a number of activities the community finds appropriate, such as singing or playing table tennis.

In all Amish communities, dating begins in the context of young-folk gatherings. A young man will not approach a girl directly; rather he will ask his sister or a female cousin to approach the girl he has his eye on to ask her if he could give her a ride home after the Sunday singing. In some of the very conservative groups, bundling, or "bed courtship," persists. When the couple arrives at the girl's home, they will go quietly to her bedroom and lie down together (fully dressed) on her bed. Other Amish groups find this practice outdated and immoral, and so the couple stays below in the kitchen, talking long after the rest of the family has gone to bed.

Ideally, in Rumspringa, Amish teenagers will decide to join the church, find a life partner, become baptized, marry, and raise an Amish family. Following the communion church in the spring, those contemplating baptism begin a sequence of nine classes, and in the fall they are baptized. Now church members, these young folk will take their place at the next Ordnungsgmay, or council church, assuming responsibility for upholding the Ordnung and passing on church teachings to their own children.

Ultimately, a life marked by Gelassenheit, or yielding to the church, is rewarded with the companionship of fellow church members to the very end. The elderly remain at home, cared for by family. When it is evident that one is near death, friends and family gather, many coming from great distances, to hold a vigil and ease the pain of the dying. The deceased are buried on land donated for a community cemetery by a fellow church member.[62]

Ties across Communities

To be Amish is to always be in church. Amish identity, encoded in the Ordnung, is the church, and because the church is the community, it is a way of life. According to an Amish woman from the large Clymer-area settlement in western New York, an Amish person is one who dresses Amish, lives Amish, and "go[es] to our church." "I like the

[Amish] way of life, that we're different from the world. It's a simpler life, though it's getting more complicated," noted a grandmother, holding her grandson. "It's a way of life; it's not our religion, it's not our faith, it's our way of life. We were born into it."

And that way of life differs from one church district to the next, even when the congregations are in fellowship. When an Amish couple moves from one settlement to another, the wife may have to remake her dresses in a new style, and her husband may need to replace his hats. They may have to get a new buggy because the one they arrived with does not meet the demands of the Ordnung. They may have to discard some tools they have come to rely on—or they may have access to technology they have never before used.

Nevertheless, as diverse as the Amish world is, there are numerous bonds and commonalities that unite the various Amish congregations. Regardless of the church district to which they belong, all conduct church services in German and sing from the *Ausbund,* a hymnbook that was first printed in 1564 and contains songs written by early Anabaptists, including a number of the first martyrs. The "Lobelied," a hymn of praise, is always the second song in the church service, although more conservative congregations sing it far more slowly than more progressive ones. The *Ausbund* does not contain melodies for the songs, and tunes are passed down from one generation to the next.[63] In nearly every Amish home, one also finds a copy of *The Martyrs' Mirror,* as well as *Ernsthafte Christenpflicht,* a collection of prayers in German for morning and evening devotions.[64]

Uniting Amish settlements across long geographic distances are a variety of publications that keep friends and family apprised of activities within the church district. Two weekly newspapers, the *Budget* (Sugarcreek, Ohio) and *Die Botschaft* (Lancaster County, Pennsylvania), publish newsletters from community "scribes," who write about the weather, that week's church hosts, what visitors were there, and who might be ill, and give details about births, deaths, travels, and everyday events. A monthly newsletter, the *Diary,* gives further information, including summaries of community events and lists of those who have moved.

There are more specialized publications as well. Church newsletters often reach far beyond the geographic borders of the settlements in which they're published, and Old Order Amish magazines focus on a variety of topics, from homemaking to clock making and bird-watching.

27

Women may read *The Little Red Hen News* or *Keepers at Home*, the first a journal filled with handwritten text and the latter a glossy publication. The Pathway Publishing Company, an Amish-owned publishing company in Aylmer, Ontario, publishes three widely read monthly magazines, *Family Life*, *Young Companion*, and the *Blackboard Bulletin*, this last a publication aimed at Old Order teachers. Together these serve to unite the diverse members of the Old Order world and help to reinforce Old Order values.[65]

Further uniting the diverse Amish communities are regular gatherings of ministers and others who meet to discuss issues of concern in the Amish world. Although the Amish remain congregationally based, many church districts send representatives to the meetings of the Old Order Amish Steering Committee,[66] a national organization that formed in 1966 to negotiate the Amish response to the military draft. At other times, Amish communities have worked together on educational issues, and in a number of states a statewide committee regulates Old Order schools.

Nevertheless, despite these intercongregational ties, just because something is done in a particular way in one district is no guarantee that it will be done that way in any other. This doesn't make one congregation any more authentically "Amish" than another. All are Amish, and as they are likely to say in explaining their differences, "That's just our way."

Amish Survival

Fifty years ago many non-Amish observers might have predicted that the Amish would not survive as a distinct cultural group. Nevertheless, today approximately 300,000 live Amish lives, more than double the estimated population a quarter century ago.[67] The Amish emphasize voluntary membership in the church, and there are always those who choose not to join. A survey of the world's largest Amish settlement, the diverse community in the Holmes County area of Ohio, found that nearly 40 percent of New Order Amish left the church community, while only 2.6 percent left the far more conservative Andy Weaver affiliation. Nationally, the percentage of Amish young who do not join the Amish church is roughly 10 to 15 percent. The percentage of those who leave after joining (and are thus subject to excommunication and shunning) is much smaller. In general, the more conservative the community, the higher the retention rate.[68]

The Old Order Amish do not proselytize, and the number of outsiders who have successfully joined Old Order communities remains low. Those who desire to become Amish must first learn to work hard. As the late sociologist J. A. Hostetler put it, "For a young man who is a prospective convert, Amishness begins with the horse stable and a pitchfork. For the young girl, it begins with the work at hand—scalding tomatoes, preserving apples and fruit in glass jars, and preparing family meals."[69] The prospective convert must learn to communicate in German, adopt a different culture, and learn new ways of interacting with the larger society. For this, the convert is offered only the hope that this new life, lived in the name of Christ, will be worthy of salvation. Not many join.

Ultimately, maintaining the health of the church depends on keeping young folk from leaving the community. This means that churches must successfully reconcile faith, tradition, and history with current community and individual needs and with the requirements of the surrounding, non-Amish society. Engaged in the ceaseless attempt to resolve the competing demands of church and world, each Amish church district defines itself through the choices it makes in dress, lifestyle, and technology use.

In coming to New York, Amish church groups have found room for growth far from crowded settlements and away from groups with different practices. They have found ample farmland, which has allowed them to reaffirm the commitment to the agrarian lifestyle that has traditionally sustained them. Through migration, church members have removed themselves from the site of possible conflict before disagreement resulted in schism. They have left behind unpleasant relationships with non-Amish authorities.

The Amish have come to New York to practice their faith and preserve their heritage. As new Amish settlers arrive in the Empire State, they contribute to the diversity that strengthens it.

2

Cattaraugus and Chautauqua Counties

Amish Pioneers in Western New York

Eight farms . . . have been bought for what is believed the first
Amish colony in the extreme southwest part of the state.
—*New York Times*, February 4, 1949

"Go west!" may have been the advice given nineteenth-century
pioneers, but for twentieth- and twenty-first-century Amish settlers, the
direction of choice is often east. In 1949, more than one hundred years
after the arrival of the first Amish settlers in New York State, Amish families from the Enon Valley in Pennsylvania and from Holmes and Wayne
counties in Ohio arrived to start a new settlement in the Conewango
Valley in Cattaraugus County, east of Chautauqua Lake. A short article
in the *New York Times* about Amish real estate purchases announced
the settlement to the non-Amish world. The Amish probably learned
of it when the settlers announced their new community in letters to the
Budget. The first appeared in the February 17, 1949, issue and noted the
arrival in the area of three families, including Enos J. Miller, a minister
from Wayne County, Ohio.[1] By the time letters announced the ordina-
tion of Joe E. Miller, the son of Bishop Eli J. Miller, less than two years
later, the community was already robust, with at least fourteen families.

These new New Yorkers thrived. Writing to the *Budget* in March 1976,
one community member charted the settlement's growth:

> In 1950 a few moved in but in 1951 fifteen families moved in from vari-
> ous localities. . . . In 1952 five families moved in and one moved back to
> Ohio. In 1953 eleven families came. In 1954 there were three, in 1955 two
> moved in and one family moved out again. In spring, 1953, the church
> was divided, North and South. Later the South district was divided again
> being east and south. In 1960 the North district was divided, being now
> North and West. There have been 15 preachers, 7 deacons and 5 bishops
> ordained, some of these moving to other states.[2]

In 1966, there were six church districts, and when another settlement resident wrote to the *Diary* in January 1999, he noted that there were ten church districts, approximately 235 families, and seventeen schools.[3] By 2006, there were eleven church districts. Today, with fifteen church districts, the Conewango Valley settlement is both the oldest extant and the largest Amish settlement in New York State.

Since the founding of the Conewango Valley community, other Amish groups have moved east into Cattaraugus and neighboring Chautauqua County, and nowadays this region offers the Amish world in microcosm, with some of the most conservative Amish living near some of the most progressive. Moving from one church to another, the careful observer can see differences in dress and buggy styles. In more subtle ways, Amish families distinguish themselves from Amish in other groups and from their non-Amish neighbors.

Like their counterparts who arrived in Lewis County in the nineteenth century, these Amish settlers to New York State have remained committed to the Anabaptist values of their forebears. Nevertheless, the settlements they have founded show the myriad ways in which these values can be realized in everyday life.

The Decision to Migrate

The Amish who arrived in the Conewango Valley in 1949 were not fleeing war or religious persecution. Instead, believing that farming was "the most ideal occupation for Christians,"[4] they were looking for a place where they could peacefully live and farm. Western New York offered cheap land.[5] More important, the move allowed the settlers, who were members of the very conservative Troyer Amish faction, to avoid potential conflicts. Even though the search for sufficient affordable farmland to keep the church agriculturally based is a major reason the Amish migrate, religious problems are often the root cause of migration.[6]

Moving to New York allowed these Troyer Amish settlers to distance themselves from the dissension that had afflicted the large Ohio Amish settlement since 1913, when an ultraconservative faction under the leadership of Bishop Sam E. Yoder (1872–1932) broke away from the Old Order Amish church because of what Yoder saw as lax enforcement of the Meidung, the shunning imposed on those in Bann (excommunication).[7] Nearly twenty years later, in 1932, Yoder's insistence on Bann and strong Meidung for even minor infractions of the Ordnung brought about another schism. Recalling

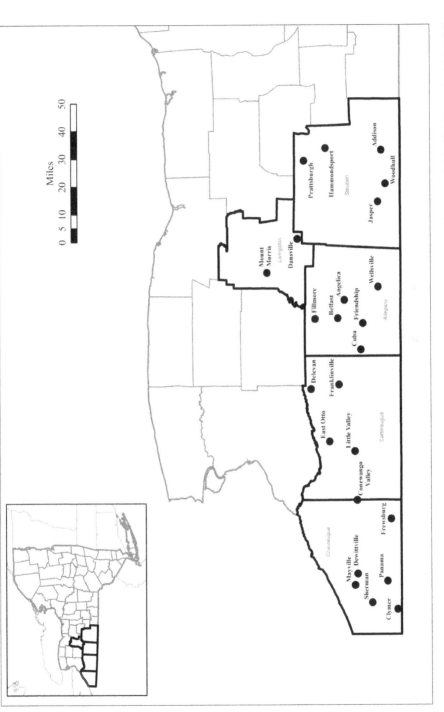

Map 2.1. The Conewango Valley region in western New York. The second Amish settlement in New York was established by Troyer Amish in 1949 in the Conewango Valley, Cattaraugus County. In 1976, Old Order Amish and Byler Amish settled in Clymer and Mayville, and Mayville/Dewittville, respec-

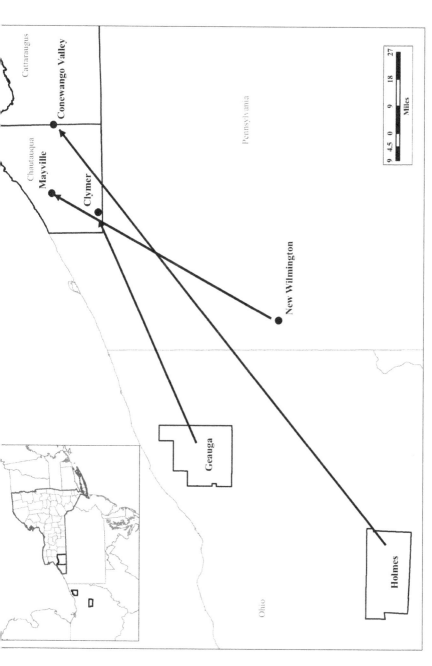

Map 2.2. Amish from Ohio and Pennsylvania established the first settlements in western New York.

events years later,[8] a member of Yoder's church noted that "some church members, boys, did not have their hats like Bishop Sam Yoder thought they should be and he wanted to put them in the 'Bann' but could not get an *einige Rot* [consensus of church members] so [he] told those who were not agreed to leave and he then put the boys in the 'Bann'. . . . [Bishops] Jacob Stutzman and Eli Troyer did not think he should have acted that way and broke fellowship with him at the same time."[9]

The new group that formed under the guidance of Bishops Stutzman and Troyer was first called the Stutzman Gmay, or Stutzman Church, but later become known as the Abe Troyer Church or, simply, the Troyer Amish. Whether the disagreement over hats was the main cause of the schisms is unclear, and Jacob Stutzman does not appear to have been long associated with Sam Yoder's church.[10] Nevertheless, the fact that, more than sixty years after the schism, its descendants continue to cite the incident as the cause of the rupture demonstrates the importance of the symbols that mark Amish appearance and Amish life.

The Troyer schism illustrates the ongoing struggle in Amish churches to define what it means to be Amish and the tension that has been inherent in the quest to maintain the purity of a church of believers ever since Menno Simons dealt with the issue of strong Meidung. On the one hand, one's role as an obedient church member is demonstrated by one's willingness to follow the Ordnung. Failing to change one's hat to meet the demands of the group can thus be seen as a sign of stubbornness and unwillingness to give up one's personal desires in order to follow the church.[11] On the other hand, putting someone under the Bann and shunning that individual for what would seem to be a minor infraction suggests a formalistic reliance on man-made rules. Many of those who disagreed with Yoder's decision felt that he had been too extreme. One woman who left the Old Order church commented that being overly strict in enforcing the Ordnung and exercising Bann and strong Meidung was un-Christian. "It's nothing but the devil making them do it so [those banned] don't come back. The Bible said you're supposed to discipline with love."[12]

Mainly of one mind about church discipline, the Troyer Amish who chose to move to western New York found respite from problematic interactions with other Amish. In a homogeneous settlement, the church does not have to worry as much about the influence of more progressive—or more conservative—ways of being Amish. There are fewer concerns that young people will be attracted to technology or patterns of social interaction that are off-limits in their own community.

Since then, other Troyer Amish families have come to the Conewango Valley, finding not only cheap land and like-minded neighbors, but also relief from threats to their way of life caused by events in the outside world. The sociologist Marc Olshan noted, for example, that "at least one Canadian family moved . . . in the wake of a decision by the Ontario Milk Marketing Board prohibiting the use of cans for storage and shipping of milk," a decision one Amish farmer has characterized as "a long-term plan by the Canadian government to get rid of the small farmers who shipped milk in cans."[13] For all who joined the new Troyer settlement, the Conewango Valley became a haven, close enough to the newcomers' settlements of origin that they could easily visit with their former neighbors or return home for family events or emergencies, but far enough away to lessen the impact of conflict in the home community.[14]

The Conewango Settlement

Today, New York's oldest Amish community remains one of its most conservative. Troyer Amish houses reflect Ordnung decisions made decades ago to forbid linoleum floors, carpeting, sofas, and other upholstered furniture. There are no indoor toilets, and homes are lit with oil lamps instead of gas or battery powered lamps. Moreover, activities in the settlement seem more a part of the nineteenth century than the twenty-first. One woman wrote to *Die Botschaft* to announce that "after a week of spring-like weather we have an inch or 2 [of] snow again. . . . I heard some icehouses have been filled when we had our other cold snap. . . . Ours is still empty, so still hoping for cold."[15]

Nestled in the rolling hills of the Conewango Valley, the Troyer Amish have managed to maintain an agriculturally based lifestyle on land that is rarely used for agriculture by their non-Amish neighbors.[16] Further, they have become an economic force in the community, and numerous small Amish shops dot the landscape. The travel website for Enchanted Mountains/Cattaraugus County features an "Amish Trail Map" that provides ample evidence of the economic diversity of the Troyer community.[17] For example, going north from the Valley View Cheese Factory on Route 62, you can pass a harness shop, a blacksmith shop, and a homestead offering wheel repairs and, on Fridays and Saturdays, baked goods. South and east of the cheese factory, along Youngs Road, you pass signs directing travelers to small shops where they can buy quilts, cabinets, cedar chests, rocking horses, or lumber.

Tourist publications and travel articles have featured the region, high-lighting the chance to return to the past while driving through Amish country. The *Toronto Globe and Mail* announced that "the Amish live in Cattaraugus County, about one hour south of Buffalo, along route 62, near the village of Leon. Bring money for handicrafts and come in a car large enough to handle quilts, rugs and rockers."[18] The *Buffalo News* chimed, "With over 40 shops located in the town of Leon in Cattaraugus County, where over 75% of the town's population is Amish, it is a wonderful place to find unique, hand-crafted gift items for the upcoming holiday season."[19] Offering personal tours of Amish country, the Amish Trail Brochure and Map urges tourists to "immerse yourself in a simpler way of life."[20]

The Valley View Cheese Company is an example of how the Troyer Amish settlers to the Conewango Valley have remained committed to their Ordnung while forging an economically strong community. The

Figure 2.1. An Amish schoolhouse. This schoolhouse is in the Conewango Valley, the oldest Amish settlement in New York. As the Amish have founded new communities, these small, one-room schoolhouses have become a common feature. Photo by author.

factory operates with milk produced on Amish farms and delivered in cans that are picked up twice a day by a non-Amish driver. It also offers an outlet for Amish-made goods and so serves to foster interaction between the Amish community and the non-Amish world.

Perhaps more important, the Valley View Cheese Company also provides employment for Amish youth who are out of school but not yet independent of their families. As in other Old Order Amish groups, children attend school through the eighth grade and then work, either at home or for other community members. In the eyes of many in the community, this apprenticeship period is as important—or perhaps even more important—than the school years, for it provides the on-the-job training Amish young people will need to earn a living, raise a family, and become contributing members of the church.

Home-based craft production and numerous small shops also provide employment for the growing number of young people, and the income they generate augments farm earnings. One elderly Troyer Amish couple is typical. In addition to their farm, both husband and wife work with their son to make woven baskets. While the son nails framing staves to wooden bases, the husband finishes the product, weaving lighter lengths of thin wood through the staves to create baskets in a variety of shapes. Bundles of basket webbing in different colors are piled up on the floor. While her menfolk make baskets, the woman folds long strands of webbing into stars, trinkets destined for a tourist shop and, perhaps, a spot on a Christmas tree in a non-Amish home.

Through small home businesses like this, Amish families support themselves and, at the same time, reinforce family ties. As they work together, the Amish talk; their conservative lifestyle does not mean ignorance of the world. The old man reads Anabaptist history and subscribes to a variety of different Amish publications, including the *Budget*, and the *Diary*. He also gets *Hiwwe wie Driwwe* ("Here Like It's There"), a magazine written in Pennsylvania German and published in Germany.[21]

The family's youngest son is married and, with his wife, has a "dishes store," a type of small shop common in Amish communities. Catering to an Amish clientele, it offers melamine dishes, decorative glass berry sets, drinking glasses, pots and pans, canning jars and lids, and homemade key chains, cards, and bookmarks. There are also flashlights for sale, and replacement parts for oil lamps and other household objects essential to a nonelectric life. Stores like these do not take the place of the larger discount retail stores found in the non-Amish world, where the Amish occasionally shop, but in rural Amish settlements, they provide daily essentials and serve as a meeting place for members of the community.

Other Amish Arrive

In the years since the first Troyer Amish families moved to the Conewango Valley, other Amish have established settlements in the region. These new settlements, while close to each other, are not overlapping, which safeguards their respective Ordnungs. In January 1976, Amish families from New Wilmington, Pennsylvania, settled north and west of the Conewango Valley in the Mayville/Dewittville area near the northern end of Chautauqua Lake. Called Byler Amish,[22] they are part of a group that originated in Mifflin County, Pennsylvania, in 1849 when their leader, Bishop Samuel B. King, broke fellowship with the larger Amish church. The Byler Amish, like their Troyer Amish neighbors, are more conservative than many of their Old Order brethren. Commenting that "religious tradition in this community in western New York [is] conservative even by Amish standards," a *New York Times* article noted that plumbing in the houses is cold water only and that oil lamps are used in place of electricity.[23]

In April 1976, only a few months after the first Byler Amish families had moved in, a different kind of Amish arrived from the Middlefield area in Geauga County, Ohio, to establish a settlement on the western side of Chautauqua Lake in Chautauqua County, only a half hour's drive from Conewango Valley. More progressive than either the Troyer or Byler Amish, the Old Order Amish in this third settlement, which now spans the towns of Clymer, Sherman, and Panama, are employed as carpenters and housecleaners in the surrounding community, notably at the nearby Chautauqua Institution. There, during the ten weeks in summer when the institution is open, guests and speakers from all over the world rub shoulders with bearded Amish men and plain-dressed Amish women.

Like the Troyer Amish in the Conewango Valley, both the Byler Amish in Mayville/Dewittville and the Old Order Amish in the Clymer area were attracted to western New York by the availability of cheap farmland. Located an hour north of Pittsburgh, the New Wilmington area in Lawrence County, Pennsylvania, has a large and growing Amish population, and the desire for cheap farm land has led a number of Byler Amish from the area to form new settlements elsewhere.[24] To the Old Order Amish, Geauga County, Ohio, felt equally crowded. A rapidly growing Amish population in Geauga County, coupled with industrial growth in the region, made it increasingly difficult for the Amish to find farmland, and so many of the settlers who arrived in the Clymer area had been employed in nonfarm occupations prior to their move to New York. They found Clymer to be a particularly attractive setting because it offered both a local market for milk and lower land prices.

For the settlers in the Mayville/Dewittville area, finding affordable farms meant saving a lifestyle threatened by overcrowding. Similarly, the Old Order Amish newcomers to Clymer hoped that the move would allow many families to hang on to and even reestablish the farming lifestyle that they saw as essential to an Amish way of life. It represented a final chance to teach their children crucial farm skills, to ensure that agriculture would still be an option for them.[25] "Farming is coming back," asserts one Clymer Amish housewife. "I think the men want to be home earning their own money." Arguing that the move was good for the entire family, she added, "In my opinion, if the men are home, they can help raise the children."

For these Ohio Amish, the move to New York was only the latest attempt to find farmland and an agricultural setting in which to raise children. The Geauga County settlement itself, for example, had grown out of a perceived need on the part of Holmes County Amish for new farmland. A 1966 clipping from the *Budget*, reprinted in *Der Gemeinde Brief*, notes that "the factor which influenced the Samuel Weaver family to migrate from Holmes County to Geauga County in 1886 was neither school nor church difference but purely his desire to better his farming status."[26] One hundred years after the Weavers moved to Geauga County in search of land, their descendants were moving east for the same reason.[27]

While not all those who moved to New York have stayed,[28] the settlements in the Mayville/Dewittville and Clymer region, now among the oldest Amish settlements in the state, have been very successful. The Mayville/Dewittville community currently has two church districts and approximately forty-three families, while the Clymer settlement, including Panama and Sherman, now has nine church districts and more than two hundred families.

More recently other Amish have arrived. The Little Valley/East Otto settlement in Cattaraugus County was started in 2006 by Troyer Amish from Union City, Pennsylvania. Byler Amish from New Wilmington, Pennsylvania, started two new settlements in 2011, one northeast of Mayville and another in Frewsburg, both in Chautauqua County. Finally, also in 2011, ultraconservative Swartzentruber Amish moved into the Delevan area in Cattaraugus County. Writing in 2012, one of the new Swartzentruber settlers noted that "the first families of our group moved here in late October of 2011 and there are 6 families here right now and 2 more have bought land." By January 2016, there were fifteen families.

Amish Diversity in Western New York

Although each of the groups who have settled in western New York is Amish—and all are descended from groups that remained devoted to the Alte Ordnung during the nineteenth-century Diener-Versammlungen—they are not all the same. A quick glance at buggies is enough for the casual observer to perceive obvious differences. The Troyer Amish buggies of the Conewango Valley community are black, without windshields or a rear window, and the side and back panels can be rolled up on warm days. When the panels are down, they are fastened in place with heavy snaps. There are no reflectors in the rear other than the slow-moving-vehicle triangle. An oil lantern emblazoned with a red reflector hangs on the left-hand side, a meager warning to motorists at night. The top corners of the buggy are squared off, giving the buggy a rectangular shape when seen from the rear.

In contrast, Byler Amish buggies have a black base and brown sides and tops. Again, the sides roll up, and the top corners are squared off, like those of their Conewango Valley counterparts. On the Byler buggy, however, the roll-up panel in the back has a small window in it that lets occupants see out. The orange slow-moving-vehicle triangle is flanked by two red reflectors.

Clymer Old Order Amish buggies present a third variation. Again, the sides are roll-up panels, but the top does not meet the sides squarely. The slight overhang makes the top look like a small house roof with eaves. The Clymer buggy is black, like the Troyer Amish variety, but with a small window in back, as in Byler buggies. It is brighter and more traffic friendly than many Amish buggies, sporting battery-powered flashing yellow lights, along with multiple strips of gray reflecting tape on the front and rear, in addition to the slow-moving-vehicle triangle. There is a windshield, sometimes with battery-powered windshield wipers, and mirrors on the sides so that the driver can check for cars coming from behind.

Finally, drivers through the Delevan area will note that Swartzentruber Amish buggies look much like those of the Troyer Amish, but they lack the orange slow moving vehicle triangle. The Swartzentrubers affix strips of gray reflecting tape around the back frame of the buggy and carry a single lantern at night.

Other types of vehicles also provide evidence of the different Ordnungs that govern these neighboring communities. In the Clymer-area settlement, farm wagons and even the wagons used to transport church benches from one house to another have rubber tires. Wagons in the more conservative Troyer, Byler, and Swartzentruber settlements have steel-rimmed wooden wheels.

More personal matters, such as dress, also distinguish the settlements. Dresses are longer, usually ankle length, and hat brims wider among the Troyer and Swartzentruber Amish. In the summertime, little boys in Clymer wear straw hats that are painted black, while their Troyer, Byler, and Swartzentruber counterparts wear unpainted ones. Clymer men and boys wear buttoned-down shirts with turned-over collars, while their Troyer, Byler, and Swartzentruber neighbors have pullover shirts with standing collars.[29] In winter, Clymer schoolboys wear knitted caps, while their more conservative counterparts don brimmed felt hats. Unlike the more conservative Troyer, Byler, and Swartzentruber women, the Clymer Amish women wear "suits," meaning that their capes and aprons are the same color as their dresses. They also wear lighter colors, including light blues, green, and slate, whereas women in the more conservative groups stick to black and darker colors such as navy blue. Yet there are limits. One teenage Clymer girl I spoke with complained that her mother would not let her have a lavender dress. "It's too light," replied her mother. In all of these communities, girls and women wear caps at all times, white for those who are married, and black for those who are not. Those worn by women in the more progressive Clymer churches may sit farther back on the head, which allows more hair to show in front. In the more conservative communities, cap strings are likely to be tied at all times rather than being left to hang loose.

Homes also reveal the varying ways in which these different communities have defined Amish life. Although the Troyer, Byler, and Swartzentruber Amish all eschew linoleum, upholstered furniture, indoor plumbing, and gas lamps, all these things can be found in a Clymer area Amish house. Yet the Clymer homes also show that Amish groups can vary from one church district to another, even within apparently homogeneous settlements. For example, gas stoves are allowed in some but not all of the church districts in the Clymer-Sherman-Panama region;

most Amish use wood stoves or rely on kerosene. Nor are propane lights permitted in all districts. Nevertheless, the different districts remain in fellowship with each other. As one Clymer Amish woman put it, "It's not all exactly alike, but it's basically the same Ordnung. Each district has its own idea."

Tourist maps of the region showing the location of Amish shops hint at the deeper diversity of the settlements in western New York by suggesting the various ways in which Ordnungs shape economic interaction with outsiders. For example, like the "Amish Trail Map" for Cattaraugus County, the "Amish Map for Northern Chautauqua County," home to the Mayville/Dewittville Byler community, and the "Amish Map for Western Chautauqua County," site of the larger Clymer settlement, suggest Amish shops where one can find lawn furniture, farm produce, maple syrup, and quilts.[30] These little businesses, run from outbuildings on family farms, allow family members to be employed close to home and parents to work with children. Catering to passersby and offering products grown or made on the site and by the family, these home-based enterprises also allow parents to control the interaction between children and outsiders.

In the Clymer settlement, however, one also finds much larger businesses. For example, a local harness maker in Panama, New York, notes that he has made more than seven hundred harnesses in the past eleven years. "I had a big shed with nothing in it. My harnesses were wearing out, and there was no one to fix them. So . . . I got me a sewing machine." In addition to making harnesses to order for Amish and non-Amish customers, this shop owner offers a variety of items, including grooming supplies, gloves, liniments, and in an upstairs room, black and natural-color straw hats in a variety of styles. Not far from the harness shop is a bulk food store that offers shopping carts for the convenience of its customers. While most who shop here are from the Clymer community, the store may serve Amish from other settlements and non-Amish shoppers as well. In addition to staples such as flour and sugar, one can purchase packaged foods including mustard and ketchup, as well as cleaning supplies. The store also sells toys, coloring books, story and cookbooks, community directories, and other types of Amish literature. In a cookware section one can find utensils, pots and pans, and dishes, and a stationery section offers school supplies. Fabric is for sale, but so is ready-to-wear Amish clothing, suggesting that many Clymer Amish women no longer do as much sewing in the home.

Figure 2.2. This Clymer-area Amish "department store" offers shoppers an assortment of books, toys, and notions. Businesses in Amish communities reflect the Ordnung of the church. Photo by author.

The Clymer area is home to a number of businesses that not only allow interaction with the outside world but also clearly cater to the tourist market. According to the "Amish Map for Western Chautauqua County," the Weaver family runs a craft store and offers buggy rides, while the Brickers run an "Amish family-style Restaurant by Reservation." The Millers give quilting demonstrations by appointment. Other businesses, such as Bender's Small-Engine Repair Shop, serve both Amish and non-Amish customers, while Miller and Sons Carpentry advertises decks and interior and exterior remodeling. Employing a number of workers from within the community, the Amish-owned Eastern States Metal Roofing is a family company on a much grander scale than the little quilt shops found elsewhere in the region.

The map directing folks to shops in Clymer, Sherman, and Panama suggests an even more important lifestyle difference between the Clymer area community and its neighbors, for it provides phone numbers for many of these family businesses. More conservative Amish groups, such

43

as the Troyer and the Byler Amish, believe that a church that permits telephones in or near Amish dwellings or businesses is conforming to the world in ways it should not. The Swartzentruber Amish generally do not talk on the phone unless they have to, preferring that the owner of the phone place the call. The Clymer-area Amish churches, however, allow members to have telephones, as long as they are not located in the house proper. A note on the map cautions customers to "allow phones to ring at least 10 times when calling the Amish."

The Old Order Amish in the Clymer area are more economically dependent on the surrounding non-Amish community; many Clymer Amish families rely on wages earned from non-Amish employers, while others are engaged in businesses that serve non-Amish needs and advertise beyond community borders. An ad in the *Chautauquan Daily* classified section, for example, reads "Amish craftsman with crew. Available for any and all carpenter work. Also do restorations. Call for estimate." Consequently, in the Clymer settlement, the telephone has become a necessity. "[My husband] lost half a day because [his excavator] broke down and he couldn't call," reported one Amish housewife. Although the Clymer Ordnung forbids church members to install telephones in their homes, many families have installed phones in a nearby shop or a phone booth located just outside the back door. Some church members even have cell phones, bringing the world even closer within the confines of the community.

Interaction with the World

The telephone is only one sign of the way in which increased interaction with the non-Amish world has made Amish life in the Clymer-area different from Amish life in the neighboring Byler, Troyer, and Swartzentruber settlements. Working for non-Amish employers and operating businesses that offer services and goods on a larger scale to the non-Amish world, the Clymer Old Order Amish have more opportunity to interact with people outside the community and the income to fund this interaction. Many in the community go over the border to shop in Pennsylvania, a trip for which they must hire a "taxi"—that is, a non-Amish driver who will charge between twenty and thirty dollars to make the trip. "Taxis" might be hired to take community members to doctor's appointments, to job sites, and even, one Amish girl said, "to the laundromat if it's raining."

The result is a growing interdependence between the Amish and non-Amish. While members of the Amish community become more dependent on their non-Amish neighbors for transportation, more willing to leave their community to accomplish everyday tasks, and even more accepting of social relationships outside the church, Amish dollars support a service economy outside settlement boundaries. This is unlikely to change soon because opportunities to earn more by working away from the farm are tempting, particularly for younger members of the community. By working outside of the Amish community, one woman noted, "newly married families now make more money than established families. Some are earning $700 a week." Nowadays, in the Clymer settlement, married women can be found working for non-Amish employers outside the home, a stark contrast to the Ordnung of their nearby Byler Amish neighbors, who do not even permit unmarried girls to do so.

Higher wages outside the community mean higher wages within the community as well. Because young girls most likely to be called on to teach have other work options, schools in the Clymer-area Amish settlement pay higher salaries for teachers, necessitating either higher tuition or fund-raising.[31] The community holds an auction on the last Saturday in July and a "bow shoot," in which men pay for target practice with bow and arrow. There is also a benefit auction every year to support the special-education class. "We have a dinner to help pay for our school," noted one mother. "That helps keep tuition down, ideally below $100 per family each year." All these events depend on the participation of non-Amish neighbors.

There are further consequences. For example, supported by wages and less tied to the land, the Clymer-area Old Order Amish are able to engage in activities for which there would be less time and acceptance in more conservative communities. For example, writing to *Die Botschaft*, a Clymer scribe noted that one of the community schools had "had a haystack lunch for the grandparents." It was also, she added, "dress-up day for the students and teachers. So we met cowboys and Indians, a nurse, Pippi Long Stockings, and Davey Crocket, to name a few."[32] Adults, too, engage in past times that would be rare for their less progressive counterparts. A Clymer Amish carpenter, whose work takes him regularly to the Chautauqua Institution, is also an artist who sells his paintings locally. "I always liked to draw," he said. "I entered a contest in *Grit* magazine when I was twelve years old and won a three-year scholarship to [an art school] in Connecticut. The guy came out to see me, but my dad wouldn't let me go." In a Christmas letter, his wife wrote that his painting now keeps him busy. "He's been doing a lot of painting this year, on slate and oil on canvas. He still has orders to fill." His paintings, which depict wildlife and rural events, hang in local Amish shops, as well as in non-Amish retail outlets in the area.

The willingness to engage more closely with the world outside the church has also helped to shape the way the Clymer-area Amish educate their children. For example, Amish children living too far away to walk to one of the local one-room Amish schools in the settlement are welcome to ride a local town school bus. The Clymer, Panama, and Sherman school buses pick up Amish children living within their respective boundaries. Not only may Clymer-area Amish children see more of their immediate world than their more conservative counterparts, who must walk to school, but they may also take an end-of-the-year field trip to sites far from home, including Niagara Falls.

Children who get on a bus to go to the Amish schoolhouse may already be quite familiar with non-Amish school ways. According to one Amish mother, children will often begin their education in the public schools. "Generally, kids go to kindergarten," she says, adding, "All of mine did except one." She also recalled a child with diabetes who went to public school until she was old enough to take care of herself. "Otherwise we would have had to educate the [Amish] teacher [to provide medical care]."

This interaction with the public schools is particularly important for children with special needs. While there is a special education class in one of the Clymer Amish schools, most children who need special help go to public school. One mother, whose ten-year-old son was far behind his grade level in reading, decided that he should go to public school rather than simply repeat a grade. In his new special education class, he has four classmates, two of whom are also Amish. When the boy comes home from school, he does his homework before tending to his thriving business raising rabbits.[33]

Greater access to the non-Amish world means young children in the Clymer-area settlement are likely to use English at an earlier age than their counterparts in Troyer, Byler, or Swartzentruber communities. One teenager said the teacher she had in her local Amish school "spoke Amish" to the youngest students in some of the lessons, but most parents try to prepare their youngsters to use English before they start school. "We have a lot of English mixed in with our German," commented one mother. "I spoke a little English to [my children] before they went to school; it [wasn't] so strange for them."

Being Amish Differently

Increased interaction with the world thus has educational and linguistic consequences. These, in turn, further reinforce the economic interdependence between the church and the surrounding non-Amish society. The result is that being Amish in the Clymer-area is different from being Amish in the neighboring Troyer, Swartzentruber, and Byler settlements.

These differences, encoded in the Ordnungs of the various churches, shape how Amish communities interact with the outside world and how they will interact with each other. Two Amish church districts will continue to dien, or fellowship, so long as they perceive their Ordnungs to be essentially the same. And as long as two groups are in fellowship, they will be "back and forth" with each other, meaning that ministers from one will preach at church services in the other, and members of the communities will date and marry across church district lines. However, when the Ordnungs differ significantly, the groups will no longer dien with each other and there will be limited social and ceremonial interaction.

The Troyer and Byler settlements are in fellowship with each other, but neither diens or fellowships with the Clymer settlement. "We would dien," said one Clymer woman, "but they won't." In this woman's eyes, interaction between the groups would only be natural, for "all the Amish are linked. Everything goes back to Menno Simons." Her husband added that "it bothers a lot of us [that there are so many different kinds of Amish]. It all goes down to different Ordnungs." In contrast to their tolerance, however, a minister raised in the Byler church drew an important line. "We would fellowship with a group that keeps the Amish ways. There are some fringe groups that decide we don't do right. They take themselves out of fellowship. I think that we should fellowship with those that have the same core values, that keep the Bann."

The willingness to shun church members who violate the Ordnung is a key "core value" that serves to maintain the church's separation from the world. Nevertheless, although all Old Order Amish groups practice both Bann and Meidung, not all do so in the same way. In the 1950s, the large Old Order Amish community in Holmes County, Ohio, experienced a schism when the majority of church members agreed not to excommunicate and shun members who left the church, as long as they affiliated with another plain, Amish-related community. More conservative-minded Amish withdrew from fellowship, determined to enforce both the Bann and strong Meidung. At the same time, they rejected changes in technology that the majority appeared willing to accept. Similar schisms took place in other large settlements as well.

These differences still mark the churches in Chautauqua and Cattaraugus counties. For the Troyer, Byler, and Swartzentruber Amish, leaving the church for a more progressive group such as the Clymer-area Amish would result in Bann and Meidung. The Swartzentruber Amish continue to observe the strongest Meidung, cutting off all interaction with any who leave after being baptized in the church. On the other hand, someone from the Clymer-area Amish community could move much more easily. As one Clymer woman put it, "If they left to go to a Mennonite or Beachy Amish church, there would be Bann, but if they stay with the Old Order Amish, then there would be no Bann." "The New Order,"[34] she added, "are still like the Old Order. We wouldn't put the Bann on them." In Clymer, the woman added, "The Bann can touch a lot of different topics, and the ministers decide. It [can] be for behavior, lack of [church] attendance—we'd talk to them first about [their attendance]—drinking, if they went to a bar and didn't want to confess." As one man noted, "When we Bann someone out of church, we turn it over to the Lord and let the Lord take over." Emphasizing the "tough love" character of Bann and Meidung, and the hope that it will help those who put themselves out of fellowship with fellow church members, the man added, "It's the last love we can show for them, to try to get them back."

At the same time, unlike in more conservative groups, the Amish in the Clymer area settlement do not practice strong Meidung, and so a church member in Bann can still engage socially with those who have stayed in good standing in the church, albeit with some limitations. "Shunning has changed over the years," the woman cited above commented. "My sister is in Bann. She can eat with us, but I'll fix [put the food on] her plate." Those in Bann will not help out in church members' homes.

By allowing telephones, permitting greater interaction with the non-Amish world, and practicing a weaker Meidung against those who have left, the Clymer-area Amish have, according to more conservative groups, "drifted," or allowed the line between the church and the world to become blurred. In other words, they have failed to guard core values. One Clymer woman is optimistic that the future will bring these diverse groups closer together. Talking about the Byler Amish community, she said, "Now the young folk greet us and are glad to see us. The older ones stiff arm us a bit. The differences [though] are being dissolved a bit." For the Byler, Troyer, and Swartzentruber Amish, however, fellowship is unlikely as long as the Ordnung of the Clymer-area Amish is so different from their own.

Daily Life

Letters to the Amish publications the *Budget*, *Die Botschaft*, and the *Diary* (a monthly Amish magazine) provide friends, relatives, and members of other settlements glimpses into the daily activities in these diverse communities. Writing in May, a *Die Botschaft* scribe from the Conewango Valley reported that "the birds were busy at feeders today. We had our first hummington [*sic*] bird and oriole at hummingbird feeder. A red-breasted grosbeak was at the feeder of sunflowers." Another Conewango Valley resident, writing to the *Diary* in July, noted that "lots of very nice dry hay was put in to the barns but since the rains started hay making has been pretty much at a stand still. Most corn is over knee high and looking nice . . . gardens are doing good and strawberries are over their peak."[35] Seven months later, the same writer related: "We have snow, winter is here finally. . . . Temperature at 12 deg. this morning and forming ice on the ponds. People are getting excited about putting up ice for summer use."[36] In the same issue of the *Diary*, a correspondent from the Mayville/Dewittville settlement noted that "some have put ice away. But lots of ponds got water between the ice on the amount of snow we got last week." A Conewango resident wrote, "Today it was cool and cloudy till mid P.M. it cleared off and the sun shone most of P.M.," adding that a group had gotten together to butcher chickens and that the writer had then gone home to paint windows.

All news fit for an Amish public, good and bad, is shared. Writing to the *Diary* from the Byler settlement in Frewsburg in November, a scribe lamented that "the silos in the area have all been filled. Well the corn is all in the silos that people plan to put in, some of the corn wasn't very good. Only a few farmers have corn to husk as most of the corn was either too late or too poor to husk." More optimistically, in the same issue a scribe from the Troyer community in Little Valley/East Otto noted that "the children are having a two-week break to husk corn, so that is our work at present."[37]

Other letters tell of family and community events. A note from Conewango announced "a quilting . . . for the community teachers, all except for the menfolks. Well they could probably help in with the talking, but hardly with the stitching. I'm looking forward for the occasion." A *Budget* scribe from the Clymer area described a "short and enjoyable evening" one September at a family gathering in Ohio for a fish fry.

There is news of funerals. "A death message came to the area . . . on Monday," wrote one scribe. "I don't know who all went to the funeral on Wednesday."[38] Other letters tell of happier comings and goings. In the first hint of a new Byler settlement, a 2011 letter from New Wilmington, Pennsylvania, to the *Die Botschaft* noted that "there were land shoppers in NY; sounds like they found ebbas [something] close to Jamestown, NY, is that right?" Similarly, a letter to the *Budget* from Gilman, Wisconsin, reported that "on Monday was the auction at Andy P. They are moving to Delevan to start a new settlement." Three years later, in a letter to the *Diary*, a newcomer to the Delevan settlement wrote, "Greetings from Cattaraugus Co. The month of November brought us a sample of all sorts of weather. The first part was fall like and very nice to do outside work, then we got about five inches of snow the week of the 12th." This didn't stop him or his family from settling in, for he added that, despite the snow, they had the first floor on the shop built by the twenty-first.

Although these reports of mundane activities are hardly "news" to non-Amish readers, they provide evidence of the well-being of the group, reinforcing bonds of friendship and ties between churches separated by distance and differing Ordnungs.

Despite these differences, each settlement is tied in multiple ways to other Amish communities in New York and elsewhere, a network of Amish family and church relationships that is sustained through visits, letters, and intermarriage. "We're back and forth with the Richfield Springs settlement," said one Clymer Amish woman, meaning that the communities are in fellowship.[39] The settlement is also "back and forth" with other New York settlements, including the community in Burke (Franklin County) and the settlement in Fillmore (Allegany County). In addition, the group maintains close ties with the parent settlement in Geauga County, Ohio, and has connections to settlements in Mumford, Kentucky. The Troyer and Byler settlements fellowship with the settlements in Fort Plain and Fultonville-Glen in the Mohawk Valley. There are ties as well to the Amish settlement founded in 1999 in the Lowville area and to settlements in Ohio and Pennsylvania. The Swartzentruber community in Delevan is back and forth with Swartzentruber settlements in New York and elsewhere.

The networks have expanded as new settlements have been established elsewhere in western New York. In 1982, for example, the community in Friendship in Allegany County was started by Amish who, like those in the Mayville/Dewittville settlement, came from Lawrence County, Pennsylvania. Fillmore, also in Allegany County, was founded in 1988 by Amish from the LeRaysville–Warren Center area, just over the New York border in Bradford County, Pennsylvania.

These two communities grew quickly. Writing to the *Budget* about the Friendship settlement in October 1982, a settler there reported that "this settlement started in the Spring. There are now 10 families here and 3 widows."[40] By January 2005, the community was considerably larger. Writing to the *Diary*, another community member informed readers that "we have 50 families, 2 church districts (25 families in each) 3 schools, 11 babies born, 4 girls and 7 boys, 1 wedding and 2 funerals. One family moved in this week and one had moved out last December. We have 40 youngie, 14 girls and 26 boys."[41] Ten years later, the community had "58 families, plus 2 widowers, 3 widows, and 3 single girls, 29 young folks, 65 pupils in 3 schools, 3 church districts,"[42] and by January 2016, there were 63 families. In sign of continued healthy growth, the scribe reported "17 births, zero deaths, four baptisms, two marriages."[43]

The Fillmore settlement has been similarly active. In the *Budget* at the end of January 1992, one of the new settlers noted that the settlement had "2 families moving in, making 15 in all, 3 babies, 1 boy and 2 girls; 8 youngfolks, 3 boys & 5 girls; 30 scholars, 14 boys and 16 girls; 9 inbetween [*sic*] scholars and youth, 5 boys and 4 girls. There are 105 persons in all."[44] Only eight years later, another community member wrote that there were "30 households, with the one that just moved in. Reports are 2 more have bought, from Sugargrove, PA. 4 weddings, one boy was from out of state and the couple now lives there. . . . 12 youngfolks [*sic*]."[45] By January 2015, there were four church districts and 75 families.

The Amish population of Allegany County continues to grow. In a repeat of history, members of the older, increasingly crowded communities in Chautauqua and Cattaraugus counties, faced with either changing their Ordnungs to allow new types of economic interaction or moving to maintain an agrarian lifestyle, have chosen keep the lifestyle of their forebears. In 2009, for example, settlers moved from the Conewango Valley to found a new Troyer Amish settlement in the Angelica area of Allegany

County. Noting the event in a September 2009 letter to the *Budget*, the scribe wrote, "Today is truck loading day [for a neighbor]. They will be the first to move to the new settlement. Their marrieds [married children] are also moving along." In 2013, Troyer Amish families also began moving to the Wellsville area, also in Allegany County. By January 2015, the new Wellsville community had "1 church, 13 households, 1 school with 30 pupils, 20 children under school age, 11 young folks . . . a few saw mills and 1 furniture shop, 1 produce grower, and 1 leather shop."[46] Only a year later, the community had sixteen families. Western New York continues to attract new Amish settlement, and the pattern of life is changing as different kinds of Amish arrive. In 2012, the Pulteney/Hammondsport region of Steuben County, just to the east of Allegany, saw the arrival of Nebraska Amish from Pennsylvania.[47] Sometimes known as "white toppers" because their buggies have white canvas tops and sides, the Nebraska Amish are, like the Byler, Troyer, and Swartzentruber Amish, very conservative. The Nebraska settlement joined Amish communities established earlier in the Jasper/Woodhull region (1983) by Amish with roots in Geauga County, Ohio; in the Addison area (1990) by Amish with ties to Lancaster County, Pennsylvania; and in Prattsburgh (1979) by Swiss Amish. North of Allegany County in Livingston County, Swiss Amish established a settlement in the Mt. Morris region in 2010, and Troyer Amish established a new community in the Dansville region in 2011.

New settlements build on bonds already established through family ties, marriage, church relationships, and movement from one community to another can strengthen the connections. A scribe from the Conewango Valley, wrote in May 2006 to *Die Botschaft* that a local family had "loaded truck a week ago today and headed for Fillmore area to make that their home." In 2006, shortly after Amish arrived from Union City, Pennsylvania, to settle in the Little Valley area of Cattaraugus County, they were already on the path of New York visiting. Writing to the *Diary* in August 2006, a Little Valley settler noted that visitors from Lowville had spent the weekend in the area while others from Pennsylvania had passed through on their way to a funeral in Conewango Valley. Writing from the Dansville settlement in Livingston County, the scribe noted that one elderly church member had gone to visit his daughter in Conewango "since he couldn't work in his shop anyways" due to a sore foot. She also noted that her mother had gone to a wedding in the Conewango Valley and would visit her sister and granddaughter.[48]

The Amish world has changed considerably since the first families came to Conewango in 1949. Amish groups in this region suggest the diversity of the Amish life characteristic of New York's Amish communities. At the same time, New York Amish settlement in Chautauqua, Cattaraugus, and surrounding counties demonstrates the patterns of interconnectedness that typify Amish settlement across the state.

3

St. Lawrence County's Swartzentruber Amish

The Plainest of the Plain People

> We don't like to change. When you change, that's when you get into trouble.
> —A Swartzentruber Amish minister, 2009

In a November 1974 letter to a friend, one Amish man wrote about "a new settlement . . . starting in Canton, NY by some of the Holmes-Wayne Swartzentruber people." "Must be they like Canton," he joked, noting that the Swartzentruber Amish had earlier established a settlement in Canton, Minnesota. The man commented further that he would "watch the Budget a bit, but . . . [that] Nov. '74 would go down as the founding date," and he added that "the one family—the father comes from Conewango Valley, NY but joined the Swartzentruber church in Ohio for his wife."[1]

Like other Amish settlers, the Swartzentruber Amish families who began to arrive in New York State in 1974 came because there was affordable land available. Land in Ohio "was too expensive. It was hard to make a living just with farming," said one Swartzentruber woman, explaining her family's decision to move to St. Lawrence County. As another put it, "They're moving out of Ohio. It's so full there, and land is about as cheap here in New York as anywhere."[2] According to George Field, a cooperative extension agent in St. Lawrence County, "One day . . . they arrived by Greyhound Bus and walked into my office and wanted me to drive them over to DePeyster to look at some farms. That was how they got their start."[3]

Although the availability of cheap farmland was a key factor in their decision to move to New York, many Swartzentruber families, like the Troyer families who moved to the Conewango Valley, were also motivated by the desire to raise their children in a homogeneous community, away from the influence of different, often more progressive Amish groups. As one Swartzentruber woman recalled, "It was so crowded in Ohio, and there were so many different kinds of people." New York offered space for those who "don't want to move too close to the others."[4] Finally, like it did for the Troyer Amish who settled in the Conewango Valley, the move allowed the Swartzentruber Amish newcomers to distance themselves from the larger Ohio Old Order community and a history of conflict and schism.

With large families, often with as many as fifteen children, the Swartzentruber Amish are among the fastest-growing groups in North America, and the new settlement expanded quickly. Only thirty years after the first Swartzentruber families moved into the Empire State, the settlement in St. Lawrence County had more than 100 families and 9 church districts.[5] By 2014, there were over 270 families, with 50 having moved into the area in the past year.

The Swartzentruber Amish

The ultraconservative Swartzentruber Amish originated in a schism that occurred in the Holmes County, Ohio, Old Order Amish community between 1913 and 1917. The issue was whether to excommunicate and shun those who left the church in which they had been baptized to join another congregation that did not *dien*, or fellowship, with the first one. More conservative church members argued that leaving the church in this way was breaking the baptismal vow and that those who did so had to be placed in *Bann*. However, others thought that this was unnecessary as long as those who left joined another plain Amish or Mennonite church. In 1913, bishops visiting from Indiana and Illinois attempted to restore unity by proposing that members who wished to leave the church should be admonished not to do so. The visiting bishops asserted that, if the member still wished to join another congregation, then church members should feel that they had done their duty and leave matters to the church districts involved and to God. Finally, the bishops agreed that, if a church member were excommunicated by his former church and then taken out of the *Bann* "in a scriptural way" by his current church, then the original *Bann* should be removed and shunning should cease.[6]

Most of the Old Order Amish church members in Holmes County accepted the recommendations of the visiting bishops, but Bishop Sam Yoder, outspoken leader of the conservative faction, did not. In an

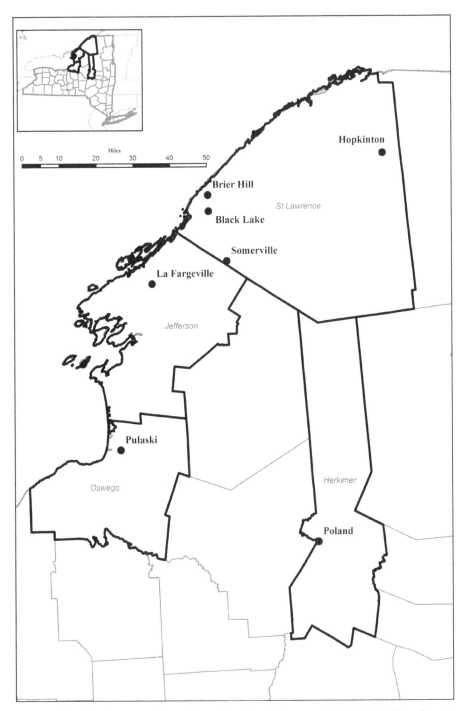

Map 3.1. The first Swartzentruber settlement in New York was established in 1974, in the area around the village of Heuvelton in St. Lawrence County. Since then, the Swartzentruber Amish have started a number of new settlements in the state.

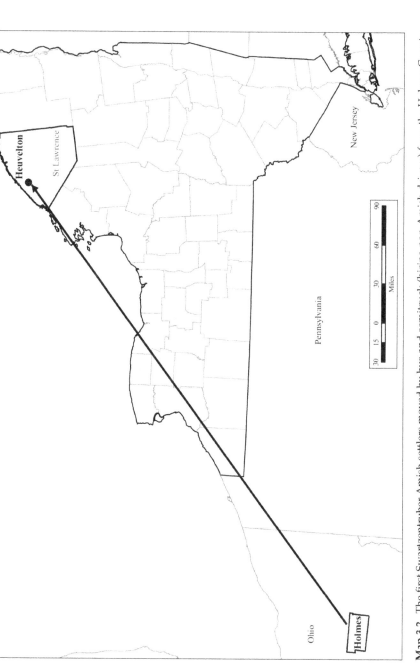

Map 3.2. The first Swartzentruber Amish settlers moved by bus and semitruck (hiring non-Amish drivers) from the Holmes County region of Ohio to upstate New York.

attempt to ease the continued tension, the Holmes County Amish congregations adopted guidelines designed to appease the Yoder group, including restrictions on the length of men's hair and on clothing styles. More important, the church leaders agreed that church members should not change congregations and that young people should marry within their own districts unless they had first met with leaders of both congregations to ensure that all were in agreement. This seemed to resolve the conflicts, and so the two church districts that looked to Sam Yoder for leadership agreed to fellowship with the other Old Order congregations. Nevertheless, the peace did not hold, and by 1917 the schism between Yoder's group and the Old Order Amish churches was complete.[7]

Although an outsider might not have noticed much change in daily life, for the Amish the schism caused a profound change in the settlement. From this point on, the different factions ceased to worship together, a divide that separated neighbor from neighbor and split families. No longer did all share in such important events as baptism, for ministers from one group could not preach at the services held by the other. Social relationships were altered because a young person from one side of the split could not marry someone from the other.

Only two years later, the Yoder faction again faced conflict when a member of the Geauga County, Ohio, Old Order Amish settlement confessed to having had sexual relations with Sam's daughter. When Sam did not place his daughter under the Bann, approximately half the families in the Yoder group left and, under the leadership of Minister Dan Wengerd, formed a separate group. In 1922, ministers from the Dan Wengerd group met with Old Order ministers to try to resolve differences between all the Holmes County factions. They invited Sam Yoder and his ministers to join them, but they did not attend.[8] Unlike the Dan Wengerd faction, the Sam Yoder group never reconciled with their Old Order Amish counterparts.[9]

In 1931, the Sam Yoder group experienced another schism when bishops Jacob J. Stutzman and Eli A. Troyer disagreed with Bishop Sam Yoder, again over discipline within the church. Their breakaway faction, known first as the "Stutzman Gmay," eventually became known as "Troyer Amish."[10] Sam Yoder died not long after this schism. As the Dublin, Ohio, entry in the May 5, 1932, issue of the *Budget* reported,

The death angel has again been in our midst and called away bishop Samuel E. Yoder. He was born in Holmes Co., Ohio, May 28, 1872 and died at his home near Maysville, O. April 25, 1932 at the age of 59 years, 10 months and 27 days. He was failing in health the last few years with high blood pressure and on Monday morning, April 25th, he had a stroke of paralysis and died the following night. He leaves to mourn his departure, 3 daughters and 1 son, namely Mary, wife of John N. Petersheim, who lives at home; Katy, wife of Andy J. Miller, who lives about one-half mile from the home; Lovina, wife of Yost N. Hershberger of near Wilmot, and Henry at home. He also leaves 20 grandchildren, 5 brothers, and 1 sister. Two wives and a few of his children preceded him in death.

Perhaps reflecting how contentious a figure Bishop Sam Yoder had been in Holmes County, a rumor spread after his death that he had committed suicide by hanging himself in a chicken coop. Nearly forty years later, John Y. Schlabach, deacon of one of the largest Old Order church districts in Holmes County, felt compelled to dictate a rebuttal asserting that Yoder had, in fact, died of natural causes. Typed and printed for wide distribution, Schlabach's statement read:

> While a rumor is circulating about Bishop Sam E. Yoder's death, I would like to state the following: About nine o'clock in the morning his [Yoder's] grandchild found him in the henhouse, sick with a stroke; then he was carried to the house and a doctor was fetched who said he is seriously ill with a stroke; then about a little after midnight on the first day of his illness he died on April 25, 1932 just like other people also die. John E. Yoder was present when his brother Bishop Sam E. Yoder died.[11]

Following Yoder's death, each of the two Sam Yoder church districts was led by a bishop surnamed Swartzentruber, and so the Sam Yoder group soon became known as Swartzentruber Amish. Over time, various families from other regions moved to Ohio to join the Swartzentruber church, many attracted by the more conservative Ordnung that was guiding Swartzentruber practice. By 1936 there were three Swartzentruber church districts and by 1957, five, with approximately two hundred families. There are now Swartzentruber settlements in fourteen states and one Canadian province.

Further Division

A century after Sam Yoder and his followers ceased to fellowship with their Old Order Amish neighbors, the divide between the descendants of each faction has only widened. According to the Amish historian

David Luthy, the Old Order Amish in Holmes and Wayne counties make fun of the long hair and untrimmed beards of Swartzentruber men and boys, calling them *gnudle Woola*, after the kinks found in sheep's wool before shearing.

For their part, although the Swartzentruber Amish recognize their Old Order Amish counterparts as different from the "English," or non-Amish, they also see them as "not like Swartzentrubers." "I think we're more in the Amish side [in comparison to more progressive Amish groups]. They [those other Amish] are strange or different," commented one young Swartzentruber mother. Another Swartzentruber woman classified Old Order Amish friends in Holmes County, Ohio, as *sotleit*, or "others," noting that "they're still Amish because they don't drive cars. Those that drive cars are Mennonites." Commenting on a trip to a wedding in an Iowa Old Order Amish community, an elderly Swartzentruber man expressed some amazement about the service: "They had just about the same scripture we do, and they sang the same songs, but faster. I could still understand them. They started later (about 10 a.m.), but they finished church at the same time." He added that his father, who had moved the family from Iowa to join Sam Yoder's group, would have found it familiar. "[It was] just about like we have it only faster."

Further complicating the widening cultural gulf between the Swartzentruber Amish and their Old Order counterparts have been internal conflicts that have caused schism in the Swartzentruber world. In the early 1980s, for example, disagreement over Bann and Meidung led several church districts in Minnesota, Tennessee, and Ohio to stop fellowshipping with Swartzentruber church districts elsewhere. The breakaway faction, today known as the *Jeck Jecky Leit*, or Jeck Jecky people, continues to fellowship with Nebraska Amish church districts that are in the Big Valley area of Pennsylvania and elsewhere.[12]

Even more devastating to Swartzentruber unity was the conflict that developed in the early 1990s over what many in the group saw as unruly and inappropriate behavior among Swartzentruber young folk, particularly in the Ohio church districts. The issue came to a head when several young Swartzentruber men disturbed a Swartzentruber minister by playing loud music on a radio. Having the radio was a violation of the Ordnung, and playing it only made the infraction worse. When the minister tried to chastise the young men, they struck him and fled.[13]

This incident caused uproar in the Swartzentruber world. At first, the minister claimed not to have recognized the boys, but, when a passing milk truck driver identified them, the minister agreed with him. Later, when one of the boys attempted to join church, the minister refused to baptize him unless he made confession. Denying his involvement, the boy refused to do so. At that point, another young man, already a church member, said that he had been one of the group and that the other boy had not, and he offered to put himself under the Bann. The minister refused to accept this second man's confession, and his recommendation that both young men be excluded from the church threatened to divide the Swartzentruber community.[14]

In the following months, the Swartzentrubers made a number of attempts to resolve the conflict, but neither side was willing to give in. While one faction feared that leniency would encourage wild behavior among the youth and therefore supported the hard line taken by the minister, the other was concerned about what appeared to be an overly strict and intolerant application of the Bann. Finally, under the leadership of Joe Troyer, one of the oldest of the Holmes County Swartzentruber bishops, the majority of the bishops agreed that it was "unscriptural to be so strong in one's thinking."[15] Accordingly, the one boy was baptized and the other was no longer shunned.

In response to this decision, two bishops, Eli Hershberger and Moses (called "Mose" or "Mosey") M. Miller, withdrew from fellowship with the others. As one Amish observer put it, "They felt the other bishop has taken two liars into the church." Other bishops, notably Isaac Keim and Andy Weaver from Lodi, Ohio, joined Hershberger and Miller, and the Swartzentruber churches across North America divided as church members took sides.[16] The larger faction became known as the "Joe Troyer church," or simply "Joe church."[17] The smaller, dissenting group, under the leadership of Moses Miller, became widely known as the Mosey Mosies because there was more than one "Moses" in a position of leadership.

In 1998, the Mose Miller church districts underwent another schism, this time in response to a conflict between the Lodi bishops Andy Weaver and Isaac Keim. While Bishop Mose Miller sided with Bishop Isaac Keim, other leaders took Bishop Andy Weaver's part, and the church membership divided accordingly, resulting in three nonfellowshipping Swartzentruber groups: the Joe Troyer churches, the Mose Miller/Isaac Keim churches, and the Andy Weaver churches.

Commenting on those involved in the Mose Miller/Andy Weaver schism, a member of a Joe Troyer congregation suggested, "There'll be a split again in a year or two. They could have stopped it [the division]. Some folks just can't get along." She was right about further dissension. By 2011, following the death of elderly bishop Mose Miller, conflict had split the Mose Miller/Isaac Keim faction. In New York, the Isaac Keim faction is known locally as the Dan Yoder church, while the Mose Miller faction is known as the Pete Hershberger church, indicating the local bishops leading each group. One woman, a member of the Hershberger/ Mose Miller faction, suggested that the conflict had been "brewing for years. . . . The other group wants more things. Dan Yoder is crowding the fence [becoming more progressive and wanting change]." She went on to claim that Bishop Isaac Keim "had English shoes and boots" and that, after the death of Bishop Mose Miller, these had become "OK."[18] Currently, the Pete Hershberger faction and the Dan Yoder faction no longer fellowship with each other, a split that, like earlier schisms, has divided families. This saddened one member of the community who said, "They wouldn't have acted like that if the old bishops were still here." The Swartzentruber settlement in the Heuvelton area of St. Lawrence County reflects these divisions. Originally home to a single congregation, seven of its fourteen church districts are now with the Andy Weaver church, two are with the Pete Hershberger/Mose Miller group, one is with the Dan Yoder/Isaac Keim faction, and four are with the Joe Troyer church.[19] When starting new settlements, the different church groups do not mix. Families moving into the Brier Hill/Black Lake area extension of the original settlement have been from the Andy Weaver group. In 2004, Swartzentruber Amish from the Mose Miller/Isaac Keim group started a second Swartzentruber settlement in the Hopkinton area, along the border between St. Lawrence and Franklin counties. As a result of church schism, this settlement now has one Yoder/Keim district and a Joe Troyer church district.[20] In 2005, Andy Weaver Swartzentruber Amish started a settlement in the Lafargeville area between St. Lawrence and Jefferson counties. In 2006, another Miller/Keim church, now with the Hershberger/Miller group, was established in the vicinity of Pulaski, in Oswego County, and Joe Troyer Swartzentrubers have started a settlement in Poland, in Herkimer County. In summer 2007, several Joe Troyer Swartzentruber families left the Heuvelton area to begin a new settlement in Presque Isle, Maine. Not long afterward, Andy Weaver Swartzentrubers began a new settlement in Sherman, Maine. In 2011, Andy Weaver Swartzentrubers also began a new settlement in Delevan, New York, and in 2013, one in Somerville, on the border between

St. Lawrence and Jefferson counties. As of fall 2016, several Andy Weaver Swartzentruber families from the Heuvelton area have bought land in Westport in Essex County and are preparing to move.

The Swartzentruber Ordnungs

Once a division occurs, each separate affiliation, or group of fellowshipping church districts, begins to develop in different ways in response to challenges it encounters—or at least others perceive it to be developing differently. For example, a bishop in the Andy Weaver church noted that the Jeck Jecky group had changed after the 1983 division. They "went further," he asserted, "They wanted more modernisms. There's always some wanting more modernisms." Implicitly commenting on change in other groups, an Andy Weaver Swartzentruber woman asserted that "I think we should stay like we're raised [and] keep things the same as we're taught when we're young." But this has not happened, and small changes begin to divide the groups.[21]

Today, the different Swartzentruber groups do not dien with each other; there is no intermarriage between the groups, and ministers of one faction will not preach at religious gatherings of the others. Of the four Swartzentruber groups that have evolved since 1990, the largest, the Joe Troyer church, may also be said to be the "highest," or most progressive, while the Andy Weaver church is, perhaps, the least. The Dan Yoder/Isaac Keim and Peter Hershberger/Mose Miller groups are in between, with the Yoder group being somewhat "higher," or more progressive, than the Hershberger group. Nevertheless, church lines cut across family relationships, and so there continues to be considerable interaction between the different factions. For example, having just received a wedding invitation from her husband's brother, who is a member of a Joe Troyer church district, a member of a Hershberger congregation commented that the Joe Troyer group was "everywhere. They're about the biggest church, though old Joe is dead." She went on to note that her father is a member of an Andy Weaver congregation. But, she added, "That's not what we people call them." Asked what Swartzentrubers said when they talked about each other, she replied "Oh, we just say 'our church' and 'their church.'"

The various Swartzentruber churches continue to be governed by Ordnungs that are virtually identical across affiliation boundaries, with differences evident only in small things. For example, the Joe Troyer and Dan Yoder/Isaac Keim groups have adopted LED flashlights and flashlights that can be worn on the head, while the Pete Hershberger/ Mose Miller group and the Andy Weaver group have not. One member of the Yoder faction thinks this will change. As she said to her sister, a member of the Andy Weaver group, "Sometime you'll all be using the LED lights because they're not making [the other kind] anymore." Her sister just shook her head.

Still, unless someone is carrying an LED flashlight, it's difficult to say which church he or she might be in. The groups maintain nearly identical dress patterns, although members of one group often claim that dress standards in the others are changing. Asked how one could tell groups apart, two women in an Andy Weaver congregation suggested that the women in the Joe Troyer church made their caps with narrower pleats in the back. They also asserted that capes were wider and dresses were shorter in the Joe Troyer group. Nevertheless, another member of the Andy Weaver group admitted that "people that we don't know, we have to ask [what group they're with]. In a funeral where people come from all over, we have to ask."[22]

Regardless of church affiliation, Swartzentruber homes follow the same general architectural design, with a large living room, kitchen, pantry, and bedroom on the first floor, and four large bedrooms on the second. There is no upholstered furniture, nor is there carpeting or linoleum. Hardwood floors are never varnished; instead they are regularly coated with linseed oil. Unlike many of their more progressive Old Order brethren, none of the Swartzentruber Amish factions use pressurized gas or propane lanterns, favoring oil or kerosene lamps instead, nor do they have indoor plumbing. Clothes are washed in wringer washers powered by small gas motors. They are hung to dry.

All the Swartzentruber Amish drive black buggies without windshields, rear windows, mirrors, or lights, and none will use the slow-moving-vehicle triangle. Gray reflecting tape outlining the back of the buggy and a lantern hanging from the rear left side of the buggy provide the only warning to motorists that there is a horse-drawn carriage on the road.[23] Further, the Swartzentruber Amish will ride in automobiles only in an emergency or when there is no bus or taxi service available and the distance is impractical for horse and buggy. While all will use telephones in an emergency, they prefer to ask a neighbor to make the call for them. Keeping "slow time," many Swartzentruber Amish do not move their clocks ahead when daylight savings time starts, although some will keep "half fast" time and set their clocks half way in between.

Figure 3.1. Home for a Swartzentruber family. Governed by the Ordnung, the interior of a Swartzentruber home is plain but warm, with plenty of room to welcome family and guests. The quilt in frame is covered with a sheet to keep it clean when it is not being worked on. Photo by author.

The four Swartzentruber groups have also maintained the same worship practices. Regardless of affiliation, for example, the dinner served after the church service is always bean soup, bread, beets, and pickles. Seated at tables grouped by gender and age, members of the congregation each have a spoon and a fork with which to help themselves from the large bowl of soup and dishes of pickles and beets that are placed in the middle of each table. Finally, in all Swartzentruber church districts, farming remains the principal source of income, the one deemed most conducive to leading a Christian life. Farming, a Swartzentruber dairy farmer notes, is "a good way to keep the boys out of trouble. And I can be at home with my work. I want my boys to grow up to be farmers." As a mother in the same community put it, "It's easier to teach [children] on a farm."

Ordnungs do permit Swartzentruber Amish men to operate small, home-based businesses, and outsiders can easily find Swartzentruber furniture shops, harness makers, sawmills, or window makers. Nevertheless, if the demands of the business are such that they impinge on one's duties in the home or to the church, church members will be asked to curtail their activities. One successful Swartzentruber furniture maker, faced with a backlog of orders and the need either to hire help from outside the family or to cut back, removed the sign advertising "Chairs for Sale" and replaced it with one that said "Worms 3 Cents," a boost to his young son's new business. In the home-based Swartzentruber shops, small diesel engines turn crankshafts connected to belt power to run saws, sanders, and other machinery. Firmly holding the line against technological change, none of the Swartzentruber Ordnungs permit air or hydraulic power. In response to the suggestion of an English visitor that some new things could save them time, one Swartzentruber couple was dumbfounded. "Save time for what?" the man asked, adding, "We can do without." "What would the children do if there weren't chores?" asked his wife. Batteries are used for flashlights, but, as noted above, only in the Troyer and Yoder factions are LED lights allowed. These similarities link the different Swartzentruber communities, a bond strengthened by restrictions all the conservative Swartzentruber Ordnungs place on interaction with the non-Amish world. Reinforcing an agrarian lifestyle that emphasizes family and tradition, these restrictions enable the Swartzentruber Amish to preserve many practices lost by more progressive groups.

Swartzentruber Amish raise their children with as little exposure to society outside their own community as possible. Infants and toddlers may go along on trips to town or out of state, but schoolchildren rarely travel, and so, unless there is a medical emergency, a child may be fourteen or fifteen and finished with school before he or she again ventures into a nearby town.

The Swartzentruber Amish also scrutinize carefully any books and magazines that come into the home, to ensure that children don't see or read material their parents consider inappropriate. Magazines such as *Family Life* or *Young Companion*, which are published by the more progressive Old Order Amish and are commonly found in Old Order homes, are off-limits to the Swartzentrubers.[24] Although Swartzentruber mothers enjoy having brightly illustrated calendars, they examine the pictures before hanging them up so no offensive images come into the home or the local Amish school. One woman was especially taken by the bright flowers on the front of a calendar that a non-Amish friend had given her. With her daughters looking over her shoulder, she flipped through the pages to see the pictures for each month. January, offering a photo of Rockefeller Center Plaza taken over the shoulder of the giant statue of Prometheus, was a disappointment. Although the photo only showed the back of the shoulders and head of the statue, it was, to the woman's mind, clearly inappropriate. "This can go," she said, ripping it off after checking to make sure that the picture was indeed printed on the back of the previous month's calendar and could be safely discarded. Perusing the rest of the pictures, she was delighted with the images of flowers and mountains. Only when July showed a picture of the Statue of Liberty did she again stop. "This will have to go too," she said, ripping out the picture, unacceptable for its portrayal of the human form.

Religious material from non-Amish sources can be especially suspect, for it might lead one to begin exploring the Bible on one's own, challenging church and family authority. One father thanked a non-Amish neighbor for his gift of a children's illustrated Sunday School Bible storybook, but, when the neighbor had left, he threw the book into the fire. His children would hear the scripture read from the family Bible itself, without the pictures.

In school, children are similarly protected from potentially dangerous ideas. In their eight years of formal education, they learn English reading and spelling, arithmetic, and German reading and spelling, a more limited curriculum than that of schools in more progressive communities. Further, the children are expected simply to do their best, which is considered far more important than getting good scores. A good Swartzentruber "scholar," the term the Swartzentruber Amish use to refer to schoolchildren, will learn to get along with others, to help when help is needed, and to be obedient.[25]

Daily Life in Swartzentruber Communities

For the Swartzentruber Amish, daily life is grounded in the seasons, and family activities reinforce family and community bonds. Within the family, men work the fields and take care of the livestock; women sew clothes, garden, cook meals, and preserve the harvest to feed the family through the winter; children do chores, boys generally helping their fathers and girls their mothers, but all working where they are needed.

When there is a task too large for the single family, they expect help from friends and neighbors. "Frolics," or parties where everyone comes to help accomplish some task, punctuate the year, and offer opportunity for fun and social interaction. Commenting on the work involved in getting the corn in, one farmer noted that "several guys go down the rows with a small knife that will slice the corn from the stalk. Then they throw it in the wagon." Asked if anyone ever got hit by an ear of corn, he laughed. "Not usually by accident." There are frolics to fill the silos, to butcher pigs when the weather turns cold, to build houses or barns when spring arrives, and to clean the schoolhouse before the new term starts. An unmarried woman living alone invited her nephews to a frolic to fill her woodshed.

Frolics allow Swartzentruber families to accomplish large tasks, but they bring obligations. One woman noted that her brother-in-law had told them that they didn't need to come to his silo raising frolic because the brother-in-law hadn't been able to help them move into their new home. Still, she thought her husband would go over to help. Similarly, a farmer, invited to a neighbor's frolic to build a barn, was told that he didn't actually have to show up because the fellow building the barn had been borrowing the farmer's horses. Still the barn builder hadn't wanted to leave the farmer out since it was a neighborhood frolic. Already indebted to the farmer, this was the barn builder's way of paying him back. A farmer who can't go himself to a neighborhood frolic will send a son or two or even his hired hand.

Frolics involve women's work as well as men. For example, preserving home-butchered beef and pork by canning or smoking it is a labor-intensive process that begins with butchering. Generally, families—either groups of neighbors or parents with married children—take turns to help each other. While men do the actual slaughtering and heavy lifting, women cut up slabs of meat into smaller chunks, reserving less desirable portions for grinding into sausage. Later, they all work together to mix the ground meat and season it, and then, while one person holds the sausage casings, another cranks the machine to fill them. Throughout, older girls serve coffee and schnitz pies to the workers while younger children bring in wood, first to keep the kettle boiling and then to smoke the finished sausages.[26] Later, the family will work together to render the fat, mix it with lye and borax, and, much later, grate the dried bricks of soap to make powdered laundry detergent.

Data collected by Victor Stoltzfus nearly fifty years ago, at a time when most Amish communities were still largely agrarian, suggested that

Figure 3.2. Washing machines for sale at a Swartzentruber Amish auction. Appliances, like all home furnishings, are governed by the Ordnung. Photo by author.

Amish farmers might spend as much as thirty days a year in such labor exchanges. Among the Swartzentruber Amish, this pattern has changed little.[27]

Swartzentruber children are part of the community from birth, which, ideally for the family, occurs at home with the mother's own mother and, perhaps, her mother-in-law in attendance.[28] Like most other Amish groups, the Swartzentruber Amish do not have insurance and so avoid, if possible, incurring major medical expenses. If necessary, a Swartzentruber woman will go to the hospital to have her baby, but she hopes that she won't have to. She will likely have had at least one checkup before giving birth, which makes getting the birth certificate easier. Only if it appears that there might be problems (such as *Rh* incompatibility) will parents make arrangements to have a doctor in attendance or to give birth in a hospital.

Pregnancy and childbirth are never discussed in the presence of children and particularly not in front of young, unmarried girls. When it is time for mothers to deliver, children who are very young will likely spend some time with their cousins or neighbors and then simply arrive home to find a new brother or sister. A new baby is immediately incorporated into family life, taken to church as soon after its birth as weather and health permit and held by all, from the youngest siblings to the oldest church members. The Swartzentruber Amish expect even the youngest children to participate with older siblings and adults in family and community life. By age five, children are doing chores and contributing to the well-being of the family.

Swartzentruber children begin school around age six or seven and attend through the eighth grade. It is their first foray alone into the world outside the family home, but they are never away from the influence of the Ordnung. Teachers are expected to reinforce the teachings of parents and church. The practices of rote memorization and drill in Swartzentruber schools downplay diversity, reinforce authority, and ensure that schoolwork gets done but does not usurp the important lessons—how to manage a farm and a household, how to raise children, how to be responsible and work hard—which are learned at home, where children participate in work, play, and ceremony to the extent of their abilities.

From the time children leave school, at the end of the eighth grade, until they reach the age of seventeen, they are home, working with their parents and siblings. They may be hired to do chores at a neighboring Amish farm where there are no "big boys" or "big girls" to help and so, in that way, continue their education in the things that count in the Swartzentruber world. Children under twenty-one are considered minors in Swartzentruber eyes, and so their wages are paid to the parents, who are, of course, responsible for all their expenses. At age twenty-one, even if a person is still living at home, he or she will begin paying the costs of room, board, clothing, and health care.

At age seventeen, Swartzentruber boys and girls join the "youngie," or young folk, and in the context of this peer group, begin an independent social life. On Sunday evenings, there will be singings to go to, and eventually, a young person will begin dating.[29] For the Swartzentruber Amish, dating is part of a process of finding one's life partner; dating more than one person at the same time or having many short-lived relationships is frowned on. Bundling, or "bed courtship," rejected by many Old Order Amish, is the norm among most of the Swartzentruber communities, including all those in New York. Late on a Sunday night, following the singing, a dating couple will go to the girl's home and, in the darkness of the sleeping household, up to her bedroom.[30] Once there, the girl will remove her outer dress, keeping on the under or "courting dress," which is never "sheer, low cut, or otherwise suggestive."[31] "Underdresses can be almost any color, but not white, or pink or yellow," said one Swartzentruber woman. "Girls just make it [so] it's new and not worn out."[32] The couple will then lie on the bed together and talk. Although they may kiss, the couple is expected to refrain from other sexual activity.[33] To enliven the dating season (and, perhaps, to help ensure that the couple do not engage in forbidden sexual activity), friends of the young man and sisters of the young lady—members of the young folk but not yet dating—will make every effort to "drop in" on the couple. But they must do so quietly so that they don't wake the family.

In addition to having dates following the Sunday singings, a young Swartzentruber couple will often write to each other. Although this is especially important when one lives far away or in another settlement from the other and dates are infrequent, even those who are close neighbors send notes, and young folks are often teased about how quick they are to bring in the mail. Shortly after joining the young folk, one young girl made sure to purchase pens that wrote in different colors so that she'd be ready to carry on a lively correspondence when she started to date.

Although it is often common knowledge when a boy and girl are dating, couples try to keep it quiet. If both have been baptized and at least one of the two is twenty-one years old, then there will be widespread speculation about when they will "be published," or have their engagement announced. One Swartzentruber woman writing to a friend about her niece's wedding predicted, "One more [niece] to go I expect. She isn't published *Yet*! And I hope that's the last one of my nieces for this winter."[34]

For the Swartzentruber Amish, wedding season lasts from the end of the harvesting in the fall to the beginning of spring planting. It is a practical span of time, a period in which there is less work to do on the farm and cooler temperatures for preserving large amounts of cooked food. The engagement is announced at the end of the Sunday service, and the wedding generally takes place on a Thursday eleven days later.

Swartzentruber neighbors from other church districts, who would not have been at the church service when the wedding plans were announced, nevertheless have their own means of finding out when a couple has gotten engaged. "I knew Jacob and Susie were published," said one woman laughing. "Barbara saw them go by in a buggy Sunday morning about the time church let out." As the woman's daughter explained, "If you see a[n] [unmarried] couple riding together in the daytime, you know something is up."

Weddings are a time for joke playing, and the fun begins on the Sunday when the couple's friends think they are likely to be published. The boy and girl try to make a quick getaway once their wedding plans are made public, and their friends try just as hard to ensure that they will not get away easily. One woman recalled that the unmarried girls always took turns going first as they took their seats on the bench for church. She laughed as she recounted how, in order to keep the upcoming announcement of her marriage secret, she had to go in first, even though that meant that she would be sitting by the wall and would have a hard time getting out quickly. Her husband added that his married cousin, to whom he had confided his plans, had told him he could use the cousin's horse if he needed to. It was a good thing, he said smiling, describing how the other boys, suspecting something was up, had put the harness on backward on his own horse. If the couple can't be teased right after church, then they may be in for more "fun" later. According to one married woman, "One trick is to put an onion under the girl's bed the night she is published." Laughing at the thought of how the onion smell would affect the bundling couple, she added, "the stronger the onion, the better."

In contrast to wedding celebrations in more progressive Amish communities, which may involve caterers, rented dishes, and napkins professionally printed with the couple's names, Swartzentruber weddings are do-it-yourself affairs that bring together family and friends to do the cooking and prepare the house. While her father and brothers put up temporary walls on the family porch to make room for the long tables that would accommodate the two hundred to three hundred wedding guests, one bride-to-be ironed her new wedding dress, which was the traditional dark blue color. Her sister, married to the brother of the groom-to-be, was sewing nearby. "How does it look?" asked the bride. "Good enough for who it's for," answered her sister. The bride smiled sagely to the others in the room. "She's just jealous."

"Well my brother decided to get married, so we will be eating chicken next week," was how one Amish man announced an upcoming wedding in his district. The Swartzentrubers call weddings *Hinglefleisch* frolics, or "chicken parties," a reference to how much chicken is eaten. The wedding begins around 9:00 a.m. and takes place at a neighbor's house. Often the mother of the bride is not there to see the ceremony because she's busy supervising the cooks—female friends and relatives who are invited to help prepare the meal. The bride's family will serve two meals, a large noon meal following the wedding and supper that night. Chicken butchered the day before has to be first boiled, and then rolled in butter and coated in crumbs before being baked. Meanwhile potatoes must be mashed, and a salad made. Cakes and pies for the noon meal and jelly rolls for the supper are prepared several days before the wedding. The bride and her family set the table long before the day of the wedding, covering the plates with a white cloth to keep them clean. The bride's mother puts the prettiest bowls and water glasses on the corner table, where the newlyweds sit, flanked by their "side sitters." The side sitters, two girls and two boys, are the Amish equivalent of the bridesmaids and groom's men, and serve as the couple's witnesses. When they choose their wedding party, the Amish couple will often try to match up their unmarried friends. For example, the bride's sister might be pared with the groom's cousin from another state. Couples try to keep secret the identity of the side sitters, and much guessing goes on about who will be chosen when a couple is published.

It may take several seatings to get everyone fed. The cooks eat first, at about 10:30 a.m., then clean up after themselves and refill the serving bowls. They will have been working since well before dawn, and the meal comes as a welcome break. Then, when folks arrive at the house after church, they are seated in groups according to gender and age—men in one room, women in the other, older before younger—and table waiters, girlfriends and female relatives asked by the bride to help out, begin to serve the meal. Bowls of fruit and vases of celery decorate the tables, and there are plates of sliced homemade bread. Dishes go by loaded with cheese slices, chicken, gravy, mashed potatoes, stuffing, and salad. The table waiters keep water glasses filled and offer coffee. For the supper, the cooks prepare meatloaf and turn the leftover mashed potatoes into potato pancakes.

After the noon meal, while the cooks wash dishes, the men sing. "It gives them something to do," commented one woman. By midafternoon, the cooks are snacking, the men are singing, and the newlyweds, their side sitters, and assorted young people are up in the bride's bedroom to unwrap wedding gifts.

There are jokes to be played at wedding itself and afterward as well. Following the wedding service, the cooks and early arrivals eagerly await the return of the newlyweds to the bride's home, hoping that the bride will, without thinking, step over the broom that has been laid across the front door. If she does, her new husband will be teased for having chosen a wife too lazy to pick up a broom. The bride and her new husband are, of course, all too aware of what is awaiting them and try to sneak in the back way.

Other jokes focus on the corner table and the wedding party. Sometimes, said one woman, "someone takes a needle and sews the prunes together. Then, when they [a member of the wedding party] take one, they take the whole chain." The bride's sisters, especially those who are also young folk, take particular delight in playing tricks. At one wedding, in a variation of the prune joke, the celery sticks had been tied together at the base. The butter dish in the corner had been decorated with small cinnamon hearts. One sister hid plastic spiders near the bride's seat.

Family and friends gather for less-happy occasions as well, a close-knit community from beginning to end. When one elderly church member failed rapidly one spring after suffering a stroke, several of her married grandchildren moved back home to help care for her. They were not the only ones who took on the extra burden of her care. From the time she became bedridden until her death several weeks later, there were always community members there, taking turns staying by the old woman's bedside all night so that the family could sleep.

In times of hardship, the Swartzentruber Amish turn inward, drawing on friends and family for strength and support. This is perhaps most evident in the practice of *shmates tsia*, or "pain pulling," which means taking the pain from one who is suffering and, literally, directing it to a place where no one is harmed. No longer widely practiced in Old Order Amish communities, pain pulling is considered extremely hard work. As one Swartzentruber man described it, "The men hold hands in a line. The first touches the person in pain and the last touches a wire that goes in the ground or a tub of water. The more electricity someone has, the more he feels the pain as it passes through and there are some guys that can't hardly do it." He added that it was sometimes necessary to bind or grasp the hand receiving the pain to prevent the pain from flowing to the rest of the body. Another noted that it had been necessary to ground one woman's pain outside because it was so strong.

"Not everyone can draw pain," one Swartzentruber woman claimed. "You can't if you have heart problems or other health problems." This woman had discovered that she could do it when her mother was in pain and asked her to try. She told how she had put her hand on the sore spot, and the pain went up into her arm. She said that she had put her other arm in cold water, and, although drawing the pain had hurt, she had suffered no ill effects. "One time I thought I was going to throw up, but then I washed my hands in cold vinegar water." Her husband talked about how, as a young man, he had gone to a person who could draw pain. "[He] was a good healer, one who was so strong that he didn't even need to touch him [the person] to draw pain." His wife remarked that this strong healer "had a bit of *rumatis*" (rheumatism), and noted that "there are different kinds of *rumatis*. If you have lots of copper in you, ([it's] like copper bracelets [that help alleviate arthritis pain]) . . . [you] are better at drawing off pain." She herself had the right kind of rheumatism, she asserted, noting that she had a lot of copper in her body. "People can work together to draw pain off, each holding on to each other," she added. "You can [also] string a copper wire to the person and then into the ground."

The Swartzentrubers believe that ability to draw pain runs in families. One woman reported that all three of her sisters could do it well, but one of them shouldn't "because of her heart." Whether one is helping to draw pain or one is the patient, the practice brings community members together to offer solace and support and personal contact. The patient is at home, surrounded by loved ones and old friends. No one in the community suffers alone.

When death does occur, others in the community take over the family's chores, clean the house, and set up church benches so there will be a place for all to sit as they come to hold vigil until the funeral. Fellow church members wash and dress the body, and a neighboring carpenter builds the coffin.[35] As folks come in to pay their respects, they shake hands with members of the immediate family, acknowledging their loss, but they also shake hands with every member of the community who is there, recognizing that everyone is mourning and the church as a whole is suffering. After the funeral, friends and neighbors clean the house, put away the benches, and do the last of the chores, before going to their own homes.

The Swartzentruber Economy

Because of the Swartzentruber Ordnungs' limits on technology, farming and other tasks remain labor intensive, and there is always work at home for young people. The Ordnungs prevent them from working in town, but the Swartzentruber Amish can send their manufactured goods to non-Amish dealers, and they have found a ready market for their products. As one Swartzentruber woman put it, "We quilted before in Ohio, but not like we do here."

Indeed, Swartzentruber women have always produced quilts for home use, but in New York's North Country, the women quilt much more, and the majority of the quilts they make are for sale outside the community. Swartzentruber girls learn to quilt early, and are often helping to make quilts for sale by the time they are in the sixth grade and producing their own to sell not long after leaving school. Much of their work does not stay in the region. A number of Swartzentruber women receive quilt "tops" from Lancaster County Amish quilters, who pay them according to the number of yards of thread they use to quilt the tops and create the finished product. Frequently the customers for Swartzentruber quilts, aprons, and other Amish crafts are from outside the North Country, including tourists, returning alumni from the area universities, university trustees, and businesspeople. Many are from urban areas and are in northern New York to vacation or to meet old friends. Amish products serve as good reminders of this respite in the country, far from work and urban sprawl. Other likely customers are those about to leave the region who want something locally made as a visual reminder. Still more quilts and Amish handicrafts are sold as gifts for weddings and births, events best commemorated with something traditional.

In response to non-Amish demands for Amish handicrafts, Swartzentruber women have begun to produce popular new products, including Amish aprons with pieced tops and multicolored pockets; "quillows," or blankets that fold up into pillows; place mats in a variety of designs (including the maple leaf for Canadian customers); quilted handbags; and porch furniture. The wife of a man who makes cedar Adirondack chairs combines her quilting skills and the by-product of her husband's labor to make small sachets filled with cedar shavings that she sells at local gift shops. Because they never use tea cozies, Christmas tree skirts, or toaster covers, the Swartzentruber Amish are sometimes unsure just what it is they are making. One quilter's first place mat featured a ship in the center, but the design had been pieced in such a way that the ship appeared to be sinking.

The Swartzentrubers have also learned to make traditional Amish items in new ways for the non-Amish market. For example, one young woman has begun to sell Amishlike sun bonnets made of printed fabrics. Her neighbor, a harness maker who works with nylon strap, keeps black on hand for his Amish customers and bright red, blue, green, and yellow for the non-Amish. He makes black bridles, harnesses, and reins for Amish buggy drivers and dog leashes, collars, and key chains for non-Amish customers. He's also marketing custom-made boat covers. Another harness maker produces a variety of leather belts, leather fly-swatters, and coasters.

This altering of traditional crafts for a modern, non-Amish consumer is evident in Swartzentruber quilting. Many non-Amish customers reject the combinations of dark colors found in quilts the Swartzentruber Amish make for their own use. Indeed, one non-Amish retailer of Amish quilts has estimated that fewer than half her customers want the black, dark red, purple, and green of traditional Swartzentruber quilts, preferring instead lighter colors, such as lavender, light blue, and rose. Often non-Amish customers want the quilts to include printed fabrics, which are off-limits for Swartzentruber homes. Moreover, according to one local North Country dealer, non-Amish customers want "old-fashioned," natural, all-cotton fabric, whereas the Swartzentrubers prefer to use cotton-polyester blends because they wash more easily and don't need ironing. Quilt frames have had to be made larger to accommodate queen- and even king-size bed quilts, leading at least one Swartzentruber woman to wonder about a world with such big beds.

The Swartzentruber quilter is producing a functional object, but the non-Amish consumer is buying a work of art. In response to the demand for decorative pieces, it is now customary for Swartzentruber quilters to date their products and even to quilt their initials in the border, both unacceptable practices were the quilts to be used in a Swartzentruber home. One quilter has produced a black-and-white checked quilt for the NASCAR market.

In addition to producing crafts for sale, a number of Swartzentruber women own small stores selling such merchandise as fabric, shoes, or bulk foods. These are generally located in the home or in a room adjacent to the home and serve a mostly Amish clientele. One elderly woman sold spices in bulk, but to reach the store shelves, customers had to walk through the main house to her sitting room in the back. There was no sign to let passersby know her shop was there, and her customers were exclusively other Swartzentruber Amish women. Another woman began a fabric store for members of her extended family. Located upstairs in her home, it allowed young mothers and others easy access to fabric and notions. Yet another started a bulk food store when her daughters were old enough to help her wait on customers.

She regularly ordered flour, sugar, salt, and other staples from various non-Amish wholesale dealers, and with her daughters' help, repackaged the products in smaller amounts for her customers. In the first month of operation the store was housed in a small shed in the yard; when fall came she moved it to her cellar. Carefully managing her stock to ensure that she had enough for her own community, she allowed the women from a neighboring Old Order Amish settlement only limited access and asked that they let her know in advance when they planned to buy flour so that she could order enough.

Craft production and other economic exchange has brought the Swartzentruber Amish into regular contact with non-Amish neighbors, businesspeople, and tourists, but the interaction is not only restricted but gendered. Women usually deal through intermediaries. The domain of Swartzentruber Amish women is the home, and the non-Amish world is generally unwelcome there.[36]

Swartzentruber men, on the other hand, often meet the non-Amish world directly in shops that cater to Amish customers and to the wider non-Amish world. In the Heuvelton-area settlement, for example, one finds harness makers, at least two buggy makers, numerous sawmills, and a number of storage-shed builders. Others in the community make windows, repair furniture, or fix small engines. Indeed, as one Swartzentruber Amish man put it, "Everyone's got something." Their clientele often comes from some distance. One storage-shed builder noted that 90 percent of his product goes to Canadian buyers. Similarly, a harness maker estimated that 50 percent of his customers come from Quebec. Often Swartzentruber men travel considerable distances for business purposes. For example, a maple syrup producer remarked that he and his brother were looking forward to their annual trip to Vermont for supplies. Another farmer talked often about his trip to Quebec to find farm machinery.

The Economy and Social Change

Although sheltered from the world outside their settlement, the Swartzentruber Amish are not untouched by worldly events. Economic downturns in the national economy have an impact on Swartzentruber lives, even though, as one Swartzentruber man put it, "If you have a farm, you always have something to do." Nevertheless, the closure of the Heritage Cheese House, which was until 2008 a major economic force in the St. Lawrence County Swartzentruber settlement, challenged the community, ultimately resulting in changes to the Swartzentruber Ordnungs.

The cheese factory, located in Heuvelton, New York, was built in the fall of 1994. Before that, farmers in the Swartzentruber community had been shipping their milk to a cheese plant built by an Old Order Amish group in Norfolk, New York, about forty miles from the Swartzentruber community. Business reversals had made that plant an undependable market, and so the Swartzentruber community decided to build its own. Although not permitted by their Ordnungs to own the cheese factory or to work in it, the Swartzentruber Amish helped to underwrite the business, and they held a barn raising to help owner Dave O'Neil build the new building, with the Swartzentruber community supplying both labor and logs.

At first the plant prospered, and Heritage Cheese House cheese began to appear in grocery stores across New York State. Then the cheese plant began to experience operating difficulties. "We knew of problems with the cheese factory," said one Swartzentruber wife. "Pickups became more sporadic, and there were two or three times a week with no pickup. They blamed it on problems at the plant." Swartzentruber dairy farmers, concerned about losing a market for local milk, began to discuss options, a prospect that worried some who feared that many church members, especially more recent arrivals from Ohio, would be unwilling to invest in keeping a cheese factory going. Said one Swartzentruber woman, "Some don't let go of money very easily. People who move here need to learn how things are. We can't all go into vegetables like they do in Ohio— [there are] too many [people]."

Nevertheless, at a meeting in 2006, seventy-one Swartzentruber farmers voted unanimously to set up a trust fund to support the cheese house. According to one who was there, "We wouldn't own it—nobody would—it would be a community thing." The trust arrangement was necessary, for a Swartzentruber-owned plant could not operate with electricity, and so could not meet state requirements. As a trust, the Swartzentruber Amish man noted, the business would not be owned by any member of the community, and so it could be operated with electricity and meet health codes. Then, "after paying all the bills, the money earned would go to pay back those who put in."

An agreement was made to run the plant under oversight from a board that would draw half its members from the Swartzentruber churches and half from the non-Amish community. Despite the initial optimism, however, by spring 2008 it was apparent that the cheese plant would not survive. In response, ministers from all of the Swartzentruber groups met, and the Swartzentruber churches changed their Ordnungs to allow the building of bulk tank milk dumping stations to serve Swartzentruber farmers.[37]

This decision has elicited mixed reactions from members of the Swartzentruber community. Some are pleased. For example, watching her brother and several other Swartzentruber men construct a dumping station a short distance down the road from her home, one woman expressed her eagerness to have the electricity installed so that the farmers could once again ship milk and receive an income. One young Joe Troyer farmer laughed about the challenges the dumping station posed for his people. He noted that one dairy farmer had lost a first load of milk after he had put it in his assigned bulk tank at the dumping station. "It says 'automatically cooled,'" he said, laughing, "but it doesn't automatically turn on. Someone has to start it up." Others are nervous about the change in the Ordnung, even though they acknowledge the necessity.

In allowing the stations, the Swartzentruber Amish had to cooperate across affiliation boundaries. A woman in a Joe Troyer church community noted that the first station to open in the settlement had been built on land belonging to a member of an Andy Weaver church district, "even though they're supposed to be so low [conservative]." Asked if this meant that the different groups were now of one mind, she smiled and replied, "Just in the milk business."

More equanimously, a Swartzentruber bishop, acknowledging that the dumping stations were a sharp departure from past practice, put the change in Amish perspective. It would, he noted, make it possible for young men to keep farming, helping to ensure that life in the community would remain agriculturally based.[38] With a more secure income, there would be less need for farmers to hire out to do carpentry or other work outside the community. Finally, he argued, building dumping stations was really "a step backwards," a move away from the modern world. Because milk truck drivers would no longer go to individual Amish farms to pick up cans of milk, the dumping stations would make the non-Amish world less intrusive in the daily life of the Swartzentruber settlement; farmers would deliver their cans of milk to the dumping station by horse-drawn wagon.[39]

Figure 3.3. Like other conservative Amish, the Swartzentrubers harvest ice during the winter. These scenes have become more familiar across New York as conservative Amish families move to the state and establish new communities. Photo by author.

Growing Pains

The demise of the cheese factory is only one of the challenges the Swartzentruber Amish have faced since moving to New York. The very success of the community has posed difficulties. Writing in the *Watertown Daily Times* in the early 1980s, one North Country reporter quoted a "young Amish sawmill owner" who said that he hoped "the flow of transplants from Ohio would cease. 'It's already too crowded up here,' he said, and said that he knew of several families from Ohio who were on their way."[40]

The Swartzentruber Amish settlement in the Heuvelton-DePeyster area of St. Lawrence County is now the second largest Amish settlement in New York State. While the region offered lots of cheap farmland when the first settlers arrived from Ohio, land is getting scarcer now and prices are rising. Incoming Amish families were paying $300 to $800 an acre for farms in the early 1980s, but a 2007 advertisement in the *Budget* for a "98.9 acre Amish farm" in the Heuvelton settlement listed the asking price as $179,900.[41] More recently, talking about how difficult it was for young families to find farms, one bishop noted that one of the big commercial dairy farms was willing to pay over four thousand dollars an acre for available farmland. He added that a farm in the area had just sold for several million dollars.[42]

Still, people keep coming, and scarce land, rising real estate prices, and church division have combined to create competition and, at times, negative feelings. Problems have been exacerbated by the perception that the newcomers are different from those who came earlier. In particular, incoming settlers in the Morristown area of St. Lawrence County, just across Black Lake from the towns of Heuvelton and DePeyster, experienced difficulties as a result of their failure to secure appropriate building permits. The resulting legal conflicts caused some who had been in the North Country far longer to shake their heads.[43] "Those people on the other side of the water [meaning the Swartzentruber Amish in the Morristown area], they're not like us," commented one Heuvelton area farmer. "The new people coming from Ohio think they know everything, and they don't listen to us." He told of Ohio farmers relocating to New York who thought they could dairy farm the same way they did in Ohio. "After a couple of years they guessed we knew something after all." Calling the newcomers "arrogant," he noted further that non-Amish people ask him, "Why aren't those people like you [Heuvelton] people?" A Swartzentruber woman from a different church group remarked that "the New York folks are stricter [than the Swartzentrubers in Ohio]" and hoped that the Ohio newcomers would not bring their lax ways with them when they moved to the area. Another asserted that young folk, "especially in Ohio" were "out of control, drinking." Asked if this were a reason some were leaving Ohio, she responded yes and said she hoped they wouldn't come to the Heuvelton area. Yet another, talking about a farm the family had just purchased for a married child, expressed some satisfaction that it hadn't gone "to the English or one of the Ohio folks. . . . We need those farms for our children. They [Ohio folks] could go to Lafargeville or Pulaski or Hopkinton."

Such talk saddened one elderly bishop in the Andy Weaver Swartzentruber church, who noted, "We're all descended from the same. God made Adam and made Eve from his rib. They were the first people and the first sinners." Sighing, he added, "Man is God's most intelligent creation and the one that causes the most complaint."

4

From Lancaster County to Lowville

Moving North to Keep the Old Ways

Greetings from the land of plenty. Where the sun, moon and
stars shine and with all their light the earth is lighted up. Where
the deer, turkey and coyotes roam and the windmills spin.
Where the moose and bear pass through once in a while. One
could go on and on.
   —*Die Botschaft*, November 2006

In 1999, four Old Order Amish families from the Path Valley in
Pennsylvania arrived in Lowville in Lewis County, the first new Amish
settlers to the area in more than one hundred years. Six years later, there
were twenty-one families and forty children in the community's two
schools, and by January 2007, there were twenty-five families. Fewer than
ten years later, the settlement boasts "two church districts, three schools,
12 babies (6 boys and 6 girls), 34 young folk (15 boys and 19 girls) . . . and
lots of preschoolers."[1] More progressive than Swartzentruber and less
progressive than Clymer-area Amish, the Amish in Lowville bring to
New York's North Country traditions that have their origins in Lancaster
County, Pennsylvania, the oldest Amish settlement in North America.

For the modern-day Amish settlers in Lewis County, Lowville is but
the latest stop in a migration that has taken place over generations.
Descendants of the first Amish to make their homes in the New World,
the parents, grandparents, and great-grandparents of the Lowville settlers left Lancaster County to escape conflict with state and local authorities over their children's education. Schooling has not been a major
issue for most Amish communities since the 1972 United States Supreme
Court ruling in *Wisconsin v. Yoder et al.*, that Amish children could not be
required to attend high school.[2] But for the first half of the twentieth century, the Amish struggled with local school boards in a number of states,[3]
and these conflicts have historically been one of the major forces driving
the Amish to establish new settlements.

For the Lancaster County Amish, difficulties began in the 1930s, when Pennsylvania attempted to enforce new laws extending the school year from eight months to nine and changing the age at which children could leave school from fourteen to fifteen. The Old Order community felt under attack. On November 17, 1937, forty representatives of Old Order churches presented a plea to "Men of Authority" in the state, expressing their concerns: "If we send our children under this code until they are grown up to manhood and womanhood or to the age when they should and generally do join the church, it will get them to be devoted to the worldly things and under-mine [*sic*] our churches in the way of bring-ing our children up as we understand the Bible."[4] Leaders of Old Order congregations also circulated a petition that read, in part,

> We the undersigned, a religious country folk, pertaining to Agriculture do hereby certify that consciously we can not send our children unto the worlds nature and teachings until they are grown up. And do hereby pe-tition the boards of public instruction to be lenient with a well-meaning people.
>
> If we are granted eight months schooling in a year and the children are exempt when they get through the low grades and let us have the one-room school houses and teach the truth, we can with a free conscience send our children to public schools.

It was signed by more than three thousand Amish and Mennonites and presented to state officials on November 22, 1937.[5]

Pleas and petitions had little effect, and attempts by public authorities to consolidate the one-room public schools in Lancaster County only ex-acerbated difficulties. On September 5, 1938, the *New York Times* reported that "after a Summer long truce, the Amish 'little red schoolhouse' argu-ment promises to flare anew when school reopens in Lancaster County on Tuesday." The article went on to describe how

> buses in suburban East Lampeter Township will roll up to the Amish and Mennonite farms, ready to take their children to the $112,000 PWA-built consolidated school building at Smoketown. If the boys and girls climb in, the township school directors, the State Department of Public Instruction and even Governor Earle will sigh with relief. . . . If the children stay in the kitchens with their mothers or in the cornfields with their fathers it will mean that the Amish are firm in their defiance of the State School Attendance Law and will risk prison for the sake of their one-room schools, where "worldly" things are not taught.[6]

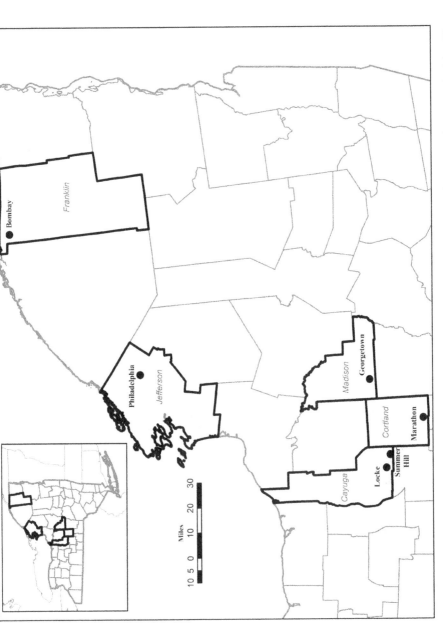

Map 4.1. The Lowville Amish. The Old Order Amish returned to Lewis County, the site of a nineteenth-century Amish settle-

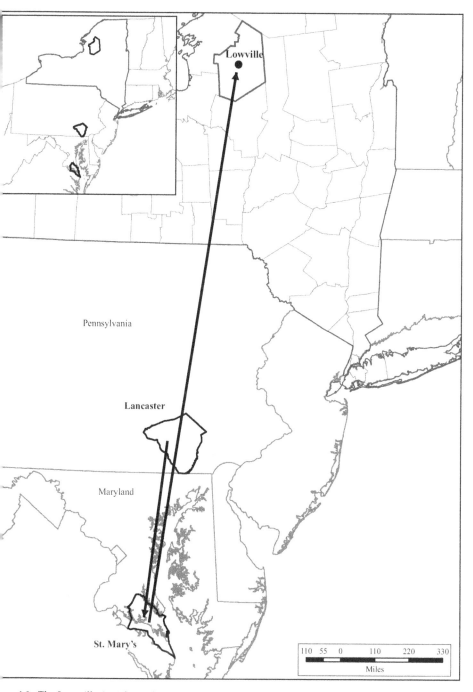

Map 4.2. The Lowville Amish are descended from Amish who left Lancaster County, Pennsylvania, for Maryland to seek the freedom to educate their children according to the values of their church.

The Amish achieved little relief through the courts. In June 1938, Judge Joseph Buffington of the federal Circuit Court of Appeals expressed sympathy for the Amish in Lancaster County and asserted that they should have "a right to educate their children according to their own views and freedom in their religious practices."[7] Nevertheless, he ruled that the federal courts had no jurisdiction over local school boards.

For some Lancaster County Amish, enough was enough. When a real estate agent from St. Mary's County in Maryland approached Minister Stephen F. Stoltzfus with an offer of good land at a fair price, Stoltzfus decided it was time to move. In the summer of 1939, Stoltzfus left Pennsylvania for Maryland, and others, similarly frustrated by the struggle, were quick to follow. As J. F. Esh noted, "soon car loads were exploring St. Marys Co[unty]."[8] Stoltzfus's son, Benjamin, moved first, on January 16, 1940, settling on a five-hundred-acre farm, and soon others followed.

The Politics of Schools and Schooling

In moving to Maryland, the Amish who began the St. Mary's settlement were not voicing opposition to public schools. In fact, until the 1950s, most Old Order children attended small, often one-room public schools with their non–Old Order peers, and Old Order parents were generally willing to let their children be educated in public schools as long as these were local institutions over which the parents had considerable influence. However, in the mid-twentieth century, state authorities began to consolidate the local one-room schoolhouses, impose longer school years, and enforce compulsory attendance beyond the eighth grade. Many Old Order parents began to resist, ultimately by establishing private schools of their own. The number of Old Order private schools grew as Old Order parents were fined or jailed for their refusal to obey new education laws. In 1940, there were only four private Old Order Amish schools, and there were fewer than four hundred at the time of the Yoder decision; today, there are over two thousand.

Having little doubt that school consolidation threatened their values and traditions, Old Order parents were unwilling to send their children to the modern, large schools in which, separated from the influence of home and church, they risked becoming assimilated to the dominant society. As the Old Order writer and publisher David Wagler put it, "The one-room country school with its personal touch gave way to the consolidated elementary and high schools with additional unfavorable elements. During the tender years of childhood, our children were . . . to receive their education and instruction in worldly schools from worldly teachers, yet it was expected that they should suffer no harm."[9]

The Amish draw an important distinction between schooling and education. Whereas many American parents expect public schools to acculturate their children and prepare them to enter society, the Amish parents expect only that schools provide book learning, the value of which varies in Old Order communities. In school, children learn to read, write, and do arithmetic. These are skills they will need to do business and sustain the community economically. Becoming educated, on the other hand, is to acquire the values of the church and community. These are what will sustain the community spiritually.

For the Old Orders, the true education on which the church depends for its survival takes place in the sharing of labor, the doing of chores, and the enjoyment of fellowship at church, around the dinner table, and even in silo filling. Voicing his opposition to sending children to consolidated public schools, one Amish leader argued, "With us, our religion is inseparable with a day's work, a night's rest, a meal, or any other practice; therefore, our education can much less be separated from our religious practices."[10] In moving to Maryland, then, the forebears of today's Lowville Amish community were, like those first Amish settlers to Lewis County, fleeing what they saw as threat to their religious identity.

From Maryland to New York

Moving to Maryland allowed the Amish to maintain their practices and to educate their children for their traditional way of life. But that traditional way of life depended in large part on agriculture, and as the community grew, it became increasingly difficult to find enough farmland at affordable prices. By the early 1960s, some church members were thinking about relocating.

Jacob Gunther, an Old Order Mennonite who had immigrated to Honduras in 1951, seemed to offer a solution. Writing to Samuel Hertzler Sr. in the Maryland community, Gunther praised the Honduran climate and the economic opportunities the country offered and encouraged the Amish to move south. Convinced that settlement in Honduras would offer a respite from "the turmoil of our modern country including draft, unreasonable school laws and high land prices," Hertzler and his sons left for Honduras.

Unfortunately, the Hertzlers did not find what they were looking for. As they reported back to their St. Mary's neighbors, "In Honduras people are poor and stealing is common. The continuous heat, the cheap market and poor transportation (except along the coast) would soon discourage the most ambitious Amish. Also the diet eaten and raised locally would not suit us." Disheartened, the would-be emigrants concluded that, although "the Amish could start as their fore fathers did," it would not be good to do so. "The Amish would no doubt improve all this a lot [in Honduras]," they added, "but [they] would find it a lot easier the way they have it [in the United States]."

The Hertzlers warned those who might still be thinking of moving that they should stay in the United States "as long as there is a Christian government" and warned that there was "no telling how soon a country like Honduras would go Communist." In short, according to the Hertzlers, while Honduras had seemed to be an ideal place, "coming back to the U.S.A. and home seemed like entering Paradise where they speak English and its [sic] easier to speak and get along with people."[11]

When they returned home, according to rumor, one of the Hertzlers said, "Boy that took the ants out of the pants,"[12] suggesting that their short stay in Honduras had dampened the urge to move. Yet families continued to search for land. Some moved back to Pennsylvania, settling in the Path Valley in Franklin County, west of Lancaster County and just over the Maryland border. Then, when land there became scarce, families moved north to Lowville, New York.

Milking Cows and Maintaining Tradition

"We moved to Lowville so that we could farm," said one Amish woman. "In [Pennsylvania] there were just no farms available. We had one, but we had boys." Having boys meant that they had to find more land for their sons to farm, ideally close by so parents and siblings could help one another other, and so the family, with others facing similar pressures, moved north.

"People ask how it goes not to milk cows, well I don't handle the greenbacks, but on my part it's fine. Its [sic] not as if we'd have no chores all of a sudden, as the barn is still full with heifers, horses and pigs. One sow had a litter of eleven live piggys [sic] on Thursday night, have two sows." So wrote a newly arrived Lowville Amish man to *Die Botschaft*, about his having given up dairy farming. As of January 2007, he was in the minority, for, as one woman noted, "Every one in Lowville is in dairying but two." Dairy farming has become the Lowville Amish community's economic mainstay.

In 1924, the United States Public Health Service enacted the Standard Milk Ordinance, known today as the Pasteurized Milk Ordinance, which governs the production, processing, and sale of grade A milk.[13] Since then, dairy farming has posed special problems for Amish farmers because of requirements concerning the refrigeration of milk. Without electricity, Amish farmers cannot keep milk cold enough to meet the grade A standard, and so many ship grade B milk, which can only be used in cheese making. Furthermore, lack of electricity has kept nearly all Amish dairy farmers milking by hand, which means that herds are small, often only ten or fifteen cows. However, the Lowville Amish dairy farmers have worked with the farmer-owned Dairylea Cooperative, with nearly three thousand members throughout the northeastern United States, to overcome at least one of these limitations. As one woman put it, although the Amish in Lowville "don't have our own bulk tanks on our own farms. We have our own tanks in a dumping station owned by Dairylea." Built on private property and wired for electricity, the dumping station allows the Lowville Amish, like the Swartzentruber Amish in St. Lawrence County, to ship grade A milk, giving them a greater return on their financial investment in farms and dairy herds than would be possible were they shipping grade B milk in cans. In addition, their arrangement with Dairylea gives individual Lowville Amish dairy farmers a guaranteed market for the relatively small amount of milk they produce and, thus, some financial stability.[14]

In short, membership in Dairylea has enabled the Lowville Amish to remain farmers and, thus, to retain practices and traditions lost or threatened in their parent settlements in Pennsylvania and Maryland. By moving to Lowville, the Amish have been able to maintain their commitment to farming as a way of life.

The Amish who remained in the parent settlement in Lancaster County have followed another path. Suburban encroachment, increasing tourism, and new industry have combined to make land in Lancaster County scarce and increasingly expensive, and hard economic times have driven many to other occupations.[15] In a December 2006 letter to the *Diary*, a writer from Lancaster County lamented that the "main stay [*sic*] of the

Figure 4.1. A fall ride in an open buggy. The agrarian Amish of Lowville are a common sight on local highways. Photo by Tina Thomas.

Amish church is fading fast. Probably less than 35 percent are real farmers."[16] He went on to assert that

> now days seems farmers can make it if they No. 1) farm tobacco (and cause many who use it to lose their health). No. 2) Farm this organic or grass fed or pesticide free style (is that always as advertised?). No. 3) Have the home farm sold to them at long go [*sic*] prices. No. 4) Go at it big, use all the latest equipment and crowd the fence [push the limits of the Ordnung]. No. 5) Have the children work away and provide extra income. And cheat young farmers out of hired help. No. 6) Sell the farm at a high price, then development will follow. Seems here in Leacock Twp. The Amish are the biggest developers. Many are building big houses with many extra roofs [more rooms than necessary], carving out a chunk out of the home farm.

By 2000, two-thirds of the Amish men in Lancaster County were no longer farming, and 40 percent were working away from home. The shift from farming to work in manufacturing, construction, and the hospitality industry is a considerable threat to the Amish way of life. Writing in the *Mennonite Weekly Review* in 2002, columnist Robert Rhodes mused that "as work takes more Amish away from their farms, other traditions may have to be reexamined, such as resistance to higher education, use of certain kinds of technology or restrictions on long distance travel, especially by air."[17]

Today Lancaster County Amish businesses serve a diverse clientele, both within the local Amish settlement, and in the non-Amish world. Shops take advantage of the tourist trade to offer a variety of craft items produced in home-based manufacturing. Larger businesses offer goods and services, including welding, machine repair, upholstery, construction, foundry work, cabinetmaking, and roofing. Women, too, have entered the workforce. Although married women generally stay home with the children, many have quilting or craft businesses. Others run produce stands, greenhouses, or bakeries. Single women often find employment off the farm in the hospitality industry or clerking at local shops.

This economic change has brought lifestyle changes. Since the end of World War II, the Amish in Lancaster have adopted electric generators for welding and bulk tanks, air and hydraulic power to run a variety of manufacturing equipment, electrical inverters, modern manufacturing tools, indoor bathroom facilities in homes and businesses, modern kitchen cabinetry, and contemporary house exteriors. Many Amish homes sport solar panels, generating electricity to run small appliances. There is greater use of telephones, and some even carry cell phones. In the fields, horses tow modern machinery, and in the kitchens, women use modern gas appliances. Perhaps most important, Lancaster Amish of all ages encounter the non-Amish world daily.[18]

"Lancaster has changed more," claimed one Lowville Amish woman. She pointed out that the Lancaster Amish had now accepted bottled gas refrigerators and freezers and gas stoves and that the women's bonnets were smaller and dress sleeves "poufier." The Lowville Amish have kerosene refrigerators but no deep freezers. "We cook on a woodstove usually," the Amish woman noted. "We have a small wood lot, but you can only get into it in winter. You have to wait until the ground freezes."[19] Like the Amish in Lancaster County, the Amish in Lowville have indoor plumbing, but there is no running hot water. It's acceptable to have linoleum on the floors but not carpeting, and furniture may be upholstered as long as sofa and chair arms remain uncovered.

Figure 4.2. Gray Lowville buggies. The gray buggies of the Lowville Amish are testimony to their Lancaster County roots. Photo by Tina Thomas.

Even the pattern of language use in the Lowville settlement marks it as more isolated and more conservative than its parent community.[20] In Lowville, noted one community member, "they're not as strict about English [as they are in Pennsylvania], and they use German on the playground. [And] they use more German [in school] than in Pennsylvania. It used to be that parents would say to learn German at home [and English in school], but they weren't learning [German] at home, so they have to learn it in school." Moreover, she noted that, in Lowville, children begin the school day by singing two or three songs, twice a week in English and the rest of the time in German. The Lord's Prayer, which follows the singing, is always said in German. Whether this was good for education or not, the church member couldn't say. Still, she suggested, using more German in the school made the singing better.

As one writer to the *Budget* put it, a key difference is, perhaps, that staying "more on the agriculture side . . . slows down the fast pace of our society today." This is not to suggest, however, that the Lowville Amish have remained unchanged over the years or have grown more conservative in their lifestyle. For example, unlike those in more conservative Amish groups, most of the Lowville Amish have Social Security numbers. Many even have nonphoto identification cards.[21]

The Lowville Amish are exemplary of how a local environment can shape a community's Ordnung. For example, because the community is smaller than its parent in Lancaster and there are fewer small businesses that rely on ties to the non-Amish world, there is less need for telephones. One woman noted that, although there had been a telephone at the end of her lane when she lived in Pennsylvania, "We don't have one, not up here. It hasn't been necessary."

As a result, the Lowville Amish have managed, at least for the time being, to avoid the problems that the telephone has posed for Old Order groups since its invention. The telephone certainly offers convenience. An early twentieth-century tract circulating among the Old Order communities in Lancaster County acknowledged the ease with which "worldly news" circulated among "worldly people" via telephone. The tract warned that the telephone would link families in "a sinful network" and reminded church members that "as Paul teaches us in 2 Cor. 6, 14–17, Be ye not unequally yoked together with unbelievers, etc." Further, the tract admonished,

> there is much talking through the phone which amounts to nothing, worldly joy, as it says in 1 Timothy 1:6. . . . [S]ome people claim that they might save a dear life when a member of your family suddenly takes sick. How is this? Do you trust it to this network to save a life? But I say such trust have we through Christ to God. . . . Never seek elsewhere for any part of that which Jesus loves to bestow; but remember, Christ is all.[22]

Seeing the telephone as a link to the (sinful) world and reliance on the telephone as evidence of a lack of faith in Christ, Old Order groups could not help but reject it.

Today, in a number of ways, use of the telephone marks one's place in the Old Order world. Some communities permit the installation of a telephone booth at the end of a church member's lane for family and Amish neighbors to use, and others, like the Clymer-area settlement, allow telephones in Amish-owned businesses. In the most progressive communities, church members may even carry cell phones. Clearly, in regulating access to the telephone, Amish groups reinforce a distinction between their church and the surrounding non-Amish society. The willingness of more progressive groups to allow the telephone into the community has strengthened the resolve of more conservative communities to keep them out.

The Lowville settlement has yet to permit telephones in shops or even to put up a phone booth for use by community members. Yet, while the Lowville Amish have, at least so far, managed to keep the telephone out of their small settlement, the parent community in Lancaster County and other Lancaster daughter settlements have accommodated the telephone in different ways. Although telephone policies vary among church districts in Lancaster County, phones are ubiquitous in the commercial center of the district, and cell phones are increasingly common. In more rural areas, it's not uncommon for farmers to install a phone in a discreet location such as inside a barn or tobacco shed, and they may use it daily for such practical matters as calling for the day's weather forecast.[23] Similarly, a *Washington Post* article announced that the Amish in St. Mary's County had put up at least twelve private phone booths, hiding them "behind barns, in the woods and, in one case, inside a former chicken coop."[24] While the easy access to private phone booths allows Amish in the Maryland settlement to maintain business ties, the community has prohibited the placement of phone booths close to homes and has outlawed the use of amplified ringers, in an effort to keep the telephone at a distance and minimize its use for social purposes.

Despite these lifestyle differences, Lowville and the other daughter settlements have continued to fellowship with those who remained in Lancaster County, and the historical and family ties between the communities remain strong. At the same time, each group has been able to change in response to differing environmental and social conditions. Thus, like any offspring, the Lowville church resembles its parent, but is not the same.

Connections

The Amish settlers to Lowville are linked to other Amish communities by blood, friendship, and history.[25] One community member traced her family back to the Maryland settlement, but she herself was born in the Byler Amish settlement in New Wilmington, Pennsylvania, the parent community of Byler Amish settlements in Chautauqua County and elsewhere, which are known for their brown-topped buggies.[26] Others maintain connections to the large Byler Amish settlement in the Mohawk Valley, and folks from Lowville often visit friends and relatives in other settlements around the state, such as those in Friendship, Bombay, Little Falls, Locke, Philadelphia, and Georgetown.

The back-and-forth visiting between church districts that are historically related helps to maintain and strengthen ties of friendship and mutual support. Writing in *Die Botschaft*, a correspondent from Locke, New York,[27] reported that visitors with ties to the Lowville community had helped the group at Ordnungsgmay, or Council Church, the service for reaffirming the Ordnung. Later that year, members of the Lowville community again traveled to the Locke settlement, this time to help rebuild a house that had burned down. Members of the Lowville congregation have more recently been back and forth to help in the new settlement of Philadelphia, in Jefferson County, which was founded by Amish from Taylor, Wisconsin, in 2012. Writing to the *Diary*, the Lowville scribe announced that "some men also went to help take down a barn for someone to rebuild in Philadelphia, NY. The barn to take down is not far from here."[28]

Visitors to the community are always welcome, and the arrivals and departures of visiting friends and relatives are reported in letters to the *Budget* or *Die Botschaft* or community reports in the *Diary*. One scribe noted that "we went to Ava area over Sun. and attended church there. We are invited to a wedding in Bombay next week. We'd like to go, depends on the weather and health."[29] "We had a load from [Pennsylvania] with us, which is always a highlight," reported another scribe one February. Only three weeks later she reported that there had been visitors in church earlier in the week and that a group from Romulus, New York, had stopped in that morning. "Every one is on the go," she remarked. The Lowville community does not fellowship with the Swartzentruber churches in neighboring St. Lawrence Jefferson, Oswego, or Herkimer counties, so Lowville ministers do not preach at services in these other communities, and Lowville young people do not date the young people in these churches. Nevertheless, Lowville church members do visit these settlements occasionally to attend church or assist in barn raisings, weddings, auctions, or other community events. Several of the churches with which Lowville does fellowship, including the Byler churches, have a somewhat more conservative Ordnung than the Lowville group, which suits the Lowville Amish. As one Lowville community member put it "We wouldn't want to go with those who want modernisms but the other way [fellowshipping with more conservative churches] is OK." Her hope is that exposure to more conservative groups might help the Lowville community "hold the line."

Yet while geographic isolation may help the community to resist change, it makes leaving the community, for a day trip or for an extended visit elsewhere, difficult. When traveling, the Lowville Amish ask non-Amish neighbors or, more frequently, hire non-Amish drivers to take them to destinations too far away to reach by horse and buggy. It is an economic arrangement that generally suits both parties well, providing income for drivers, who are often retired, and increased mobility for the Amish. Nevertheless, there are some drawbacks. For example, at least one driver proved unsuitable for trips to the obstetrician because he had a habit of commenting to those riding with him about where he had driven folks on past trips. Like other more conservative Amish groups, the Lowville Amish rarely discuss pregnancy. An expectant mother will only talk about her condition with her mother and, perhaps, a close woman friend or sister, provided the friend or sister is married. News of pregnancy is never bandied about in the community at large. "We try not to get that driver to go to that doctor or everyone would know," said one woman succinctly.

Much of the adventure of a trip may be in the coming and going itself. The Lowville scribe commented in a November letter to *Die Botschaft* that she, along with several friends, had headed to Pennsylvania to attend a wedding. Recounting the various stops along the way, she listed the other passengers in the van and the different family connections each had to the bride and groom. Her letter, however, said nothing about the wedding itself.

Amish Settlement and the Larger Community

Writing in the *Diary* in April 2006, J. L. Stoltzfus noted that seven years had passed since the first family in the Lowville church arrived in the region. In that time, he remarked, "42 babies were born, 8 new houses were built, 2 new schools and 12 barns." In his January 2007 letter to the *Diary*, Stoltzfus described the settlement as "one church of 25 families, 13 young folks, 2 schools with 48 children." He added that there were currently 53 children under school-age and noted sadly that "our little granddaughter that died the second winter we were here from crib death . . . is in a new graveyard over along the West Road all by [her] self." Now, nearly twenty years after the founding of the community, the settlement has grown to two church districts.[30]

As the Lowville Amish community has expanded, local government and business leaders have made an effort to welcome and to get to know their Amish neighbors. In 2002, the Cornell Cooperative Extension of Lewis County and the Lewis County Chamber of Commerce sponsored a seminar entitled "Working with the Amish" to allow area businesses and other leaders to meet with some of the new settlers. Asserting that "they [the Amish] are part of our population base, and there's not a lot of information out there," organizers invited a community development extension agent from Holmes County, Ohio, to present the workshop and expected several Old Order Amish from the Holmes area to attend.[31]

Subsequent offerings have included a workshop on small-scale sustainable farming, featuring as keynote speaker David Kline, a New Order Amish bishop, farmer, naturalist, and author. Further, the Amish have featured in the region's plans for economic development. The plan adopted by the Lewis County Comprehensive Economic Development Strategy Committee in August 2006 and endorsed soon after by the Lewis County Board of Legislators listed the promotion of "Green Lumber Manufacturing/Amish" among measures to strengthen the forest-products sector. The report suggested that "large companies are not the answer[;] the marketing of small homespun products is. There is a significant population of small woodworkers, including Amish, that could be [promoted]."

Meanwhile, the Amish have already met a friendly reception from the Lowville business community. A local bank and the village of Lowville joined to install hitching posts in front of local shops, and a speaker invited to address area business leaders urged them to make use of the local Amish populations to "create unusual local products."[32] In June 2007, the Lowville Town Council voted unanimously to waive the building permit fee for a schoolhouse the Amish were planning to build. As Town Supervisor Arleigh D. Rice noted, "They pay school taxes, and they don't get that much for their money." The move was endorsed by the town's code enforcement officer.[33]

Casting the Amish as "sustainable farmers" and "small woodworkers," Lewis County has welcomed them as productive community members who can contribute much to the county's understanding of itself as historically rich, environmentally committed, and focused on family, hard work, and the values that make a community strong. A writer to the *Watertown Daily Times* commented that "seeing the Amish buggies, to me, is a good omen. It is knowing our vacant lands and farms will have excellent stewardship. It is realizing these people can show us a way of life, long forgotten."[34] In an interview in the same newspaper about an upcoming quilt show, a resident from nearby Sackets Harbor noted that "with their wagons coming to our area, we're more conscious of their existence," and she expressed her admiration of "the Amish sense of community and cooperation."[35] In the same article, a Pamelia, New York, resident asserted, "Their life is way better than ours. They worry about simple things." His wife added, "We like the Amish and everything about them." Commenting on the behavior of Amish children she had seen in the local stores, the Mennonite historian Arlene Yousey noted that she was "very much aware of how well behaved those children are and how they stay with their parents. I just admire the characteristics that are forming in those children. One of their chief aims is to keep their own within the church." Upon his retirement in 2011, Lowville Town Supervisor Rice highlighted the Amish population, "which tends to contribute taxes without draining social programs," as one of the town's positives.[36]

In other regions of New York State the relationship between the Amish and non-Amish neighbors and local governments has not been so positive. Not far away in Cayuga County, for example, officials in the town of Locke charged local Amish families with violations of a junkyard ordinance and for using a mobile home for agricultural purposes (a chicken coop). More problematically, town officials insisted that building contractors provide proof of workers' compensation and liability insurance, neither of which Amish builders can supply.[37] And while Amish builders had problems in Cayuga County, Amish fishermen to the south in Madison County have been accused of overfishing the lakes.[38]

Perhaps the most notable conflict between Amish settlers and local authorities is that which began in just to the north of the Lowville settlement, in Morristown in St. Lawrence County, when in 2006 newly arrived Swartzentruber Amish ran afoul of building code requirements. By 2007, the conflict had reached the courts. Representing the Amish, Assistant St. Lawrence County Public Defender Steven G. Ballan argued that the citations for building code violations issued against eight Amish men were a violation of the Amish men's religious freedom. According to local newspaper reports, "Mr. Ballan also requested dismissal of the charges for . . . the defendants on grounds of discriminatory enforcement and lack of speedy trial, as a violation of a federal statute on religious land use, or as a matter of justice." Since the Amish use their homes as churches, Mr. Ballan argued, they should fall into a separate category.[39] By 2009, the number of Amish men cited for building code violations in the town of Morristown had risen to eleven, and the Becket Fund for Religious Liberty had filed a lawsuit on their behalf in the U.S. District Court for the Northern District of New York. Only in 2013, after depositions had already been taken, was a settlement reached.[40]

These controversies, like others involving the use (or nonuse) of the orange slow-moving-vehicle triangle, child labor, and even horse droppings in parking lots, pit Amish religious beliefs and practices against the secular government and their neighbors' understandings of civic responsibility. They also reveal the very different ways in which the non-Amish have come to understand their Amish neighbors. As the historian David Weaver-Zercher noted in his study of the representation of the Amish in popular culture, the non-Amish have invested the Amish and their way of life with multiple meanings. Some see the Amish as quaint, simple folk who, having rejected the cars, telephones, television, and other trappings of modern civilization, remain somehow more "real" and honest than their non-Amish neighbors.[41] For many mainstream Americans, the Old Order Amish demonstrate the stability and traditional values of a pioneer past—values that they see disappearing from the modern society.[42] Others point out Amish imperfections, suggesting that the Amish are in some ways flawed, not the innocent God-fearing folks of tradition, and certainly not worthy of any special consideration. Many, not understanding the Amish willingness to use technology they refuse to own (e.g., accepting rides in private automobiles), consider the Amish hypocritical.

Letters to the editors of local newspapers capture the competing narratives. Writing to the *Syracuse Post-Standard*, one local reader was incensed about the difficulties the Amish were facing in Cayuga County and ended by inviting them to come to her neighborhood. "If they choose to move away from the unfriendliness they are experiencing now, I hope the Amish will resettle in Onondaga County. It would be a privilege to have them as neighbors."[43] Another wrote to express dissatisfaction with the Town of Locke's "manipulation of power and small-minded, intolerant discrimination" and proclaimed that "Amish character is more noble than what we see as commonplace in our lazy, materialistic, self-centered American society, and it would be a wonderful influence if they would be allowed to populate."[44] Another man began his letter by reminding readers of the killing of five Amish schoolgirls in Pennsylvania in the fall of 2006, and how the Amish had forgiven the murderer. He continued, "Whatever one's religious or humanitarian perspective, one must respect the Amish and their kind and gentle ways. They tend to practice

101

what many other people in our society preach: Love thy neighbor; do unto others; respect the land; do no harm; avoid selfishness." Implying that the Town of Locke had been less than welcoming to the newcomers, he argued that "[the Amish] do all they can to avoid hurting others, and they try to be good neighbors. We need more neighbors like the Mennonites and Amish in Central New York and should be good neighbors to them as well."[45]

Others, however, feel that the Amish have been allowed to skirt rules. Quoted in an article on the controversy that appeared in the *Syracuse Post-Standard*, the Locke town supervisor asserted that "everyone is welcome in Locke. I don't care who you are or what you are. As long as they follow the rules. . . . But they have to follow the rules like everyone else. The rules are the rules."[46] Some letter writers make the same argument more forcefully, suggesting that, under the guise of religious freedom, the Amish seek to avoid responsibility. Argued one, "The Amish are not 'being targeted.' Any other contractor in town would be required to follow the rules. It's not enough to be law-abiding only when it is convenient for you. The 'rules are the rules' for a reason." He asserted further that the issue was not one of religion but rather one of public safety and that exempting the Amish would, in fact, harm the general population.

> The people of Locke suffer when a special class of people is set up to do contracting in the town. Homeowners will be left unprotected. Legitimate contractors will not be able to compete because of the higher cost of doing business. Buildings will be built without proper engineering and oversight. I urge the people of Locke not to be sucked into a discussion about religion when the real issue is public safety. Let your town officials know you expect the rules to be the same for everyone.[47]

A fellow letter writer concurred, saying that perhaps the Amish were being disingenuous in their insistence on religious freedom as grounds for exemption from the requirement that they purchase liability insurance. "This issue has nothing to do with religion. Unless these contractors are truly helping their neighbors and working for free, they should earn the trust of their customers by operating a business under time-tested guidelines."[48]

In response to letters, articles, and photographs commenting on the simplicity of Amish life and how picturesque it is, other letters to the editor focus on the drawbacks of the Amish presence. Commenting on the *Watertown Daily Times*' publication of a photograph showing an

Amish buggy driving down the road on a snowy day, one reader wrote, "Anyone who travels these North Country roads every day knows all too well that an Amish buggy on a snowy day is anything but dashing through the snow, or picturesque. When I looked at that picture, all I could see was an accident waiting to happen."[49] A subsequent letter writer agreed, arguing, "It is time that the residents of New York state demand that the state require the Amish equip their buggies with the same visual safety devices as automobiles. Additionally, they ought to be required to pass written rules of the road test just as automobile drivers are and abide by the same age requirements."[50]

Folks were equally vehement—and divided—over whether the Marathon Central School District in Cortland County should provide separate busing for Amish students. In response to a local news article on the subject, some readers asserted that "running separate buses for the purpose of keeping one group of children from having to interact with another group only because they differ in religion, color, ethnicity, language, disability, etc is illegal" and that providing separate buses for Amish students was tantamount to an endorsement of segregation. Others attacked the Amish themselves ("But let's keep claiming they are such a simple folk. It is crap.") Still others felt compelled to remind readers that the Amish "pay SCHOOL TAXES and Property taxes . . . that alone should entitle their children to SAFE transportation to school . . . and even to a private school within the district" and that "the Amish have already provided economic growth to the area."[51]

Even seemingly minor issues, such as horse manure on public road, can excite passion.[52] When the village of Gouverneur in St. Lawrence County debated an ordinance that would have required the local Swartzentruber Amish to diaper their horses, some claimed that the Amish were being discriminated against, while others complained about the smell. In the end, the proposed village ordinance failed, and local Amish said they'd pay more attention to cleaning up after their horses.

Perhaps in part because they settled in a region with an Anabaptist past, the Amish who came to Lowville have found their adjustment a bit easier. Arlene Yousey, a descendant of the nineteenth-century Amish settlers to Lewis County, has written that the Lowville Amish tend to remain separate from other residents of the region. "Several came in and bought my book and I see them in stores. They do not speak unless they're spoken to." Nevertheless, a healthy economic and cultural exchange has developed between the newcomers and longtime residents, and many people buy produce from Amish neighbors. In Yousey's opinion, the presence of Mennonites and an Amish history has made people in the area more welcoming, and she too invokes the horse stalls and designated buggy parking in Lowville: "In the IGA there's an open area; they built a horse shed at the Agway [a feed store selling products for the farm]. I feel [Lowville] has made wonderful provisions for the Amish."[53] One Lowville Amish woman concurred, noting that "three, four, five people a day stopped in to welcome us. Every day, Mennonites would just come in and visit." She added, "There's a difference between the Mennonites and the non-Mennonites. Mennonites are more like we are in their thoughts and ways. Their language is better, so much like we are, clean spoken."

The Lowville Amish appreciate the region, and, having come to the North Country to farm, they feel that they have found a welcome among the other farmers in the area. Commenting on all the region had to offer, one Amish woman said, "We have one lady here with fabrics, and another one sells herbs. We have a Mennonite couple in Croghan that has bulk foods. We send them an order every other week. The feed store delivers." She joked that the community would be "all set" if Wal-Mart also delivered, and added sadly, "Of course, there's no banking by mail."

The friendliness on the part of their neighbors has, at times, even overwhelmed the Amish settlers. As one member of the Lowville community asked rhetorically in a note to *Die Botschaft*,

> What do you do when someone leaves two geese on your doorstep on a Sunday afternoon? With a lot of counseling we decided to skin them, gut them, and set them in water! Now I hope to roast them this afternoon! Does not look like there was a lot of meat on them, but for the breasts. The guy [who left them] had once asked if we would eat them. We said we would, but did not think to add, not on a Sunday though! Have a good week.

Twenty-First Century Amish Life in Lowville

Since the arrival of the first Amish families, the Amish settlement in Lowville has expanded from four families to nearly forty, and with nearly one hundred children in school or not yet started, the community is clearly growing. Nevertheless, as charted in letters to the *Budget* and *Die Botschaft*, rural life in Lowville continues to be governed by the same seasonal activities that would have been familiar to their nineteenth-century predecessors in the North Country. In November, these include hunting, corn husking, clearing fields, and making Christmas gifts. Writing to the

Diary in August, a Lowville resident noted that "the sun is shining in a clear sky, which will put smiles on the threshing crew."[54] Later in the fall, threshing gives way to husking. A *Budget* scribe wrote, "I believe everyone is glad to see the last of November. . . . The man of the house filled all of his tags on Saturday morning and was back in the house by eight o'clock with three. Today he is setting up the husker shredder to shred and husk corn in hopes the field is not too soft to get through and I have six runners to quilt yet before Christmas, so plan to . . . try that out today. See how it goes."[55] When winter comes, there are chores to do even in the coldest weather. "Ice harvesting is about done," wrote one community member to the *Diary*, adding that a neighbor "still wants to fill his ice house once it's ready. The thickest ice was 14 inches, nice ice, no green frozen in."[56]

Summer and fall bring their own tasks. Writing in August, one woman, involved in canning like so many other rural farmwives, noted that "right now I have a cooker of green beans and one of peas on. A cake in the oven and bread dough rising. And peas and green beans with ham on for lunch. I want to cut up some onions and put salt, sugar, and vinegar on and that will be our meal."[57] Later that autumn, she wrote, "There are bins of apples to be made into sauce too. . . . Also have comforts and quilts to be made. More weddings coming up, so we are not putting our feet up yet. Is time to get the noon meal on the table for the Cornhuskers and [the baby] has gone to sleep here on a pillow taking his bottle." Some chores go on throughout the year. Writing to *Die Botschaft*, one correspondent documented wash day:

> Cheery greetings. A very windy day. Seems to sweep the earth. Saves me a job although it is not so fun on a wash day. I only hung three loads out and saw [it was] just not very smart. As the hem tore off one tablecloth, I put coloreds on hangers and hung [them] under the roof and a basket of denims wait in hopes it will soon die down. Is not cold and they are not calling for cold yet. We had thunder storms last evening.

Seasonal activities are punctuated with special events. Periodic frolics, or work parties, offer fellowship, solidify bonds between community members, and teach children that they can enjoy work and accomplish much when they work with others. "Frolics are still on the go," commented the scribe to *Die Botschaft*, noting that the week before a group had helped put siding up on a new house. And as newcomers join the settlement, building is ongoing. In spring 2014, one Lowville Amish woman wrote to her *Diary* audience that there would be a "fence frolic" at the home of a family recently arrived from Maryland and another the day after in "south dale."[58]

When there are young folks, there will be marriages. Weddings are welcome opportunities to visit family and friends. In the same report to *Die Botschaft*, the writer mentioned that a group would be leaving for a wedding in the Path Valley and that others had been attending weddings in Maryland and Pennsylvania. The Lowville wedding feast differs a bit from the dinner served in other Amish settlements. One mother noted that the dinner served after the wedding church service featured "mashed potatoes, stuffing, gravy, celery with sweet and sour sauce, cole slaw, pineapple tapioca, roast chicken, cherry and pumpkin pie and donuts." For supper there was "meat loaf and layer cakes."

Not everyone born in an Amish community decides to become baptized and join the church, and not all who do join stay with the church after baptism. For those who do, being Amish is a way of life shaped by tradition. The Amish do not study their faith or question the scriptures; they simply live as they believe the Bible says Christians should live. They are what the anthropologist Edward T. Hall called a "high context culture," meaning that group members leave many things unsaid. The important messages—the group's values and beliefs—are conveyed in the daily behavior of group members. Children learn by doing, not by being told how to do it. In a high-context culture, it is the group that is important, and tradition and consensus are favored over individual desires.[59] As a Lowville resident commented, "What makes someone Amish is they're born that way. My sisters [who are no longer Amish] are still Amish in ideas and ways of cooking. [It's] a culture I would say. It's so different with the non-Amish. Their attitudes in the home. Maybe if you raised a child Amish they would be. When you meet people, you can just tell." The fellowship that is at the base of frolics and wedding celebrations is implicit in her notion of Amishness, however. "You'd almost have to speak German," she asserted. "If there were a bunch of us cleaning a house and there's someone who can't speak German, you just can't think right. You just can't visit."

In the Lowville Amish community, as in Old Order settlements elsewhere in New York State and across North America, people live a faith expressed in their clothing, their visiting, their daily activities, and their language. Neither saints nor scofflaws looking to avoid inconvenient regulations, the Old Order Amish, much like their non-Amish neighbors, seek to raise their children to hold dear values, traditions, and faith handed down across generations.

5

The Mohawk Valley Amish

Old Order Diversity in Central New York

This settlement started in March 1986. In the foothills of the
Adirondacks, where the coyotes howl and the wind blows
freely.
　—*Diary*, March 2002

Whether Amish life is truly slower, calmer, or as often depicted, simpler, is debatable. Certainly, having to earn a living, feed numerous children, build homes and barns, milk cows, grow much of one's own food, do laundry, and preserve gallons of fruit and vegetables each year, all without the aid of many of the labor-saving devices mainstream America deems essential, makes for a challenging and sometimes complicated life. That the Amish must do all these things while remaining separate from a fast-paced, dominant society presents challenges few outsiders can begin to appreciate.

Each Amish church meets these challenges differently. As a result, each Amish church must negotiate, not only with the non-Amish world, but also with other Amish congregations. In the Mohawk Valley, not far from Albany, the state's capital, several Amish groups from several different states have started settlements. Each encodes in its Ordnung its own particular approach to life, and as these various Amish groups settle near each other, they face the most difficult task of all—learning to live together.

In Search of Cheap Land

In the mid-1980s, Amish families from the New Wilmington area of Lawrence County in Pennsylvania began to settle in Fort Plain, about thirty miles southeast of Utica in Montgomery County. A visitor to the new community in July 1986 wrote that the "new settlement of Lawrence Co. folks . . . have a real nice little valley there between the Adirondack

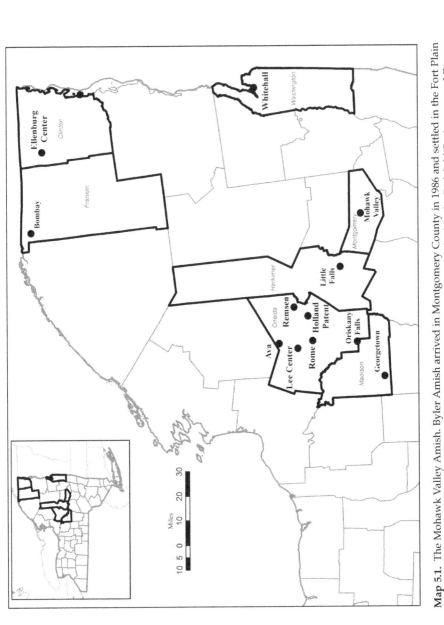

Map 5.1. The Mohawk Valley Amish. Byler Amish arrived in Montgomery County in 1986 and settled in the Fort Plain area (A). In 2001 and 2002, two different Old Order settlements were established in the Richfield Springs area of Otsego County (B), and in 2005 an Andy Weaver Amish settlement was established in the Fultonville-Glen area of Montgomery County (C). In 2007, Swartzentruber Amish began a settlement near Poland, in Herkimer County. New settlers continue

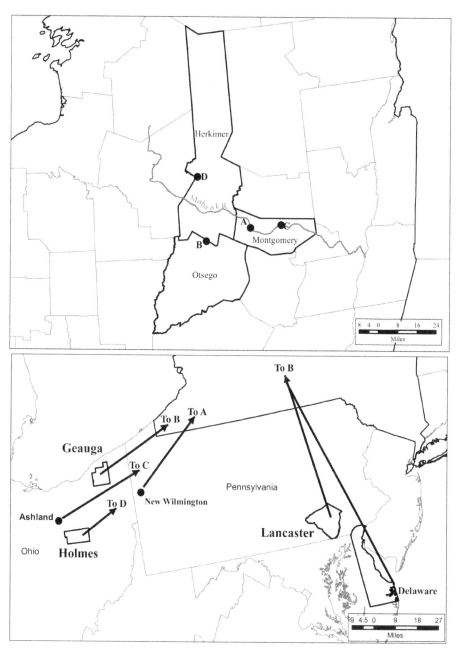

Map 5.2. Central New York's Mohawk Valley region is home to Amish settlers from three other states.

Figure 5.1. Byler Amish buggy. Brown buggies seen in both Fort Plain and Mayville are a visible sign of the connections between these two Byler Amish communities. Photo by author.

Mts., and the Catskill Mts. Eight families are there and they expect one more . . . from Mayville." Belonging to the Byler Amish, like those in the Mayville/Dewittville settlement of the Conewango Valley, these families came in search of "cheap land and plenty of it."[1]

By 1988, there were at least fourteen families in the region, and the settlement was growing steadily. Writing in the *Diary* in February 1999, not quite fifteen years after the arrival of the first families, a scribe from the community asserted that there was "no Amish settlement farther east" and wrote that "we now have 42 families, 2 church districts, 92 adults, 153 children, more or less, total 245 people." By that time, there was also a cemetery for the community, with "3 adults, 1 boy 16, and 2 stillborns" buried there, and each church district had a full complement of ministers.[2] Only three years later, according to the same scribe, there were approximately thirty families in each of the two church districts, a substantial increase. By February 2006, there were eighty-seven families in the settlement, and by February 2007 the scribe to the *Diary* reported that "statistics for 2006 . . . are as follows: 36 babies born, 21 boys, 15 girls, 1 funeral, 5 weddings, 1 widower, 4 families moved in, 5 church districts, 7 schools, 47 young folks, 98 families."[3] By January 2013, the *Diary* scribe was reporting "106 families, 75 youngie, 5 church districts, 6 schools, 2 families moved in, 3 families moved out, 1 death, 7 marriages plus 1 widower married elsewhere and moved here. 16 baptisms."[4] The arrival of the Amish was a sign of good things to come for some non-Amish residents, who hoped that tourist money would follow Amish settlement and give the region a much-needed economic boost. As an article in the *Poughkeepsie Journal* demonstrated, the county needed it.

> Montgomery County, the gateway to the Mohawk Valley . . . has the highest percentage of residents over 65 in New York State, and the highest percentage of unwed mothers. A Planters Nuts factory is closing soon, taking at least 150 jobs. Coleco Industries in Amsterdam is foundering. The collapse of the Thruway bridge over Schoharie Creek a year ago cost the county $600,000, of which only $125,000 has been returned.[5]

The headline of a 1990 *Albany Times Union* report got right to the point: "Amish Resurrect a County."

At the same time, however, few were eager to exploit their new neighbors. County Administrator Charles Bigler was openly unwilling to endorse "a Lancaster Pennsylvania-Dutch tourist gravy train." Speaking to the *Poughkeepsie Journal*, he commented, "I don't think that we should be gawkers or intruders. What if they stood around and watched us mow our lawns? I leave it up to them. If they want to open farm stands, fine. But to jump out of your car and begin taking pictures."[6]

Hoping the Amish could help revitalize the county but wary of turning their new neighbors into tourist attractions, Montgomery County residents have, for the most part, simply made the Amish feel welcome. As a scribe from Gettysburg, Pennsylvania, wrote about Montgomery County to *Die Botschaft*, "The English [non-Amish] people have really welcomed and accepted [the Amish]. They weren't there long till different business places have put up hitching posts, and even installed public telephones for their convenience." The scribe concluded, somewhat sadly, "That is more than we can say of our section [region]."

Welcomed, but not exploited, the Byler Amish in Fort Plain found economic success. The Gettysburg scribe marveled that "one remarkable thing about the Fort Plain settlement is the baking trade they have started up after being there less than, or not more than, three months. People come to their homes and pick up bread and pies. Some of the women said they use 100 lbs of bread flour a week. It's good work. I, too, like to bake." Moreover, non-Amish neighbors quickly found that they could work with the Amish in mutually beneficial ways. "In the past 30 years, the valley has languished economically," claimed Earl Spencer, a non-Amish dairy farmer in the area interviewed not long after the Amish arrived. "And the hardworking Amish have been an inspiration to the local farmers. I tell them [the Amish] 'You must sleep with your hammer,' they are going at such breakneck speed," he added.[7]

By 1990, only four years after the settlement began, the Amish had worked with Spencer to establish a dumping station for their milk, a backup plan after an initial attempt to start a cheese plant on their own fell through. Later, again in partnership with Spencer, the Amish community in Fort Plain started the Palatine Valley Dairy, an enterprise they ran jointly until 2001, when Spencer bought out his Amish partners and moved the cheese plant to its current location between Utica and Albany.[8] In 2002, the Dairylea Cooperative, working with the local Amish dairy farmers, constructed twelve milk dumping stations in the Palatine Bridge area. By 2005, Amish farmers had nearly doubled the amount of milk they were shipping each month, from 450,000 pounds to 800,000, and the number of Amish families shipping milk had grown from thirty to forty-five.[9]

More Amish to the Region

The success of the Fort Plain settlement did not go unnoticed. An Amish man from Christiana, Pennsylvania, commented in a 1997 letter to *Die Botschaft* that the Amish in that region lived "a carefree life." There was, he noted,

> no bottle gas, no mantel lights, no milkers, no mechanical coolers, no chain saws, no engines in fields. One farmer paid $46,000 for 100+ acres and erected buildings quite cheaply, such as wooden cow stalls. They pre-cool

milk in a homemade water trough and are equipped to cool it further in an insulated box type cooler. Nothing fancy or expensive. . . . In mid-summer when they want to make ice cream they get ice out of the saw-dust-insulated icehouse. One farmer supplements this income with 2 green houses and a baking business.[10]

Motivated primarily by the need for farmland, but attracted, at least in part, by these idyllic reports of life in the Fort Plain settlement, other Amish began to think about settling in the Mohawk Valley region, and non-Amish in the area began to think about how they could attract Amish settlers.

Otsego County, like neighboring Montgomery County, is a region of rolling hills, small towns, and farms. The county's website characterizes it as "rural" and notes that it has maintained "its agribusiness, farming, and forestry base."[11] For some Otsego County officials, Amish settlement seemed to offer a means of economic renewal that would not jeopardize the rural character of the region. As Hartwick Planning Board member Orrin Higgins asserted, "What's happening [in Lancaster County] is the Amish are being priced out of the market. The area is being developed so fast, they're under a lot of pressure trying to stay in farming. Now here, we have lots of farmland and almost everyone I know wants to see the land stay in farming."[12]

Higgins began to promote Otsego County at auctions in Lancaster County, Pennsylvania, distributing a one-page flier that listed farms for sale and noted the prominent role played by agriculture in the county's economy. He argued that if the Amish were to move to Otsego County, it would be a "'no-lose situation'—the Amish [could] maintain their farming heritage and Otsego County [could] keep its rural character. In his words: "It would be a plus for our community if we could encourage these people to move in. This is what I am hoping for: we could get an Amish community going."[13]

In fact, Otsego County soon had two. By the end of 2001, settlers from Delaware had bought land in the Richfield Springs area and were moving in. Writing in the *Diary* only a year later, the scribe from the new settlement commented that "we now have 13 families living here with 3 or 4 making land deals. So far [they are] all our original DE folks. In the past year we had 3 births, no deaths. We have 4 ministers here and do appreciate the good help of our many visitors."[14] His daughter, a scribe to the *Budget*, reported twenty families in the settlement only six months later.[15]

Not long after the Richfield Springs settlement was started, families were also moving into the South Columbia area from Geauga County, Ohio, again in search of land. By spring 2002, the second Otsego County Amish settlement had three families.

At first, the older Richfield Springs church did not wholeheartedly welcome the new arrivals from Ohio, for the newcomers had a different Ordnung. Starting a new community so near another only recently established appeared invasive, especially when the two groups lived by different rules. In a letter to an Amish friend, one Richfield Springs church member wrote plaintively about Geauga families who had bought farms close to those of the settlers from Delaware and would even have Richfield Springs addresses. "I complained bitterly," he wrote,

> even before they bought and moved, that they decide to move so near us, yet do not plan to join us nor have the same church standards. I personally spoke to the leader. But all to no avail. [The most] recent family to move in lives only 8½ miles west of us, right here on our road. . . . To date, they have 4 familys [sic]. A Bish[op] from OH comes out every 4 weeks to hold church services. Only 1 ordained living there, a Deacon. . . . I have not seen any letter from there in Budget-Botschaft.

He went on to note that, although most of those in the newer settlement were, in fact, in South Columbia Township, he did not know how they would be identified in *Die Botschaft* or the *Budget*.[16]

Letters to the Amish newspapers soon confirmed the new community's South Columbia identity. In 2003, the *Budget* scribe from Middlefield, Ohio, in Geauga County reported that families continued to arrive in the South Columbia settlement and that there was a teacher for the new school. The scribe wrote that the settlement would "go under the South Columbia, NY heading."[17]

Since their founding, the two Otsego County settlements have grown and stabilized. Writing in the *Diary* in January 2004, a minister from Richfield Springs reported that his settlement had "29 families [and] 2 church districts . . . 2 families moved in, no families move out, 10 births, 7 boys and 3 girls, no deaths, 4 baptisms, no marriages." By 2007, the entry in the *Diary* noted "a total of 33 families" and added, "This past year we had 1 family move in. No family moved out, 3 weddings, 5 baptized, 5 births, no deaths."[18] By 2009, *Raber's Almanac*, which annually updates the list of Old Order Amish communities, was reporting that the Richfield Springs settlement had two church districts, each with its own bishop. Six years later, according to the *Diary* scribe, the settlement at Richfield Springs still had "two church districts, full ministry now in each."[19]

Although smaller than the Richfield Springs community, the settlement in South Columbia has also seen its numbers increase. The community scribe informed readers of the *Budget* in mid-January 2004 that "the statistics for 2003 in our community are 14 families, 2 births and one death." Writing to *Die Botschaft* in June 2005, the same scribe welcomed "family number 23." Since then, the population has appeared to remain steady. According to the 2015 *Raber's Almanac*, the South Columbia settlement has one district, with a deacon, two ministers, and a bishop.

More important, the relationship between the two communities appears to have warmed. Writing in the January 2007 issue of the *Diary*, the scribe from Richfield Springs included "the South Columbia group from OH to our west" among the "neighboring churches that we occasionally visit." As an Amish man not from either community put it, "There's a big highway between Richfield Spring and South Columbia; the ministers are back and forth."

A New Start: The Settlement in Fultonville-Glen

In moving to New York, many Amish settlers are signaling a devotion to a more traditional, agriculturally based way of life. With enough land, farmers can more easily resist the temptations of modern inventions that might help them increase crop yields on shrinking farms. If young parents can find farms, they will be less tempted to look for other kinds of work away from home and church. Those who move will be able to keep a more conservative Ordnung.

Moving may also enable the group to maintain an Ordnung that would otherwise be threatened by changes within the parent community.[20] In other words, rather than force a confrontation and risk a schism in the church, one faction may simply move.

For Amish families from Ashland, Ohio, the Mohawk Valley offered both land and a respite from church difficulties. The first hint of a new settlement in the Fultonville-Glen area, across the Mohawk River from the Fort Plain settlement, came in a note in *Die Botschaft* from Ashland, Ohio, in which the scribe commented, "It seems there's no end to people moving out of Ashland. The past week some men went up to the "planning to be" settlement in Glen, NY to have a milk meeting. Haven't

Figure 5.2. Quilt in frame. Amish women make quilts for use at home and to sell. The quilt frames are often set up in the main living room. While she quilts, the Amish housewife can keep track of children and baking bread. Notice the window curtain. Ordnungs decree both the appropriate curtain color and how it should be hung. Photo by author.

heard for sure who all bought now."[21] Others also talked about a new settlement that was in the works. Writing to a friend, one Amish man from Ashland noted, "There are about 9 or 10 families relocating to around Glen, NY just across the river from the Fort Plain people. . . . Think they'll wait till after Gros Gma [communion church] in late March or early April."[22] The new settlement became a reality in spring 2005. Today the Fultonville-Glenn settlement has four church districts.

For the newcomers from Ashland, deciding to pack up life in one region and start anew in another was not easy. "I wish I could put it in a few words the tremendous strain or the nights we'd be awake for hours asking if we were doing the right thing," said one of those who founded the Fultonville-Glen settlement. He said he had moved to Ashland as a preschooler. "I had a lot of good close friends. My parents are buried in the family cemetery. I was debt free. To leave all of that, that took something to make that decision."

Nevertheless, many felt they had no choice but to move. Life was changing in the Ashland settlement, and many of the more conservative members were appalled by what they saw as behavioral problems and lack of discipline among the Ashland young folk. They saw no resolution to the conflicts and feared both for the future of their children and the future of the community.

The problems in the Ashland community were not new. Nearly ten years earlier, one Amish man and his wife had expressed doubts about moving to the Ashland area because they were concerned about the behavior of the young folk. Writing to a friend at that time, the man averred, "[It] would be nice to just go to Ashland with 2 of our marrieds [married children] there. But then they have a youth problem there. Had different ones that did not get baptized and now the one boy and his girl ran off the last weekend, and the week before, one left that was banned that day. It's so sad."[23] Acknowledging that one of the reasons for leaving Ashland was "the lack of serious commitment to upholding the old way of Amish life," one settler argued that

in society as a whole, there's a break down of moral constraints, and the Amish are not free of that. We rub more shoulders with the outside because we're into other things, but that's not the only thing. [There are] more magazines on average and more opportunity to learn the ways of outside society. We no longer have over all serious convictions of upholding the Amish way of life like we used to. The Older generation are aware that things are changing. The younger generation is not as aware as we are. People are no longer seriously committed to keeping the Old Amish way.

Feeling that the problems with the young folk had become more serious over time and that the difficulties were showing no signs of abating, many in the community saw no recourse but to leave.

Difficulties within a church have a personal impact on each member. One former Ashland resident noted that he had been thinking of moving for some time before his young son joined the young folk. "I'm not saying this to condemn those left behind. I felt things what the young folk were up to were way beyond what a Christian group ought to be. Are we God's people? One of the severest trials I went through in my lifetime—that [my son] wouldn't get sucked into the bad crowd. There was a group and I thought they would remain true but they changed.

I worried that [my son] would too. I wanted to move before [he] joined the young folk. It never worked out. I decided that we weren't supposed to move."

He described the difficulties his son had experienced. "He took a lot of mockery and a lot of time his buggy was severely damaged in singings. The young folk that were wild didn't like him. The fourth time the buggy was damaged, that morning at the breakfast table I could tell something was wrong. That morning he cried and said he'd never go back to the singings again." Ultimately, he said, his son succeeded, met, and married a girl from another settlement. He added, "[She] told [my son] that out of respect for us she would agree to live in Ashland but didn't want to live there always. She was appalled at the disrespect of the young people."

Finally, the parents, their son and his new bride, and a number of other families decided that the time had come to leave. As the father noted, "The last Sunday in church in Ashland, I was ashamed of myself, but I openly cried that this was the last time. But now, knowing [this new] area, and there's a real feeling of closeness [because] pretty much all moved for the same reason. I miss some things, but I have no regrets. I don't know how it would have been with our young folk. If we parents are honest and God-fearing, then God in his mercy to us can in his power help us with the young folk staying respectful and obedient. Now I can just about cry with joy at the respect the young folk show us old folks [if we go to the singings]."

Young Folk and a Community's Future

In moving to preserve church standards, particularly in the behavior of the young folk, the Fultonville-Glen community was, in fact, reenacting its own past, for the Ashland church itself had been started by Amish who had left Holmes County in the early 1950s because of the behavior of the young folks.[24] Throughout Holmes and Wayne counties, said a Fultonville settler who had moved to Ashland as a child, "boys that joined the young folks before joining church would get a car and a set of English clothes, but they'd still be accepted at home." This was, he added, "the number one issue" that caused his father to move to Ashland.

Like the people they left behind in Ohio, members of this new settlement in the Mohawk Valley are "Andy Weaver Amish,"[25] a group that dates officially to 1952 and takes its name from Bishop Andrew J. Weaver, a conservative-minded bishop in Holmes County, Ohio.[26] Weaver came into conflict with his fellow bishops when he insisted that those who left an Old Order church should be excommunicated and shunned, even if they joined a related, albeit more progressive, nonresistant church, such as a Beachy Amish Church or a conservative Mennonite congregation. As one member of the community describes it, "The issue was the Bann. When the ministers and bishops didn't frown at members associating with folks in Bann or make it plain that Bann was recognized, then they no longer agreed with the Andy Weaver church."[27]

The Andy Weaver Church has always been more conservative than the majority of Old Order Amish churches in the Holmes County region, for, as one church member put it, "He [Bishop Andy Weaver] took a stand against drift."[28] Since parting with the Old Order Amish, the Andy Weaver Church has remained committed to a strong Bann, enforced strict behavior standards, and held the line on technological innovation,[29] a stand one church member describes as fundamental to being Amish. Being Amish, he argued, means being willing to "deny yourself whatever it takes to obtain a future, highly valued goal. If we're not willing to deny that, we're probably not ready to be a real Amish man. If you're not willing, you won't remain completely true to the Amish way of doing things. We can compromise . . . but we won't stay Amish." Commenting on the situation in Ashland that had helped to motivate his move to New York, he added, "A number of our young folk in Ashland left the Amish. They'd probably give other reasons, but that's why. Their desires got crossed with their parents and church's guidelines. They just followed their own way and came to where they had to choose, and just followed their own desires."

Because there was no schism or formal rupture with the church districts in Ashland, those who moved to the Fultonville-Glen area have continued to fellowship with family and friends they left behind, and the two settlements appear to share a common lifestyle. Both continue to reject chain saws, and although homes may have indoor plumbing, there is running cold water only. As in the Ohio community, a number of those now living in the Fultonville settlement have adopted some of the trappings of modernity—some have old box freezers in their cellars, for example. But appearances can be deceiving. The old box freezers keep things cold with blocks of ice harvested from ponds or frozen in buckets placed outside on winter days, and the interaction with the community back home is limited so that the rowdiness left behind will have less influence on the new settlement.

Most important, unlike Ashland, the new settlement has reasserted strict behavioral guidelines governing the actions of the young folk, and parents are often present at singings or other young folk gatherings. One father noted that "sometimes after church [the young folk] may get together and play games. . . . Singings are every Sunday. There's a 1 a.m. curfew." An adult couple must also accompany the young folk on any trips. "Our young folk wanted to go to the new community of Georgetown (around 90 miles s.w. of here [Madison County])," writes one of the older community members, who went on to note that his married son and the son's wife had gone with the group. "We prefer that youngie not make such a trip without a married couple along, and I guess we older ones were all a little too chicken of the wintry weather."[30]

The community has also carefully defined proper courting. The Andy Weaver Amish do not have bundling, or "bed courtship," as do the even more conservative Swartzentruber Amish.[31] Instead, there is "chair courtship," which varies from community to community. In some churches, "chair courtship" means that the young woman sits in her boyfriend's lap, and so the two occupy a single chair. Yet, as one member of the Fultonville-Glen settlement commented, "Lap-sitting chair courtship is a situation that causes a lot of problems."[32] In the Fultonville-Glen settlement, families with daughters of young folk age invest in a wide chair in which the couple can sit side by side, a purchase that can bring a lot of winks and comments as others in the community begin to anticipate a wedding. One Amish mother noted smiling, "Sometimes we parents just say we're getting a little wider in our old age." Her husband added that the couple "[could] put two regular chairs beside each other, but it's just not as comfortable."

In part to reinforce youth standards, members of the Fultonville-Glen settlement have also gone out of their way to ensure smooth relations with neighboring Amish churches. For example, anticipating that their farms might appear to encroach on those owned by members of the older, larger Fort Plain community, the settlers wrote to the Fort Plain ministry to ask if they would mind the new settlement. They were told it would be acceptable as long as the Fultonville-Glen group remained on the southern side of the Mohawk River.

These efforts have paid off. Now the two settlements are "back and forth" with each other, and the young folk from one community often interact with those of the other. A Fultonville-Glen father noted,

> We considered [the young people] when we moved. As much a priority as land—not to move close to a community that has the same kinds of problems if our young people are back and forth. A boy from here married a girl from there (Fort Plain) but they were already going together. They moved here. She just adjusted her clothes to our code. Not as difficult as it would appear. They [Fort Plain] have five districts and quite often one of their ministers attends church here and vice versa. [Their] young folk come over here three or four times a year and ours go over there.

Then he added, "There are a number of things different [between the Fultonville settlement and the one in Fort Plain]. They have brown buggies and different dress customs. But as far as what we strive for our goals are similar. Our beliefs and what we strive for are on the same level."[33]

Life in the Mohawk Valley

Leaving a long-established settlement to start a new one may mean beginning from scratch to create a new life. Homes and barns often have to be built (or rebuilt), schools constructed and teachers hired, long-fallow fields restored to productivity, economic ties established, and even drivers found to get from one place to another. Writing from the recently established settlement in Richfield Springs in December 2003, the correspondent to the *Diary* commented that the group was "still very busy getting farm buildings built before winter set in. This year we built no less than 5 large dairy barns. Some larger than others. Also 6 large shops or sheds including the latest one still in the making for a project to benefit our school fund. All these buildings plus a small schoolhouse kept our 26 families very busy while most were doing their farm planting and harvesting."[34] According to one Fultonville settler, an advantage to buying a place without any buildings is being able to "put up buildings how we want them." His wife commented that it was the only advantage. This particular couple had designed their house in such a way that the wife could work in the kitchen while her husband read, a single light sufficing for them both. The property the couple had bought was originally a cornfield with no buildings on it, although there was a dumping station for milk close by. The wife wanted to build near it, and her husband acknowledged that that would have been a good site. Still, he noted, there were no trees there, so the house would have been unprotected. In addition, the house would have been on the edge of the property, and not in the middle, which was ultimately where they chose to build. The deciding factor was the forest along the ridge that runs through their property. Commented the husband, "My greatest enjoyment is having built close to woods. Sometimes we think we're having a picnic every day."

The couple's son and his wife had built nearby. A carpenter, the son was ready to help his parents finish their home, but his father was hesitant to accept his help too often. "Everyday we keep him home to work for us, that's less money for him to pay off the principal. He pays a lot of money on interest for his loan." The father noted further that members of the settlement had "intended to have this community based as much on agriculture as we can. But just having a barn wouldn't guarantee an income. We have to stock it. Given the economy, we'd rather [our son] paid off his mortgage debt first."

As the membership in the different settlements grows, each community is attempting to ensure that the next generation will have a good start. In contrast to Amish in the long-established settlements in Ohio and northern Indiana, many of whom have continued to send their children to rural public schools, each of the Amish communities in New York State has established private schools so that their children can be educated within the Amish community. One of the first buildings constructed in the Fultonville-Glen settlement was a schoolhouse, and early discussions within the community focused on how often the board would have to meet to ensure adequate supervision.

One sign of how important the Mohawk Valley has become for Amish settlement in New York was the first Annual New York State Teachers' Meeting, held for the state's Old Order teachers in Richfield Springs in August 2007. This was the first time a school meeting of this type had been held in the state. In the past Old Order teachers who wished to meet with their counterparts from other communities had to make individual visits or attend teachers meetings in other states. The New York meeting, which attracted Amish teachers, ministers, and parents from across New York and beyond the state's borders, opened with a prayer led by the bishop from the South Columbia settlement. The first address, a discussion of the benefits of school meetings, was delivered by an Amish man from Canada who had long been active in the Old Order Amish private school movement. Other talks on subjects such as peer pressure, the harmful effects of mockery [bullying], and the first year in school, were delivered by representatives from different communities, demonstrating the evolving ties between many of the New York settlements.

The Challenges Facing New Settlements

Moving to a new region challenges the Amish, but it also challenges their non-Amish neighbors, most of whom know little about the horse-and-buggy folks who might be moving in next door. The first arrivals to a new settlement are always concerned about how they will be received. Although at least some in Otsego County actively recruited Amish settlement, the Amish are not always so welcomed. For example, an Amish man in Montgomery County acknowledged that his community had had "some problems with building permits and architectural drawings." Claiming that his group could not in good conscience pay for architectural drawings to accompany each request for a building permit because they saw the expense as exorbitant and the drawings unnecessary, the man added, "On judgment day it would be hard to say we wanted to be strangers and pilgrims with a big mansion."[35] The Amish find it impossible to meet the demands of county regulations that go in the face of the community's Ordnung. Devoted to putting faith into practice, the Amish must defer to their understanding of the wishes of a far higher authority. This is perhaps an inevitable conflict between the Amish, who ask only to be left alone, and the desire on the part of county officials for tourist dollars.[36]

Compromise is possible, though occasionally hard won. While the "picturesque" lifestyle of the Amish settlers is attractive to tourists with cameras, non-Amish neighbors must adjust to sharing the road with more slowly moving horse-drawn vehicles. Acknowledging that "there's real concern about traffic and Amish schoolchildren on the road," one Amish man expressed pleasure that the different communities were working together to come up with a solution to the traffic problem. "They're trying to come up with a plan," he noted. "Speed bumps aren't popular. They're thinking about heavy patrols and flashers." Then, he added, "The county commissioner talked to the bishop to get his input, and the bishop was humbled by the effort on behalf of the Amish. He said that the Amish would teach their children to be careful."

Flooding in the Mohawk Valley in 2006 helped to bring the Amish and non-Amish communities together. A writer to the *Record* (out of

Amsterdam, New York) specifically thanked members of the Amish community for their assistance and commented "Let's keep working together." Said one Amish man hopefully, "We realize the public needs to put up with things they don't like because of us, because of our slow ways, but maybe because of things like this [Amish help after the flood] it will even out a little more."

Ultimately, although the differing lifestyles and conflicting desires of the various Mohawk Valley communities could result in tensions, they appear more often to resolve themselves in neighborliness. Regarding the Fort Plain settlement, one Amish man said, "At first they were just tolerated by outsiders [non-Amish], but there are now about one hundred families, and they're definitely making an impact on that part of the county." The *Budget* scribe from Fultonville-Glen commented with relief that, only a few months after the first members of the settlement had moved in, "we have been largely welcomed by the natives [non-Amish] and hope it can remain so. The area is rolling, with lots of woods and wildlife."[37]

Already, the Amish and their neighbors have become economically and socially interdependent in a variety of ways. A lack of public transportation, for example, has meant that the Amish must hire drivers to ferry them to distant train and bus stations, doctors, and shopping centers. One man said he had set about finding drivers by talking to neighbors and finding out where they worked and what they did. "I don't like to ask favors right away," he said. "I don't think that's nice." But he noted whether or not someone was retired, and, if so, asked how the person kept busy. "If the man says he has a nice hobby, then I don't bother him. Sometimes he says he doesn't do much and the days get long, and I ask him if he'd be willing to do some taxi work for the Amish. We like to make it clear that they don't have to—it's up to them. Sometimes a driver is too expensive; others just want to cover expenses."

Store owners and managers, particularly those operating feed and hardware stores, have gotten to know their Amish customers, and word of mouth has spread names and addresses of Amish carpenters, quilters, and produce sellers. Amish women have gotten to know neighbors with whom they can ride to pick berries or go shopping. As Amish businesses grow, they attract non-Amish customers.

Events in the Fultonville-Glen area demonstrate how quickly a community can be integrated into the economic life of the larger community and the conflicts inherent in this. In spring 2005, only a few months after the first families moved to the region, the settlement began to work with the Dairylea Cooperative. The *Budget* scribe was able to report in August that "the milk dumping station, where our milk is to be picked up by a Grade A milk company [Dairylea], is finally getting the finishing touches, and the barns and milk houses passing the last inspections for milk to be accepted by the last of this week. A relief in more ways than one, although it will probably end the delicious surplus of homemade cheeses, yogurt and butter."[38] According to one community member, at least half the families in the Fultonville-Glen settlement are now shipping milk. He said the Amish dairy farmers are exempt from shipping milk on Sunday if they put ice in the water in which the milk cans are stored. As a result, he added, everyone in the community had plans to put ice up the following winter, and he himself hoped to put up an icehouse in the fall.

The help provided by the Dairylea Cooperative was instrumental in enabling the Fultonville Amish farmers to ship grade A milk. Indeed, Dairylea describes its role in the economic success of the Mohawk Valley's Amish churches as "pivotal." Through the cooperative's lending subsidiary, AgriFinancial Services (AFS), Amish farmers in Fultonville-Glen received financial assistance to build milk houses and purchase the necessary dairy equipment. Because the Amish will not connect to the power grid, Dairylea owns the dumping station, where milk is collected. The result, according to Dairylea, has been a revival of farming among the Amish in the Mohawk Valley. A newsletter from the cooperative asserts that "more Amish children are getting involved in dairying due to their parents' success with the cooperative. This change counteracts the recent trend of Amish offspring moving away from farming because of operational difficulties and decreased revenue."[39]

Because the Fort Plain Amish community had already forged an arrangement with the Dairylea Cooperative, it was no doubt easier for the Amish from Ohio to enter into this economic agreement than it might have been otherwise. That it allowed the Amish to maintain their agricultural base further favored the arrangement. Nevertheless, a member of the Fultonville-Glen community argues that change, whether social or economic, must be approached cautiously: "There are a lot of things that are in a gray area but history and our experience tells us if we don't make a line somewhere we'll lose our way of life. Our way is not the only way, but we feel there's a value to it. If some members don't agree and just do as they please, it will bring disunity, and we'll lose our way of life. Within two or three generations, we'll be driving a car, and you won't see any difference."

He acknowledges that standing still is not necessarily a better option. "There are groups, and there may be even among ourselves, that take rules too far. Some even depend on the rules as the only way to salvation—as long as you follow rules. [That's a] misuse." Modern life, the Amish man asserted, has become difficult because of the many choices confronting the church today. "One reason there are so many different church groups among the Amish and so many new settlements is the influx of so many new inventions. There are pressures our forefathers never experienced. The difficulty and cost of farming—we really encourage farming—will influence the Amish a few generations down the road. If we branch out into other things, we get into areas where we feel it's necessary to have new things, [then we] can no longer all see eye to eye on what's necessary to make a living and what we can do without." The difficulty, he concluded, is that "the older generation fear new things, but the younger generation can't make a living."

The negotiation between tradition and innovation that allows an Amish church to redefine itself while, at the same time, maintaining its integrity is evident even in smaller commercial ventures. Having successfully cultivated a market for his handmade wooden toys in the far more tourist-focused region of Holmes County, Ohio, one newcomer had to work to reestablish himself in a region in which he was unfamiliar with the different markets and tourist centers. "No phone, and no . . . long-distance transportation limits my interaction with the outside society," he said, and he expressed concern about what he saw as "a very real danger of being carried away from what we strive for spiritually by naturally wanting to promote our business." His solution was, he said, to "try to rely on my own conscience, and any concerns voiced by any community member. As long as I keep it to a one-man shop, and basic woodworking tools, the community is usually at ease."[40]

Although, as one man put it, "having our way of life agriculturally based is vital," sometimes conditions favor the establishment of larger businesses or business relationships that go far beyond settlement borders. Following flooding in the Mohawk Valley, two Amish brothers in the Fultonville-Glen community bought the stock of a lumber company, much of it apparently damaged and of little value in a retail market. The deal benefited both the lumber company and the local Amish communities; the lumber company was able to sell the usable wood instead of taking a complete loss on its stock, and the brothers salvaged the lumber to supply the Amish in the Fultonville-Glen and Fort Plain areas. As another member of the community noted, the brothers considered the benefit of the deal for the whole community. "If the brothers hadn't had the money," he added, "the whole community would have chipped in, but it was easier for them to do it."

Like other Amish who have started new settlements, those who have come to the Mohawk Valley have confronted situations with which they have little prior experience and for which their Ordnung provides only minimal guidance. As a result, they have had to consider doing things differently. Amish society is always negotiating, and renegotiating, the symbolic boundaries that define the church. And in such a dynamic process, the outcome is uncertain.[41]

In the Mohawk Valley, as communities that were not in close contact before become next-door neighbors, Amish families confront other Amish families that do things differently, and this both puzzles and challenges them. Even little things are confusing. Commenting on the dress of his Fort Plain neighbors, for example, a Fultonville Amish man said, "I couldn't figure it out at first. I know the women look different, but I pay so little attention." His wife clarified things for him. "The women's caps—the back part is different. Like a guinea hen," she said, referring to the little bow that sticks up a bit at the nape of the Fort Plain cap, unlike the bow on her own cap, which lies flat. Little things are important in the Amish world. As more families move into this Andy Weaver community, including some from the Byler settlements in Fort Plain and Mayville, the man and his wife worry that too many could move in too quickly. "That might lead to changes in our church because they would want to keep some of their ways."[42]

Burgeoning Amish Settlement in the Mohawk Valley Region

In spring 2003, a member of the Richfield Springs church lamented jokingly that "at present we have 24 familys [sic], a resident Bishop plus 4 ministers, with more familys making deals and plan to move in, including a deacon. How do we slow this down? Maybe our severe, harsh winter of '02–'03 will give some cold feet."[43] That has not proved to be the case. The Amish continue to come to the Mohawk Valley, a wave of settlement that shows little sign of abating. As the scribe from Richfield

Springs commented in a September 2005 letter to the *Diary*, "Our good New York farm land is being sought out."[44] A year later, describing his trip to the Mohawk Valley, a Lancaster County resident asserted that he "had to think of Moses as he looked over the Promised Land. There's much room in Mohawk Valley and Little Falls. I'd venture to say there's room for 150 churches."[45]

The Lancaster County writer did not hold out much hope that those who moved to the Mohawk Valley could succeed as farmers because of the short growing season. Moreover, he added, "[Crop] prices are low, land prices high, it's impossible to pay for a farm today unless you have additional income."[46] Nevertheless, his neighbors, selling farms at premium prices to Pennsylvania developers, found the income, for they began buying property in the Little Falls area near Fort Plain. The first families, including a bishop for the new settlement, moved to the area at the end of March 2004. A minister was ordained in the community in fall 2006, and that year the new school had nineteen pupils.[47] By February 2007, the Little Falls settlement had nine families and spread over Herkimer and Montgomery counties. As one Amish letter writer noted, "The Mohawk Valley in NY is taking off like wild fire with the Ashland people at Glen-Fultonville. The Lanc[aster] or Little Falls group is moving in close to Glen and Fort Plain, also some want to start farther north. Will have to wait till the dust settles. The Lanc[aster] People are pushing the land price up."[48]

The Little Falls community was only the first Lancaster settlement. By December 2005, more settlers from Lancaster County had come to the region to settle in Montgomery County. Only four years later, the community, which identifies itself in Amish publications as "Mohawk Valley," had forty-three families divided between two church districts; by 2013, it "58 families, 3 church districts, 18 births . . . 3 ordinations, 3 marriages, 5 moved in and 1 moved out." The only thing it didn't have, lamented the settlement scribe, was a carriage shop. This community has continued to draw families from various Pennsylvania settlements. By 2014 there were "69 families in 3 districts, 7 school houses, around 50 young folks, 15 births, . . . 8 families moved in, 4 from Big Valley, 3 from Lancaster County, and 1 from Dauphin County." The community has continued to grow. Only two years later, in January 2016, the community scribe wrote to the *Diary* that "statistics for Mohawk Valley, which is now 10 years old: 90 families in four districts, eight schools, 20 births, . . . two ordinations, one bishop and one preacher, 13 baptisms." The scribe reported that his own district now had thirty families.[49]

With their Lancaster heritage, the Little Falls and Mohawk Valley settlements tend to be among the more progressive in New York.[50] But there has been more conservative settlement in the Mohawk Valley as well. For example, in 2006, as noted above, the Georgetown settlement in Madison County was started by families moving from Woodhull, New York, a community that was started in Steuben County in 1983 by settlers from Troutville, Pennsylvania (which had been started by settlers from Ohio in 1972). In 2007, Joe Troyer Swartzentruber Amish founded an even more conservative settlement in nearby Poland, New York. By January 2015, the Poland community had twenty-eight families in a single church district, many of them raising sheep.

As settlement in the Mohawk Valley region has extended westward into Oneida County, other new communities have been established by settlers from several different states. The Orinsky Falls community, for example, was started in 2010 by settlers from Michigan and Wisconsin. The *Budget* scribe from Fultonville-Glen noted in March that "the families moving from Stanwood, Mich. to the new community of Augusta, NY [Orinsky Falls] (about 89 miles west of here) asked for help to unload trucks the 24th. A van load went to help." Helpers also came from communities in neighboring counties as well. Writing to *Die Botschaft* in May, 2010, the scribe from the new community was overwhelmed, "Last Wednesday, a vanload of men and boys and one woman from Lowville [Lewis County] came to help wherever needed and want to come again this week. Makes us feel unworthy that they just come and donate their help!" By January 2015, there were twenty-six families in a single church district. Only a year later, the *Diary* scribe noted, "27 families, two churches, four schools, occupation is mostly dairy farming." In the past year, he added, here had been "one wedding, seven baptisms, one death, 13 births (five boys and eight girls)."[51]

Also arriving in Oneida County were settlers from Atlantic, Pennsylvania, who began to settle in the Remsen area in 2011. That May the scribe from Atlantic wrote to the *Budget*, "Yesterday was the last time for our bishop and family to be in church. They are leaving us for a new settlement in N.Y., which he is starting. Sad to say, and it hurts to write this, but there are more leaving our church for the same place in the near future." By the following month, five more families had left for New York. Today, the Rome-Remsen-Holland Patent settlement has twenty-eight families. In 2012, settlers from Mercer County, Pennsylvania, arrived in the Ava-Lee Center area, and by January 2016 there were, according to the *Diary* scribe, "26 families, one school, 46 scholars, and 26 young folks."[52]

Yet, in the past decade, as the Mohawk Valley has seen new settlements, it has also witnessed movement out, for available land has become both scarcer and more expensive. Most affected, perhaps, has been the Fort Plain settlement, oldest—and largest—in the region, which has seen a number of families leave for new settlements north of the Mohawk Valley, in Bombay (Franklin County, 2009), Ellenberg Center (Clinton County, 2011), and most recently, Whitehall (Washington County, 2014). A member of the Fultonville/Glen community, writing to the *Budget* in 2009, lamented the departure of neighbors and friends.

> With our neighboring community Ft. Plain, rapidly increasing in numbers, and hardly room to expand by being hemmed in by the river and towns, 15 of their families bought farmland up in the Bombay area. Wanting to enjoy a visit yet while there was still opportunity, [my] brother invited [several of the departing families] over for Sun. dinner. It was such an enjoyable, but short day, tinged by a deep sadness that this might well be the last time that we are together like this. [They] had done much to help our own young community take root.[53]

The new arrivals to the New York's North Country were welcomed by other Amish neighbors. A *Diary* scribe from North Lawrence in St. Lawrence County wrote in 2010 that she had not yet "seen a Bombay, NY area piece in the Diary yet, so maybe . . . should write a little about them. Quite a few families moved in from Fort Plain. They live around 15 miles from here. They had 11 barn raisings this summer. Also a lot of silos were built. They plan to ship milk, or most of them are at it. Four weeks ago they had their first funeral."[54]

The relationship between churches in a particular region may be mediated as much by history as by geography. An Atlantic, Pennsylvania, area Amish man noted, for example, that several of the new settlements, including those in Ava/Lee Center and Remsen areas, "aren't or won't be communing with the parent settlements. Will probably be somewhat more conservative or restrictive, though the problem isn't really Ordnung. There has been a split here in Atlantic about 1st of December," with the more conservative moving to New York. He added that "the more conservative would commune with . . . Glen, Fort Plain, Bombay, and some newer settlements."[55]

Patterns of visiting between the different groups in the Mohawk Valley clearly reveal the ways in which each settlement is bound by its past and the Ordnung it has evolved. For example, while the Fultonville-Glen folks are "back and forth with the Fort Plain people," they have little to do with the Little Falls church. As a member of the Fultonville church put it, "After many years, we no longer work back and forth [fellowship] with Lancaster people, they have modernized so much." He listed the differences between their way of life and his own, including "larger scale farming [and] modern machinery." They have, he elaborated, "an engine with a PTO shaft on a cart and any piece of equipment they can hook up to that they do." To make a final point, he added, "They wouldn't think of doing loose hay," that is, putting hay loose in the barn for storage rather than baling it.[56] Nor was his group "back and forth" with the communities in Richfield Springs or South Columbia; ministers from one community would not preach in services held by another. But, he affirmed, "We help out with barn raisings."

Numerous accounts of visiting, not just for pleasure but to help out, appear in the Amish publications, and these show the ties that help to bind communities. In a note to the *Diary* in August 2014, for example, the scribe from Ava/Lee Center wrote,

> On the 15th a load went to the barn-raising at Whitehall, NY near the Vermont border. On the 16th I went with a load to Samuel Wagler's barn-raising in Philadelphia, NY. We helped put up a used barn, it was a very interesting day and an old fashioned setting. Amish were there from Bombay, Lowville, Glen and Ava, NY, so it was a mixed group of Lawrence, Lancaster, Swiss, Holmes, and Geauga type people. This building went up, so I guess we could all understand each other![57]

As the non-Amish residents of the Mohawk Valley become used to the mix of gray, brown, and black buggies on their back roads and hitched up outside various town businesses, it is clear that the Amish are changing life in this region. When the first Amish settlers came to live in the Mohawk Valley nearly thirty years ago, newspaper columnists expressed hope that they would bring new prosperity to the region. Yet Amish settlement appears to have yielded a far greater return. While the establishment of Amish communities in this area so close to the hustle and bustle of the state capital has benefited their non-Amish neighbors, the Amish themselves have found a home in which they can live according to their faith and express through their daily labor the values that define their particular churches. They have sought out the necessary farmland to ensure that their young people will be able to continue tilling the soil. Some have found respite from community strife. As the different churches in the Mohawk Valley interact in the years to come, the Amish will confront new challenges and will, in response, reaffirm or readjust the boundaries of their faith and their identity.

6

In Search of Consensus and Fellowship

New York's Swiss Amish

There's times when you wonder whether [you] did the wrong thing—you don't want to offend people. It's harder when not everyone agrees.
—A Swiss Amish woman in New York

Despite their common origin in the Anabaptist movement and Jacob Ammann's break with the larger Mennonite movement, today's Amish are ethnically as well as religiously diverse. The Swiss Amish began to arrive nearly a century after the first German immigrants had reached North America, and although they identified as Amish, the Swiss Amish immigrants differed in many ways from their German Amish counterparts.[1] The Swiss immigrants, who came to North America directly from Switzerland or from Swiss enclaves in Europe, including Swiss communities in Alsace and Lorraine, had few kinship ties to those who had immigrated earlier. Further, while the Swiss and German immigrants shared basic Anabaptist beliefs, they had had little interaction in Europe and had evolved different traditions, and this helped to keep the groups separate from each other as they established new settlements in North America. Often these new Swiss Amish settlers were more progressive than either earlier Amish immigrants or their newly arriving German counterparts. Finally, and perhaps most important, the "Shwitsa" German dialect that the Swiss Amish used was often incomprehensible to other Amish, who spoke Pennsylvania German (also called Pennsylvania Dutch).[2]

Most of the settlements these nineteenth-century Swiss Amish immigrants established did not survive as Amish.[3] The churches established in Adams and Allen counties in northeastern Indiana by the Swiss Amish forebears of New York's Swiss Amish settlers were a notable exception. These Swiss Amish churches continue to thrive, but they have

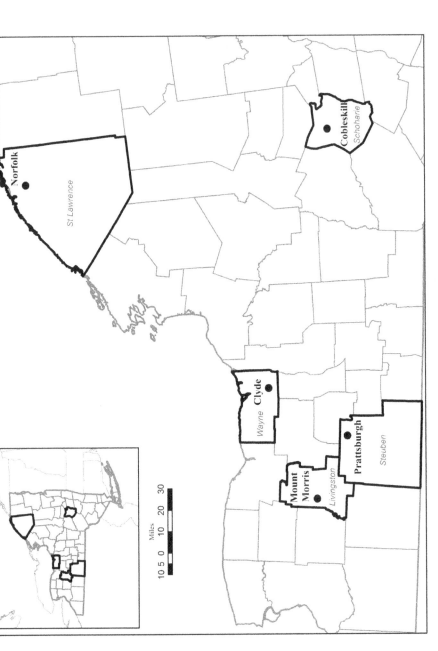

Map 6.1. New York's Swiss Amish settlements. The first Swiss Amish moved to Norfolk, New York, in 1974. A second Swiss settlement began in the Prattsburgh area in 1979. Clyde, a daughter settlement of the Norfolk community, was started in 1997.

historically had limited interaction with their German counterparts and so have evolved differently. For example, although they chose an Old Order path, few Swiss Amish leaders attended the nineteenth-century Diener-Versammlungen, which helped to define the Old Order Amish as distinct from more progressive Amish churches. Over the years, the Swiss churches have acquired a reputation for stubbornness, and their communities have been shaped by internal conflict.

Conflict and the Swiss Amish Churches

A key difference between the Swiss Amish and the German Amish is that the Swiss Amish favor "an understanding of unity as uniformity."[4] Against this "not with us means against us" backdrop, church politics are much more contentious, and events cause dissension long after they might have died down elsewhere. Comparing her German Amish church near the Indiana border to the predominantly Swiss one in New York State in which she used to live, one Amish woman asserted that "if something happens in church [here], it's done. We just don't talk about it. People do not chew it! There [the New York Swiss settlement] women would talk about it endlessly. . . . [They] never moved on with anything, and that includes the ministers, not just the people."

Perhaps as a result of this unwillingness to "move on," the Swiss communities have experienced a number of schisms, often resulting in an exodus of members from the Amish church. For example, during the nineteenth century, the Allen County, Indiana, Swiss Amish church, like the Croghan Amish community, lost membership to the Apostolic Christian Church, a movement begun in Switzerland in the 1840s under the leadership of a former Reformed minister, Samuel Froelich.[5]

The Swiss settlement in Adams County has had an even more turbulent history. In the mid-1860s, Bishop Henry Egly, who served a congregation near Berne, Indiana, began to preach that his church had become formalistic and lacked spirituality.[6] Further, he argued, the church had been lax in maintaining the old customs and had baptized those who had not experienced an individual spiritual regeneration. Those who had not felt such a spiritual regeneration, Egly preached, should be rebaptized once they had. By 1866, Egly's views were no longer compatible with those of the rest of the ministry in his community, and he, along with half of the congregation, left the Amish church and formed the Defenseless Mennonite Church.[7]

The Amish community in Adams County divided again when, in 1894, approximately two-thirds of the community left to follow David Schwartz, son of the group's bishop, Joseph A. Schwartz. Zealous in his interpretation of Ordnung and often relying on his own understanding of scripture rather than on a traditional reading, David Schwartz was unwilling to compromise and even put his own father under the Bann. In a short history of the church that he published in 1925, David Schwartz asserted that his new church was "built upon the Cornerstone of Jesus Christ. Therefore she calls herself 'Christian Church' after her Master's name. By the people she is commonly called Amish, after Jacob Ammannn [sic]. Therefore she carries the name, 'Amish Christian Church.'" He went on to draw a direct line from his breakaway group to the early apostolic church.

> This church was named "True Believers" (Catholic) in the beginning. Later, about the year 1530 to 1700 she was called "Mennonite Church." Then from 1700 until 1894 she was called "Amish Mennonite Church." Then from 1894 until this time she is called "Amish Christian Church." . . . This is, through the grace of God, the preserved and remaining Bride or Church of Jesus Christ, which has made its passage through the ages until the end of time.[8]

This belief that the group embodied the only true church led Schwartz's followers to reject fellowship with others and to condemn those who remained with the Old Order Amish.[9]

For David Schwartz and his followers, uniformity in thought and a resistance to compromise were evidence of the purity of the church. Members of the group were willing to place any who disagreed with church decisions under the Bann. It was a trait they shared with those who remained with the Adams County Amish congregation, which, favoring unyielding loyalty to particular beliefs and practices, continued to face church turmoil and schism. David's father, the aging bishop Joseph A. Schwartz, angered some in the congregation when he resisted pressure to shun one Jacob Shetler and his wife, Amanda, who had been placed under the Bann by a Holmes County, Ohio, church. Schwartz reasoned that, since his church was not in fellowship with the Ohio congregation, it made little sense to enforce the Ohio Ordnung by refusing to accept the Shetlers as members. Nevertheless, when the old bishop died, another son, Joseph L. Schwartz, took over the church leadership and proceeded to impose a stricter Ordnung that called for shunning the Shetlers. This action divided the church.

Desiring to avoid further church conflict but unwilling to compromise on their understanding of the church and what it meant to be a good church member, many Swiss Amish left Indiana to establish settlements elsewhere. Some went to Mt. Pleasant Mills in Snyder County, Pennsylvania, where they were in proximity to a number of other Anabaptist groups that had settled there over the years, including, coincidentally, the descendants of David Schwartz's Amish Christian Church.

Over time, the Amish Christian Church had evolved a rather progressive lifestyle, with church members adopting changes in dress and technological innovations such as the automobile. Photographs from the 1930s show male church members wearing bow ties and women without caps. In 1937, however, the group reorganized, renamed itself the Reformed Amish Christian Church, and began to shed its progressive ways. Ten years later the group established a settlement in Tennessee, and, in 1952, it moved to Snyder County, Pennsylvania, where, not long after, the group "dissolved."[10] The remnants of the Reformed Amish Christian Church joined with others in the area, identified themselves as Old Order Amish once again, and adopted a lifestyle far plainer than that of many Old Order Amish churches.

A common thread in all these disputes is disagreement over the nature of the church itself. For the Amish, the church is a community formed of those who have come together voluntarily to live according to God's commandments, and the Ordnung is the framework that supports the community and guides church life. Determining what and who the Ordnung will cover; when one has violated the Ordnung and must be shunned; and whether one must be rebaptized upon joining the church is, in fact, defining the church itself. This, in turn, has implications for one's eternal life, for the Amish believe that only by living in fellowship with others in the congregation and working with them to put Christ's teachings into practice can they hope to be worthy of salvation.[11]

Schism acts to distill beliefs. Each baptized church member must take a stand, committing to a particular way of being Amish. Each of the resulting factions, convinced that those on the other side have taken a wrong spiritual turn, reinforces its own practices. Relocating to avoid schism has much the same effect. It takes away from the settlement those who disagree with the direction in which the church is headed.

Coming to New York

In 1974, three Amish families moved from Snyder County to St. Lawrence County to establish the first Swiss Amish church in New York State, and others soon joined them, some coming from church districts in Indiana and Michigan. The first child in the new community was born in April, shortly after the group's arrival. By May, one local paper, the *Watertown Daily Times*, was reporting that "five Amish families have purchased property and four of them are residing in the Norfolk communities of Plumbrook and Brookdale."[12] The *Massena Observer* called the decision by Amish families to settle in the town of Norfolk one of the highlights of 1974.[13]

The settlers themselves minced no words in explaining their decision to come to New York's North Country.[14] "Farms here are dirt cheap, and it's good land," said one newcomer, who bought a farm and established a small store in the new community. He added that he had come with his wife and family from Indiana because "we couldn't hardly buy land there, while here it was going for $250 an acre."[15] Another member of the Norfolk settlement agreed. Interviewed not long after his arrival in the region, he commented that "in Indiana, farms cost anywhere from $1,500 to $2,000 and $3,000 an acre. . . . My place here I bought for $200 an acre."[16]

Clearly, however, there were other factors behind the decision to move to New York, for if land alone had been the reason families left Snyder County, the families who stayed behind could have bought the farms of those leaving, and the community would have remained stable.[17] Instead, the population of the Snyder County Amish settlement continued to decline. Only five years after the establishment of the Norfolk settlement, another group of families had left the Pennsylvania community to found a settlement in Prattsburgh in Steuben County, New York. Following their departure, the scribe from Snyder County wrote in a letter to the *Budget*, "There are only five families left here now since the others moved to New York. Our gatherings on Sundays sure seem small now compared to what they used to be. We'll really miss them."[18]

The Swiss Amish who left Pennsylvania and moved to New York were also seeking greater freedom from the pressure to assimilate to a more modern lifestyle. At least one man from the settlement, Eli Garber, undertook to find a simpler path for himself and his family. In a journey well documented by the *New York Times*, Garber was attempting "to

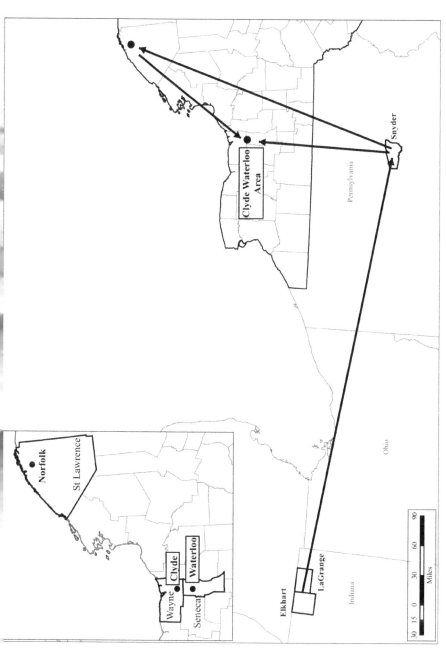

Map 6.2. New York's Swiss Amish came to New York from Indiana via Pennsylvania.

escape from the commercialism growing around his Amish community in Mt. Pleasant Mills" and to "re-create the purer life of self-sufficiency practiced by his forefathers."[19] He took his wife and four young children from Snyder County to Maine by horse and buggy. The would-be pioneers returned to Snyder County in the same way only when no other families joined them.[20]

Scarce land, commercialism, and pressure to modernize were not the only problems facing the Snyder County church. More important were the rifts developing within the Swiss Amish community itself as church members debated their response to these forces. While some responded to the growing discord by leaving the area, those who remained appeared willing to change their way of life or even to leave the Amish church in their search for fellowship. For example, one woman recounted how some in the Snyder County church had attempted to join an Old Order Mennonite church. "We tried to fellowship with the Hoover group. They're just a small batch that broke off from the Stauffer Mennonites.[21] But because [our Bishop] chewed tobacco [which was forbidden by the Hoover church] we couldn't dare."[22] She added, "We went through lots of changes to find a group to fellowship with."[23]

Small, lacking strong leadership, and eager to find fellowship with others, the new daughter settlement in Prattsburgh was, at first, also willing to change its Ordnung. The minister sent letters to those he knew were searching for a community in which to relocate. He wrote to one Amish man, who was contemplating a move,

> I saw in the Budget that you visited Stanton, Mich[igan] and maybe you live there by this time but I thought there would be no harm in writing and asking you if you would consider us if we lowered our Ordnung. We agreed with John to put away our chain saws and quit hiring drivers to go to church or visiting. There are sometimes circumstances where it is just about necessary to hire a driver such as getting a large piece of equipment from a distance, moving and such things. Also electric watches, clocks etc. we would put away.

The minister went on to add, "You had mentioned about hiring tracters [sic]. I feel we could also agree to stop that if it made a big difference to you."[24] The concessions the minister was willing to make on behalf of his congregation, particularly his offer to give up chain saws and to quit hiring drivers, would have made the group one of the most conservative.

A Strange Belief in the Snyder County Church

The conflicts that troubled the Swiss Amish communities of Snyder County and Norfolk and Prattsburgh, New York, went deeper than disagreements about technology or tobacco. In 1984, members of the Snyder County church and its daughter settlements in Norfolk and Prattsburgh found themselves struggling with each other over the issue of *Gewissheit der Seligkeit*—that is, the belief that an individual can have personal knowledge of salvation. Such a "strange belief," as many in the community called it, strikes at the heart of the Amish church, for it challenges church authority, promotes individualism, and suggests that the tradition is irrelevant. If you can know you are saved, why should you yield to the Ordnung? Arguing that only God can know if a church member is saved, the Old Order Amish consider this belief to be prideful. In response, those who believe that one can have a personal relationship with Christ and know oneself to be saved chide the Old Order Amish for privileging tradition over spiritual enlightenment.[25]

Hoping to resolve dissension, the Snyder County ministers met with the ministers from Norfolk and Prattsburgh, and in September 1984 they drew up a statement of their common beliefs. Despite the apparent agreement, however, conflict remained. As one outsider reported,

> I learned that a meeting had been held at Prattsburgh on Sept 27, attended by the ministry of Snyder Co. and of Norfolk, NY (some of them). Bish. Sam had been there, too, and a statement of faith had been drafted with regard to the assurance issue, and was apparently underwritten by all in attendance . . . a very moderate, discreetly-worded statement which nearly any Amish church would endorse. Yet [one member] now said Sam wanted to [reconsider] the idea of Kindschaft, saying we really can't know whether we are children of God or not.

The Amish generally do not talk much to outsiders about matters internal to the church. Even as the settlements were being torn apart and ministers from other congregations attempted to help, the event was acknowledged only briefly by those involved. An April 1985 letter from Mt. Pleasant Mills, Pennsylvania, to the *Budget* reported simply that "for those who know of the committee of men who were here concerning church matters, I will try to name them . . ." and went on to list the visiting ministers.[26] Writing of his visit to the Snyder County community in October 1984, shortly after the ministers had met, the author and historian

Joseph Stoll, from the Aylmer, Ontario, Old Order Amish church, commented that "for some time" younger men in the community had been attending "Fellowship services" outside their own church "because they felt they were not being spiritually nourished under Bish. Sam's direction." Stoll noted that a member of the ministry had been going with them and added that "more radical members" of the community were "already lost." Reportedly, one family was ready to join a Baptist church and another was leaning toward joining a conservative Mennonite church. Both families had been placed in Bann by the bishop. Fearing for the future of the Snyder County church, Stoll concluded, "I'm sure these young men are strongly motivated for something better in their Christian lives, and their concern is no doubt genuine. But it seems our Enemy is always busy, and that he would like to scatter these sheep hither and yon."[27]

To resolve the conflict, the Snyder County church did not follow the traditional practice of asking ministers from other churches to mediate between the different parties. Stoll noted that he had asked the minister who was leading the dissenting faction why he had not followed the "usual procedure" and gotten a "Fremde-Manner," an investigation of the issues by outside ministers. Without taking this step, the dissenting group could not hope for help from, or fellowship with, other Amish churches. According to Stoll, the minister "argued that it would be hard to put a plan into effect," apparently because the more radical members of the breakaway faction had no faith in efforts at mediation led by other Amish ministers.

The conflict within the Snyder County Amish community ultimately caused the dissenting minister and his followers to cease fellowshipping with the bishop and other church members. Stoll concluded his account of the visit by noting sadly that, while he had first thought the schism was the result of obstinacy on the part of the bishop, he had come "to see more and more that it was a group of dissatisfied young men who had high ideals and a vision of how they could run the church more Biblically."[28]

Others outside the Snyder County community agreed, for as one wrote, "I'm completely convinced that this division was only the result of a 'rebellious attitude' not recognized by the ones it possessed. It 'seems' to me, it started by being aware of the need for 'assurance of salvation' but taking it too far. Then criticizing anyone who could not quite see it that way. This in turn brought discontentment among quite a few, and soon [the bishop's] sermons were a target for criticism."[29]

Continued Conflict and the New York Settlements

By 1990, the Pennsylvania parent community was extinct, and the remaining families had moved to Somerset County, Ohio. "Some went to Norfolk. Others went elsewhere," noted one of the last to leave. "We went to Ohio." Nevertheless, the issues that had divided the church in Snyder County continued to trouble all the daughter settlements. Writing to one of the ministers who had helped provide oversight during the discussions in Snyder County, a young Amish man from Norfolk, New York, noted sadly that

> the "Gewissheit der Seligkeit" ([knowledge of salvation] church) split that happened in Snyder Co. Penna. . . . is reaching quite strongly into our churches here in Norfolk, N.Y., through family ties. One family has left for Carrol County, Kentucky already, and three more families seem to be very unstable. We do not feel that we would want any part in condemning anybody for having "gewissheit der Seligkeit" *if* their lives and works would be completely in agreement with God's commandments as written in the New Testament. But it seems, more often than not (from what we have observed) that they start leaning toward higher churches right away. This we do not approve of. The thing that really "knocked the props" [out from under] us here, is the fact that 3 of the families involved here are the *very ones* we had the most confidence in, and depended upon to help build the church and work against the forces of darkness. It still remains to be seen what these remaining families do.

The young man went on to note that he and his wife were also contemplating a move.

> We have a strong desire to be part of a sincere Christian Church, where strict, loving discipline is practiced; no tobacco, no strong drink, no bed courtship, etc. are tolerated, and where correct, scriptural teaching is to be found. Now don't get me wrong . . . we're not looking for the "perfect" church. We realize that is unrealistic, and even if we did find such a church, after our arrival it would no longer be such. But still, it's our fervent hope to find a small Old Order group somewhere, where the Bishop, ministers, and most of the members sincerely desire to live a consistent, Christian life. There's a world of difference between church members that have weaknesses, and those who just boldly and willfully try to "stomp the fence down."[30]

Writing to the same minister some time later, the Norfolk bishop expressed regret that those who had left the Amish church "feel they are now born-again Believers and led by the holy spirit and have something the average Amish man don't have. I do not believe they would consider the Amish church a church of God."[31]

Letters such as this show continued turmoil within the New York Swiss churches, and the history of the Norfolk Amish settlement bears this out. In 1981, there were twenty-seven farms and six businesses in the community.[32] By the mid-1980s the settlement had grown large enough that it had divided into two church districts, each with a bishop and a full complement of ministers. The community had also built a large schoolhouse, with two classrooms, and a cheese factory to provide a market for its milk. The growth was short lived. By 1986, the *Budget* scribe from the Norfolk community was reporting an exodus, with folks leaving to go to existing Amish settlements in Centreville and Quincy, Michigan; Ghent, Kentucky; and Beaver Center, Pennsylvania.[33] By the early 1990s, the Norfolk settlement was on the wane.

As in the past, moving became a way to avoid conflict and schism. Seeking a settlement in which they could be more comfortable, a number of Norfolk families moved to the Prattsburgh community, which seemed to both please and surprise one of the Prattsburgh ministers. Writing in the *Diary*, he remarked that another family had moved in from Norfolk and "we now have 13 families in this settlement. This is the first time in about 42 years that I'm living in a settlement of more than 12 families. Can anybody beat that? I'm now 47 years old."[34] The church in Prattsburgh continued to grow. In 2005, a letter to the *Diary* reported, "23 families, 18 young folks and 22 scholars in this settlement. We had one wedding this year and one funeral. Seven babies were born, 3 boys and 4 girls."[35] The next year the community had increased by one family, bringing the total of young folks to nineteen and the number of scholars to twenty-three. That year there were again seven babies born, this time four boys and three girls.[36] Prattsburgh numbers remained steady until 2014, with the *Diary* scribe reporting that year that the community consisted of "1 church of 22 families plus 3 young people living alone . . . 2 schools, 35 pupils."[37]

Despite the departures of community members for Prattsburgh, disagreements continued to plague the Norfolk community. "The problem is mostly internal," wrote one former member of the Norfolk community in 1997, suggesting that, unless other families moved in, the settlement in Norfolk, like its parent settlement in Snyder County, would "be history."[38] Instead the opposite happened. In August 1997, families began to leave Norfolk to establish a new settlement in the Clyde-Waterloo area of Wayne County, west of Syracuse. Recounting the decision to establish the new settlement, one woman remembers that

> there were ten families interested in moving. . . . Then, of course, there was the decision of where we'd locate. The men started scouting in the central part of New York. After checking out different areas, it was decided to settle south of Clyde, where they found enough farms for all, though it was mostly bare land. This is located just below Lake Ontario. Everyone bought bare land, except us. We found a farm with a fairly large house, in good condition. I was so thankful for this.[39]

In October 1997, a letter to the *Diary* reported, "Of the 10 families moving out, 4 have already gone." In January 1999, a new scribe from the Norfolk community wrote to the *Diary* that the Norfolk church had only "8 families . . . 9 young folks. The youngest member is 5 weeks and . . . the oldest being 58." In January 2002, the same writer noted, in a sad echo of a much earlier writer from Snyder County, "There's only 5 families to take church."

Figure 6.1. Taking a break. A young Norfolk Amish girl relaxes. Even young children have chores to do. Photo by author.

By 2010, the Norfolk community consisted of nine households in two extended families. The *Diary* scribe who lamented the departure of so many families in 2002 herself had left several years earlier with her husband, a minister, to move to a new Swiss Amish settlement in Clarion, Pennsylvania. Norfolk continued to fellowship with its daughter settlement in the Clyde-Waterloo area and the new Swiss settlement in Clarion, Pennsylvania, but there were only a few young folk in the Norfolk community. Because nearly all the students in the small one-room schoolhouse were closely related to one another, the future of the settlement was uncertain at best.

Talking about her community, one Norfolk mother worried that "there's times when you wonder whether [we] did the wrong thing— you don't want to offend people. It's harder when not everyone agrees." Still, she defends the decision not to dien with some of the communities they had fellowshipped with in the past, asserting that "the reason we wouldn't fully go back and forth [with the other settlements] is our children. The more we go back and forth, the more they would see things they want."

Perhaps surprising even the Norfolk Amish, the community hung on, and in subsequent years its population swelled. Writing to the *Diary* in January 2011, the Norfolk scribe announced that "there are now six new families here, which makes fourteen families altogether if I'm not mistaken. Also five babies were born in 2010 here if I'm not wrong and nineteen young folks. The schoolhouse had to be enlarged this season for more scholars and other improvements made and we wonder was enough done?"[40] By January 2015, however, a new scribe was reporting to the *Diary* that there were eighteen families and sixteen young folk. The previous scribe had moved his family to the Clyde settlement several months earlier.[41]

Daily Life in Norfolk

Having grown in size in the past ten years, largely because of an influx of families from Seymour, Missouri,[42] the Norfolk church continues to keep the Bann and strong Meidung, and life in this community remains grounded in the practices church members brought with them from Pennsylvania, and before that, from Indiana and Michigan. Although representative of the Swiss Amish diaspora, the Norfolk community also has multiple connections to Old Order non-Swiss Amish settlements, and Norfolk's black buggies with tops and their patterns of dress make them appear much like non-Swiss Amish in southern Michigan or northern Indiana.

Although some in the community are dairy farmers,[43] many rely on carpentry, pallet making, and various small farm enterprises to support their families. In the past, a number of the young girls and women in the Norfolk community worked for non-Amish employers, cleaning houses or babysitting, an option that remains open although there are few women with free time or girls old enough for such employment. Several of the married women have started businesses, including an organic produce business and a greenhouse.

Because the community is small, the group often works as a unit. Writing in the *Budget*, the Norfolk scribe reported one October, "We filled our silo Sept. 28. We still have 2 more to fill in the community."[44] Other letters tell of work frolics to fill woodsheds, butcher hogs, and husk corn.

The communal nature of work in the small settlement extends to other commercial enterprises as well. For example, the Norfolk Amish have been active participants at local farmers' markets. One community member or maybe two will go together to town, carrying for sale produce and baked goods provided by all the other families. One woman, widely known in the area for her organically grown berries, will also sell pies and bread made by one of her daughters-in-law or produce raised by another. Since this woman has no small children at home, she can more easily go to market, providing her daughters-in-law a source of income that they might not otherwise have. The men work together as well, building pallets or cutting wood at the sawmill they built together.

Norfolk remains a very conservative community, and the homes are plain. Houses may have wood floors, but the Ordnung, like that of the Swartzentrubers, requires that they be oiled, not varnished, and the women do this several times a year. The Amish in Norfolk do not have iceboxes. In winter, food may be placed in an uninsulated pantry or in a sheltered place outside to keep it cold. In summertime, families use ice chests or borrow freezer space from a willing non-Amish neighbor if there is one who lives nearby. Just in time for a wedding, one Norfolk mother found an old refrigerator that she could buy cheaply, and it made a good insulated storage space for the bags of ice that kept wedding foods cold.

Like their Swartzentruber neighbors, the Norfolk Amish pump water by hand, and there is no indoor plumbing. They use small gasoline

Figure 6.2. A Norfolk buggy. This buggy, a type found in Norfolk and related communities, differs from the Byler Amish or Swartzentruber Amish buggies in several ways. Most notably, it has sliding doors, side windows, and a windshield. Photo by author.

engines to run wringer washing machines. They have gas lanterns for light, and cooking is done on a woodstove. Any upholstered furniture must have wooden arms, and rocking chairs are generally set around the sitting room to provide comfortable seating for folks gathering around the woodstove and talking on a winter's evening. There is often a china closet, but, if it has a glass front, it will have a curtain so that one cannot see the dishes inside. In one home, a collection of glass baskets was arranged atop the kitchen cabinets, but they were not at eye level and so not pridefully displayed. The Norfolk Amish do not have telephones on their property nor will they own cell phones. Unlike their Swartzentruber neighbors, however, they will talk on the phone and often make dates to catch up, via a neighbor's phone, with distant relatives.

Apart from attending Swartzentruber auctions, the Norfolk Amish interact little with the Swartzentruber counterparts, but they do patronize the small Swartzentruber grocery stores.[45] Generally, one or two will make the trip, hiring a driver and taking everyone else's shopping lists along. There is also much visiting. Letters to the *Budget, Die Botschaft*, and the *Diary* tell of trips to see family members in Pennsylvania, Indiana, Michigan, and other New York settlements. Commenting in the *Diary* one February, the scribe wrote, "A load came from Clarion [Pennsylvania] . . . and we enjoyed their company." Several months later another scribe from the community wrote that her parents had had a big surprise when a son and family and several friends arrived to visit from a settlement in Michigan, not far from where a sister was teaching.

For the young folk, whose numbers have swelled with the influx of new settlers from Missouri, life has become far more interesting. At the same time, new settlers also bring new ways. As one long-time community member put it, "They came in with the idea that they could change everyone."[46] Already internal conflict in the Missouri community has threatened the Norfolk and other Swiss settlements in New York and elsewhere, and one faction of the Missouri groups has ceased to fellowship with the Norfolk community.

In preparing his study of extinct Amish settlements, the historian David Luthy, a member of the Old Order Amish community in Aylmer, Ontario, adopted a "rule of thumb" measurement that to count as a settlement there should be at least three families, two if one is headed by a minister. However, he noted that "such tiny settlements soon either grow or disband."[47] As far back as 1990, outside observers suggested that the small population of the Norfolk community would make it "difficult to find four males to fill the customary leadership positions."[48] Although members of the church worry about its future—several years ago one mother predicted that the departure of one of the community's ministers and his family would doom the settlement—the Norfolk community perseveres, demonstrating the importance of family ties.[49]

Norfolk's Daughter Settlement at Clyde

An Amish family typically decides to move on its own and has no guarantee that any other families will follow.[50] If families move because there are problems within the parent community, then the move allows those who are unhappy to leave without forcing an unpleasant issue. Since the settlement that the family leaves continues to exist, those who become disillusioned after moving or fail to entice other families to follow them may return. If the new settlers have been careful in selecting the site and are able to manage the community in such a way that others think the new settlement will be viable, then the group will attract other settlers, and the community will likely succeed.[51]

In moving to Clyde, families from Norfolk were able to avoid an outright break with their friends, neighbors, and relatives. They were also able to meet other perceived needs, notably easier access to other Amish settlements. Located in the Clyde-Waterloo region, approximately forty minutes west of Syracuse, Clyde is closer and more accessible to the other communities with which church members interact. "Norfolk is so far from other churches that we had fellowship with," commented one woman who moved with her family to Clyde. "[From Clyde] it's easier to leave and come back the same day." This did not necessarily make the move easier, the woman acknowledged, saying that "it was a great confusion to pick up and relocate, [and] a great adventure," but it was "hard to leave friends behind." Nevertheless, the move was a good one. And, as other families joined the newcomers, the community grew, becoming even more attractive to other families thinking about relocating.

The new settlement at Clyde was also fortunate in that there was a minister among the founding families. In 1999, the *Diary* entry for the community tallied "11 families in our church district, which started in 1997. All but one of the families moved here from Norfolk, NY. All but one family bought bare land, therefore lots of building was done, and still some to do. All moved in from Aug. to Nov. 1997. There are 21 scholars, 18 young folks, and 3 babies born in past year—2 girls and 1 boy. Oldest member is my Dad, who will be 90 on Jan. 22."[52] In February 2007, the community reported "28 households, 2 marriages, 2 deaths—babies. 8 births, 1 of these died at 1 week and the other still born. 8 baptisms, 50 pupils. Around 40 young folks."[53] That spring, with too many families to continue meeting as a single congregation, the settlement divided into two church districts. By the end of 2015 there were three church districts and two schools.

The presence of a large group of young folk has further helped to ensure the continued well-being of the settlement. In Clyde today the young folk group is quite active. As one young participant said, "Anyone in the young folk can plan things. Some will just get talking, get a van, and start asking the others." She was quite excited about an upcoming canoe trip planned with the young folk in the Clarion, Pennsylvania, settlement.

The community at Clyde is also economically diverse. "Quite a few raise produce," one woman said, listing various community enterprises, which included sawmills and sheep herding. "There are a couple of

Figure 6.3. The interior of an Amish school. Like homes, schools reflect the Ordnung standards, and the lessons children study prepare them for an Amish life. Photo by author.

dairies," she added. "They [the community] will be putting in a dumping station [for the milk], and there's carpentry work too." Women contribute to the economic well-being of the settlement, mostly working at home and selling baked goods and produce from small roadside stands or running greenhouse businesses. The younger girls may work at local farms picking berries.

Finally, the Amish who have come to the Clyde area appear to have established good, harmonious working relationships with their non-Amish neighbors and seem to feel a sense of the area as a "homeland," which is important for the community's survival.[54] Writing in the June 2006 issue of the *Diary*, one resident, a greenhouse owner, noted that the "flu bug was in the area and I think hit most every household." She went on to recount that she and her sister had been felled by the illness, which struck over the busy Mother's Day weekend "when we had lots of greenhouse customers." Fortunately, she added, "our good friends, 'Bubbles' and Lori came to our rescue and helped out and [we] sort of took vacation." The writer acknowledged that these non-Amish friends "have since also helped out on busy days."[55]

The Clyde community seems determined to maintain their Ordnung. Listing groups with which the Clyde group fellowships, one Clyde housewife, cited several in New York, including Prattsburg, Norfolk, and Lowville, as well as the Quincy community in Michigan, and the Clarion community in Pennsylvania. But, she added, there could be no fellowship with another community "if they allow something we wouldn't want [or] if a church steps out into modernisms more."

At the same time she acknowledged that the community has not been static. "I often wonder if we can call ourselves Amish," mused a Clyde housewife, pondering the changes that have occurred in Amish communities over time. "The world has traveled, and the Amish have walked the same trail but slower." The biggest challenge for her people, she asserted, "is to stay away from modernisms, not to keep on drifting." She pointed to Norfolk as an example of what could happen. "I came from Fort Wayne, Indiana, to Norfolk, and that church has changed a lot. [That's] probably why we made the move. I think our church has drifted more slowly. As far as I know, we're much the same." "Holding the line" continues to be a challenge, and life remains unsettled for New York's Swiss Amish, especially as new settlements are established, sometimes at the expense of existing communities. In 2010, a group of settlers from the Quincy settlement in Michigan arrived in Mt. Morris (Livingstone County) to begin a new Swiss Amish community. Writing in *Die Botschaft*, in April 2010, the Clyde scribe announced that "a van load is planning to go to Mt. Morris tomorrow again to help unload more trucks of the Quincy people who are settling there." In the same issue, the scribe from the other church district wrote that "last Wednesday we accompanied one of two loads to Mt. Morris, NY where it was moving day [for several families]. They all unloaded at the same place for the time being, until buildings can be put up. It is a large house with a big barn and outbuildings, making it possible for such a move. They are all from Quincy, MI and have several large flocks of sheep that are ready to lamb." By 2015, the Mt. Morris settlement was reporting "18 families here, one church district, 21 young folks, 36 school children."[56]

At the same time, Prattsburgh was contributing to a new settlement in Cobleskill in Schoharie County. Writing to the *Diary* in July, 2014, a community member noted, "I will try and see if I can be a *Diary* writer. We come from Prattsburgh, NY. We moved to Cobbleskill area to start a new settlement. We moved in March. [Others] moved in since also from Prattsburgh area." By January 2015, the Cobbleskill settlement was reporting seven families. The Prattsburgh community, on the other hand, was reporting only one church district of fifteen families, for eight families had moved out. A year later, there were only thirteen families.

In the New York Swiss Amish response to the turmoil in the Seymour, Missouri, settlement, there are some indications that not all will end up on the same side. Further, as land prices climb in the Finger Lakes area, farms are becoming less affordable. One Norfolk housewife whose family had contemplated a move to Clyde, noted sadly that they simply couldn't afford it. Having seen dissent and turmoil in the New York Swiss communities, a housewife in Clyde worried about the future. "We try to look ahead but maintain what we have. We want to stay the same."

7

On Franklin County's Western Border

New Settlements in the North Country

I've noticed from the migration list in the Diary that there were 70 families that moved to N.Y. last year. There are new areas filling up all around us. There seems to be a moving atmosphere in the air.

—*Diary*, April 2006

The Empire State is spacious, and the Amish have arrived to take advantage of its rich and plentiful farmland. Two of the more recent Amish settlements in New York, the Burke settlement in Franklin County and the nearby Swartzentruber settlement founded near Hopkinton in St. Lawrence County, demonstrate the diversity of the Amish world. The Burke settlers, representing one of the more progressive realizations of Amish identity, have come north from Marion, Kentucky, eager to begin farming on new land. The Hopkinton settlers, ultraconservative Swartzentruber Amish from the area around Holmes County, Ohio, also want land, but they seek a region where their young people will not be tempted as they were in the crowded diversity of their Ohio settlement.[1]

Located on either side of the city of Malone, New York, facing each other across the border between St. Lawrence and Franklin counties and embodying very different ways of being Amish, these two groups have encountered similar difficulties in finding farms, setting up schools, dealing with non-Amish neighbors and local governments, and creating markets for their wares.

The Burke Settlement

One of the earliest announcements of a new Amish community in Burke, New York, appeared in the *Budget* in a February 2002 letter from a member of the Clyde congregation: "Another group from KY is looking near Malone, which is 30 miles east of where we used to live. It is not uncommon to see 30 below zero up there. Almanzo Wilder [of *Little House on the Prairie* fame] grew up near Malone. I have seen the homestead."[2] The writer, a former resident of the Norfolk settlement, knew the area well, and her assessment of the region was, perhaps, more forbidding than that offered by a *Budget* scribe from Kentucky, who commented that those leaving the Marion settlement were "looking for a cooler summer climate" and that "in the trade they will also get colder winters!"

The Kentucky scribe clearly was looking at the pros and cons of a move to upstate New York. Although he acknowledged that the region offered cheaper land and dairy barns ready for cows, he added, "I understand [another] dark side of the trade is higher taxes to pay!"[3] Still, the North Country favorably impressed yet another *Budget* scribe. Describing a visit he had made to the new Burke settlement to deliver "2 motor carts," he noted that "the area seems very suitable for Amish farmers, being mostly a dairy area, nice large barns and many available farms for sale at still reasonable prices. The trees, etc. seemed to have leafed about the same as our area, perhaps just a tad later. I had expected to see more hills but was surprised to see a gentle rolling area with the ground nice and loamy."[4]

The first families moved to the Burke area in October 2002. Although the community grew slowly at first, after the first couple of years the number of settlers began to increase steadily, evidence that, when it appears likely that a community will succeed, "the more cautious may decide to make the move also."[5] In July 2004, the sixth family moved in. By February 2006, the settlement had ten families and one single man; only four months later the scribe to *Die Botschaft* reported that a fifteenth family had joined the community. As is often the case with successful settlements, about which word travels widely,[6] this fifteenth family was from outside the parent community, one of several arriving from Delaware to join the original settlers from Kentucky. Family number sixteen, also from Delaware, arrived a month later.

Still others have continued to arrive, and the number of families in the community soon surpassed that of the Norfolk settlement only forty-five miles away. In January 2007, the *Die Botschaft* writer commented that 2006 had "brought changes to our small far north settlement" and offered a thumbnail sketch: "Eight families moved in, one moved out in spring and moved in again by fall and one family out in October. Four babies

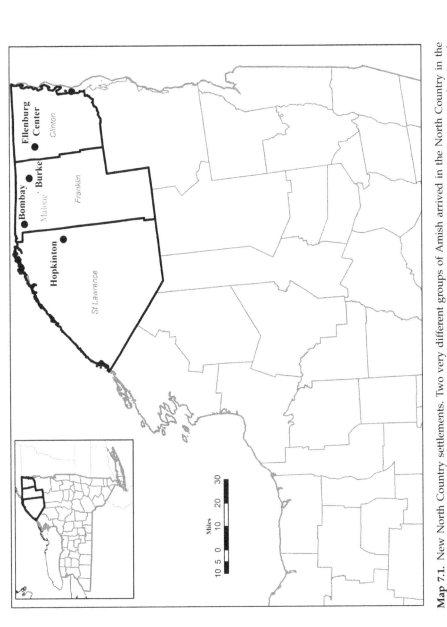

Map 7.1. New North Country settlements. Two very different groups of Amish arrived in the North Country in the twenty-first century. In 2002, Old Order Amish arrived in the Burke-Malone area. One year later, Swartzentruber Amish arrived in Hopkinton. More recently, Byler Amish have moved to this region.

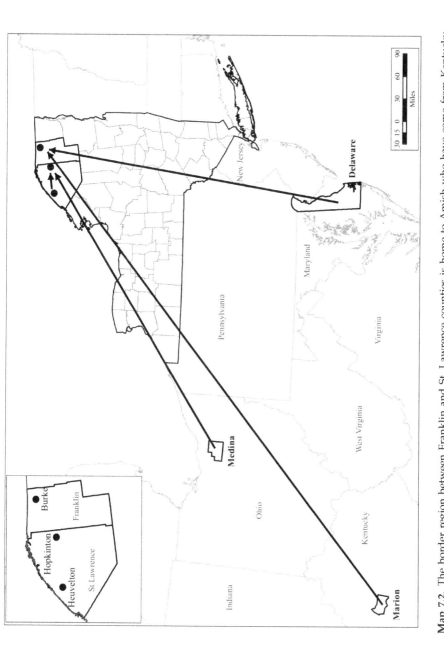

Map 7.2. The border region between Franklin and St. Lawrence counties is home to Amish who have come from Kentucky, Delaware, Ohio, and elsewhere in New York.

were born and all were boys. One lived only several hours and was buried in the new graveyard. Twelve youngie folks, six boys and six girls; 25 scholars, 12 boys and 13 girls. . . . Total of 18 families. . . . Hope my figures are correct." Six years later, there was still just a single church district, but there were now thirty-three families and two schools with a total of forty-three pupils. By February 2015, there were thirty-six families, and the following fall the settlement divided into two church districts.

"We moved to the North Country to get away from having to work in the public" [i.e., work for non-Amish employers], said one of the first settlers in the Burke area. In Kentucky, she said, "Some did farm . . . but mostly [the men] were involved in carpentry." She added that, while some of the men had found work building furniture, "not everyone could have a cabinet shop or a pallet shop." Establishing the new settlement in the North Country made it possible for her husband to once again become a farmer and for the family to work together at home. "My boys say they didn't know their father til they moved because he worked away," she said. "I didn't want to raise my boys by myself."

By 2007, approximately 50 percent of those in the new settlement were farming, according to one community member, who noted that others "want to move in, many from Delaware, where it's so congested . . . a rowdy, busy state." "The Amish in Delaware want to start farming and stop working out," asserted another Burke Amish woman. "One of these years," she added, "it will probably be like a big city all over Delaware."

Today the settlement has a diverse economy. As the *Diary* scribe put it, giving the community statistics, "10 dairy farmers, 1 metal business, 1 truss shop, 1 mechanic repair, 1 harness shop, 2 farriers, 1 variety store, 1 bake shop, market comb., 1 greenhouse, 1 store shop, 1 butcher house, 4 carpenter crews, 1 masonry crew, a few work at a local mini barn shop. . . . Oh yes, some produce growing is done."[7] Most important, all of these are home businesses. In *1001 Questions and Answers on the Christian Life*, a handbook explaining the practices of Amish life, the anonymous Amish writer comments that farming is the ideal way of life because "we have the opportunity to work together as a family. The lines of 'your work' and 'my work' become blurred so that it is 'our work.'" In moving to the North Country, the Amish in the Burke community have attempted to keep that ideal.[8]

Like the church districts in the Clymer region of western New York with whom they fellowship, the Burke Amish are more progressive than many of their Amish counterparts elsewhere in the state, a difference detectable in subtle details of their clothing. They dress much like the Clymer area Amish. Men's shirts have collars, and women wear dresses in lighter colors than those found in the Norfolk community or among the neighboring Swartzentruber Amish.[9]

There are also striking differences between Burke Amish homes and those in more conservative New York Amish settlements. In Swartzentruber or Norfolk Amish homes, one is likely to hear only the ticking of a clock that must be wound regularly, but in at least one Burke house the clock on the wall chimes Frank Sinatra's signature tune "My Way." Burke homes also have telephones in attached sheds or even in entryways. Some families, said a Burke woman, "have caller ID," although none, she asserted, "had answering machines." Women use gas irons, and families have gas refrigerators and freezers, which means community members do not need to make or gather ice in winter, and they are not dependent on their non-Amish neighbors for food storage. Burke Amish homes have indoor plumbing, with hot and cold running water. One woman pointed out that those renting homes could have electricity "if the house is in someone else's name." But, she added, "They [the community] don't want you to have it so long you get used to it and depend on it."

Outside the home, there are other indicators that the group has adopted more of the world's technology. In the fields, horses pull power carts with gas motors that run farm machinery. As one Burke resident put it, "We can mow and bale hay a lot quicker and get it in the barn." In contrast to the farm equipment used in other North Country Amish settlements, the farm wagons and other machines pulled by Burke horses may have rubber tires. Furthermore, members of the Burke community use power mowers on their lawns. All these advances are markers of a different way of being Amish, distinguishing members of the Burke community from those in other Amish groups.

The Swartzentruber Settlement in Hopkinton

In the Swartzentruber settlement on the other side of the city of Malone, only thirty miles or so from Burke, you find neither power mowers nor collars on men's shirts, and you will certainly not find phones. Like their brethren in the Heuvelton area an hour's drive away, these Swartzentruber settlers are among the most conservative of all Amish groups. New Swartzentruber settlements are homogeneous, and when they first arrived, the new settlers in Hopkinton, on the easternmost edge of St. Lawrence County, were all members of the Mose Miller/Isaac Keim church, fellowshipping with only one of the three Swartzentruber groups then in the Heuvelton area. Subsequently, however, schism has divided the community. While a number of families joined their bishop in identifying with the Isaac Keim faction of the Miller/Keim split, others took the opportunity offered by schism to join with the Joe Troyer Swartzentruber church.[10] Today this settlement has two nonfellowshipping church districts.

The Swartzentruber Amish have been the most prolific of Amish groups in starting New York settlements. Since the arrival of the first New York Swartzentrubers in the Heuvelton area in 1974, Swartzentruber Amish have started settlements in several other towns across the state. The Hopkinton community began in 2004 as a Mose Miller Swartzentruber settlement. LaFargeville, in Jefferson County, an Andy Weaver Swartzentruber settlement, followed in 2005; the Pulaski community, a Mose Miller Swartzentruber settlement in Oswego County in 2006; a Joe Troyer Swartzentruber community near Poland in Herkimer County in 2007; an Andy Weaver Swartzentruber settlement in Delevan in Cattaraugus County in 2011; and most recently, a new Andy Weaver Swartzentruber settlement in Somerville, on the border between St. Lawrence and Jefferson Counties, in 2014. In spring 2016, several Andy Weaver Swartzentruber families from the Heuvelton area bought land in Westport (Essex County), so by spring 2017, there will be yet another New York Swartzentruber community. Although there has been some movement between these different settlements (within the confines of church affiliation), the communities have grown primarily through migration from Ohio.[11]

As with the Burke settlement, the first hint of the new Swartzentruber community in Hopkinton appeared in letters to the Amish newspapers. In 2002, a scribe from Homerville, Ohio, wrote in *Die Botschaft* that members of the Mose Miller faction of the Swartzentruber Amish had been making trips to upstate New York, possibly to search for farmland. Although the region was not as popular an Amish destination as it had once been, owing, he said, to increasing property values and taxes, the writer acknowledged that the area still offered lots of job opportunities.[12] By 2007, only five years after that brief comment, the Hopkinton settlement had two church districts.

Figure 7.1. Surveying the construction. A patient horse waits by the open hole that will soon be its owner's new home. Note the rolled-up back panel on this Swartzentruber buggy—and the lack of a slow-moving-vehicle triangle. Photo by author.

For the Swartzentrubers, leaving the Medina-Holmes-Wayne counties region of Ohio and coming to Hopkinton, New York, meant leaving one of the largest concentrations of Amish settlement for one of the smallest. Today, approximately half the 513 church districts in Ohio, are found in the Holmes County region, a number that dwarfs the 128 church districts in all of New York State.[13]

One benefit of the migration for new Swartzentruber settlers is that they do not have to deal with the diversity that often characterizes long established settlements. For example, over the years, as the Amish population in the Holmes County region has grown, numerous disagreements have arisen, resulting in a number of schisms. Today, the four different factions of the Swartzentruber Amish in Ohio live in proximity to members of the Old Order churches from which their ancestors separated in 1913, as well as to members of other groups such as the Troyer Amish, Andy Weaver Amish, the New Order Amish, and the car-driving Beachy

Amish; in all at least twelve separate groups of Amish and Mennonites are in evidence in Holmes County,[14] distinguishable by dress and technology use. While some congregations have allowed indoor plumbing with hot and cold running water, others have permitted only a hand pump in the kitchen. Some have allowed a variety of safety devices on buggies, including windshields, rearview mirrors, and battery-powered flashing lights, while others have resisted these things. In the one-room schoolhouses in the large Ohio Amish settlement, children from homes with indoor bathrooms, kerosene refrigerators, linoleum floors, and battery-powered living room floor lamps play ball with children whose church districts forbid all of these "modernisms."

In coming to the Hopkinton area, the Swartzentruber Amish have also ceased to be involuntary participants in a major tourist industry. The spring 2016 homepage of the Holmes County Chamber of Commerce guide to "Ohio Amish Country" website features five revolving photos, three of which are explicitly Amish, and invites visitors to come to a place where "slowing down is second nature."[15] Although not entirely free of tourist cameras, Hopkinton is hardly a mecca for tour buses, and the Swartzentrubers do not face gawkers on every shopping trip.

As Amish settlements become crowded, tourism grows and land prices rise. In coming to the Hopkinton area, the Swartzentruber Amish have found farmland and a respite from tour buses, and although they no longer have a homogeneous Amish community, their neighbors are Swartzentruber Amish with whom they share values, history, and family connections. Fleeing Amish diversity, the settlers to the Hopkinton area, have created a community that looks inward.

Like their brethren in Heuvelton, the Swartzentruber Amish in Hopkinton have made fewer concessions to the demands of technology and modernity than most in the Old Order. They have hand pumps in the kitchen from which they draw their water, and visitors sit on hickory rockers or wooden chairs because there is no upholstered furniture. Rag rugs in the doorway are the only floor covering. Also like their brethren in the Heuvelton area, the Hopkinton Swartzentrubers will generally not work "in town," set up stalls at village farmers' markets, or work for hourly wages in non-Amish-owned factories, restaurants, or retail businesses. Generally reluctant to hire a driver for long-distance travel except in an emergency, those in the Hopkinton area settlement, like those in other Swartzentruber Amish communities, rely on public transportation to travel distances that are too great for horse and buggy. Further, like all

Swartzentrubers, the Hopkinton area settlers have kept telephones off their farms, choosing to rely on a pay phone or a non-Amish neighbor's phone in an emergency and even then preferring to ask a non-Amish neighbor to place the call.

Differently Amish

The Swartzentruber Amish and the Burke Old Order Amish do not fellowship with each other. Although both settlements are Amish, and recognize each other as such, there is no back-and-forth visiting, nor do members of the two communities work together in daily activities or gather socially. Each group acts in ways incomprehensible to the other. They dress differently, they farm differently, and they have forged different bonds with the neighboring non-Amish world. In short, despite a shared Amish heritage, they are strangers to each other.

The Burke Old Order Amish find the Swartzentruber lifestyle surprising and puzzling. One Burke woman recalled that once, when she and her husband had to attend an out-of-state funeral, they were unable to find a driver, and so they decided to go by bus, a way of traveling that she did not particularly enjoy. In remembering the trip, she expressed dismay that her Swartzentruber neighbors regularly traveled long distances that way. Her preference, she said, was for more drivers in the Burke area.

Willingly dependent on non-Amish drivers, the Burke Amish have also turned to their non-Amish neighbors in other ways equally unthinkable to the Swartzentrubers. For example, one church member asserted that she is far busier baking and selling bread, rolls, and pies than she had ever been in Kentucky, her previous home. She serves an international clientele. "Canadians come," she said. "They can't buy to take home like they used to. Now they get stopped at the border. [But] many have camps [in the North Country]." She noted that her baking business grew rapidly after she twice placed an ad in a local newspaper. Since then, she said, she has almost more demand for her baked goods than she can meet.

Swartzentruber Amish women also sell baked goods, and in summer the highway between Potsdam and Malone is dotted with small wooden stands displaying loaves of bread and sweet rolls. Generally, a Swartzentruber woman will build her business simply by putting her goods on display at a roadside stand and hanging out a hand-lettered sign reading only "Baked Goods. No Sunday Sales." She may acquire a few special customers who order in advance, but this minimal advertising and word of mouth suffice. As her family becomes more settled and she has time to for sewing, she may also produce quilts, pot holders, and other crafts to sell at the stand. Although a Swartzentruber Amish family may put an ad in a local newspaper to sell piglets or a piece of machinery, they will do this only if the item for sale is too big or expensive to sell easily at a stand or by casual word of mouth advertising. There are no ongoing, general newspaper ads for businesses. While their Burke counterparts can take orders by phone, the Swartzentruber Amish must rely on personal contact or letters for special bakery orders or quilt commissions.

Interconnected, Nevertheless

Despite their differences, the Burke and Swartzentruber settlers have drawn on similar networks of support and the experience and help of earlier arrivals. If a new Amish settlement is to survive, it cannot be isolated from family and friends. Neighboring settlements and those more distant but connected by bonds of family and friendship supply needed labor to build homes and barns. Networks of fellowshipping churches provide spiritual support. Until a new settlement has its own church leaders, visiting ministers conduct religious services and a bishop from the parent community will provide ministerial oversight. Family and friends will travel long distances to attend church services in support of the new community. The first Swartzentruber settlers in Hopkinton stayed with family and friends in the older Heuvelton settlement until their belongings arrived in the North Country from Ohio. Since then, Swartzentruber Amish from Heuvelton have regularly visited the Hopkinton area to help raise barns and houses and build schools. In their turn, the Hopkinton Swartzentrubers have traveled to provide support to the new settlement in the Pulaski region and to visit other Swartzentruber communities for barn-raisings, weddings, funerals, and auctions.

This interdependence is especially important in times of crisis. For example, when a five-year-old Swartzentruber child playing with matches burned down his father's barn, members of the other Swartzentruber churches and neighboring Old Order Amish groups came together to help the family rebuild it. While the men worked outside, women cooked for them, many contributing food from their own stores of canned goods, since the family had arrived in the North Country only a short time earlier and had not had much time to stock their own pantry.

Similarly, although far from its parent community in Kentucky, the Burke settlement is small but hardly isolated. Like their Swartzentruber neighbors, the Burke Amish have been supported both by neighboring settlements and by those far more distant.[16] The Burke congregation fellowships with communities in the Mohawk Valley, as well as settlements in central and western New York, and, as one Burke woman put it, "most other Amish groups that would want to worship with us." Reports in the *Budget* and *Die Botschaft* tell of regular visits by the Burke Amish to settlements in Delaware, Kentucky, and Pennsylvania.

The community support that sustains both the Burke and Hopkinton settlements is also evident in the myriad smaller exchanges that unite Amish communities within New York and across the United States and Canada. For example, when they lost a child through premature birth, a family in one northern New York settlement received numerous cards and letters from Amish families, most of them strangers, expressing their support and offering their prayers. More mundane exchanges provide tips for growing new plant varieties or starting a new business. For example, a Norfolk family, contemplating the raising of goats, sought advice from counterparts in Clyde, and Swartzentruber Amish in Heuvelton gave their Hopkinton fellows tips on how to raise strawberries in the North Country. Help goes across church district boundaries and travels long distances. A woman in a North Country community happily shared her expertise in raising blueberries organically with a newcomer to the Mohawk Valley.

The Amish communities in Burke and Hopkinton have each become participants in a widespread network that highlights their differences but also connects them to each other and to the larger Amish world. That they do not fellowship with each other does not mean they do not interact.

Engaging the World and Shaping the Community

Within the Amish world, one's behavior is as salient a marker of identity as the presence or absence of particular technology, the use of horse and buggy, and the type of cap a woman wears. The Amish look beyond these superficial signs for evidence of good faith. Indeed, as Nolt and Meyers have written, "in order to be taken seriously in the Amish world, one must recognize that actions not only speak louder than words—in many cases they supersede or replace words."[17]

As do all Old Order Amish groups, the Burke Amish and their Swartzentruber Amish neighbors live in a dualistic world of good and evil that suspends them between *Demut* (humility) and *Hochmut* (pride); between stewardship of the earth God created and greed for personal gain; between obedience to God and adoption of the ways of the world. Guided by the Bible, the Amish strive to remain separate from the world and unconformed to its ways (Romans 12:2).

In coming to New York, the Burke Old Order Amish and their Swartzentruber counterparts have made explicit lifestyle decisions about how their children should be raised, how they should be Amish, and how, as Amish, they should remain separate from the non-Amish world around them. For each group, this has meant renewing the Amish commitment to farming.

The Amish have traditionally seen rural life as simply better. An article in one Amish publication noted that "when Cain fled from the Lord (Genesis 4), one of the first things he did was to build a city which he peopled with his wicked descendants, filled with the smoke of industry (v. 22), and lulled with music and arts (v. 21). Cities have been degenerating ever since that time. We find in them every evil and vice known to man." Although the text goes on to acknowledge that evil can be found in rural settings as well, it asserts that "cities and towns bring evil doers closer together where they corrupt, support, and harden each other."[18] For all Amish groups, even those whose members no longer rely on farming to support themselves, the ideal lifestyle is grounded in agriculture. In farming, say the Amish, one learns reliance on "the natural order of daylight and dark, sunshine and rain, the swing of the seasons, and the blessings with which God has ordered our world."[19] Certainly the Swartzentruber Amish know this. With an Ordnung that sharply curtails employment possibilities off the farm, they ensure that the home will be the focus of family and community life. The Burke Amish know this too, for they have moved to New York in an attempt to reinforce an agrarian lifestyle, determined to give up, as much as possible, employment "in the public."

The commitment to remaining on the farm has important social consequences for the church and community, strengthening family ties and shaping gender roles. In particular, the decision to reinforce the

agricultural base of the settlement affects the way in which the group re-
solves two competing biblically based metaphors that shape Amish life.
The first sees in family and church relationships a reflection of a divine
hierarchy that positions God over all creation and man over woman. At
the same time, the second understands the church as the embodiment of
Christ, in which there is no male or female and for which each church
member is equally responsible.[20]

As long as the settlement is agriculturally based, these competing understandings of the church tend to function in tandem. Although the
formal structure of the church is hierarchical, for only men can serve as
ministers, daily life reflects more generalized gender equality. Farming
unites community members of all ages, each contributing to the success
of the whole. Moreover, in agriculturally based communities, husbands
and wives have an equal stake in common goals. When the family works
together on the farm, all labor is in the context of the church and even the
choice of tools reflects the Ordnung and community beliefs about what
is proper behavior in the eyes of God.

A job off the farm for a non-Amish employer takes the laborer away
from the home and community and its guidance and oversight. Since
married women are generally expected to care for children and the
home, it is more often the husband and unmarried adults who take
wage-paying positions. Out in the world, men engage in activities that
women cannot; they earn a paycheck, a stark contrast to the tangible
contribution of craft production, food preservation, and child rearing;
and their work, unlike that of their wives, is limited to set hours. The
result is that the distinctions between male and female suggested by the
divine hierarchy are reinforced and encoded in everyday practices. Thus
the more church members are engaged with the world, the more the social structure of the community reflects gendered hierarchy rather than
generalized gender equality. Reinforcing an agrarian lifestyle, therefore,
will have implications for the social structure of the group.

Having an agrarian base does not, of course, mean that no members of
the family will be employed outside the Amish settlement. For example,
even in the ultraconservative Swartzentruber communities, men engage
in carpentry work for non-Amish neighbors. In controlling this labor
off the farm, however, the Amish privilege particular kinds of activities
and devalue others. One Swartzentruber woman, for example, shook
her head over a neighboring Swartzentruber man, a carpenter, who was
very successful at building home additions for non-Amish in the North

Country. That he was earning a very good income did not excuse his absence from the community during the day or the fact that he was not there to eat meals with his children and to help his wife. Were his business to get too large, leading him to spend so much time away that he no longer farmed or helped to raise the children, he would risk the ire of the church and face Bann and Meidung. Family and community come first.

In the Community but Not of It

Asked if she thought of herself as a New Yorker, one Burke Amish woman responded enthusiastically "Oh yes." But neither the Burke Amish nor their Swartzentruber Amish counterparts vote, because, as the Burke woman put it simply, "That's just one of those things we wouldn't do."[21]

For the Amish, the surrounding non–Old Order society is an ever-present fact of life, necessary to their continued economic existence but a constant challenge to their religious integrity. The Amish do not judge their non-Amish neighbors, because they believe only God can judge. But they will remain separate from them, believing that it is necessary in order to serve God and be worthy of redemption. Devoted to a higher authority, the Amish define for themselves an identity that rejects many of the responsibilities, and questions many of the rights and privileges, that mainstream Americans associate with citizenship. They do not run for public office, and as noted above, do not generally vote in elections. Committed to pacifism and nonresistance, they will not serve in the military. The Amish appreciate the necessity of government and view rebellion as unchristian. Yet, while they respect civil authority, the Amish will not allow the government to assume the functions of conscience. They pay taxes but will not collect Social Security or any other kind of direct financial benefit from the government. They will also not permit the state to assume authority over the church.

Nevertheless, despite their determination to remain apart from the non-Amish world, the Burke Amish church and its nearby Swartzentruber neighbors have, in the short time since their establishment, become in key ways part of the larger Malone-area society. Each has carved out a particular niche in this northern New York region, reflecting their different ways of being Amish and New Yorkers.

For the Burke Amish, being New Yorkers means playing an active role in the civic life of the community. For example, although members of the

Burke Amish church will not volunteer as firefighters, the community actively supports the local fire department. Making rolls for a fire-station fund-raiser, for example, one Burke Amish housewife called her effort simply "a contribution." She noted that others also baked for the event and added that, in addition to her own donation, she sold rolls to others who donate them. She felt her efforts were important. "I don't know what they did for baked goods before we moved here," she commented.

This controlled participation in civic life is not unique in the Burke community. Donald B. Kraybill has noted that "the spirit of caring and sharing does not stop at the borders of Amish society."[22] Although all Amish take seriously their separation from the world, how this is realized differs from church to church. While some Amish take an active role in the Mennonite Disaster Relief organization, traveling to help rebuild homes destroyed by hurricanes or tornadoes, others practice charity on a more individual scale. In the aftermath of the 1998 ice storm, when power lines were down across much of New York's North Country, Swartzentruber youngsters readily pitched in to help non-Amish neighbors milk cows and to do other necessary farm chores.

Contributing to the support of local North Country institutions, the Burke Amish have also found their non-Amish neighbors to be enthusiastic supporters of Amish fund-raising efforts. Not long after they arrived in the North Country, the Burke Amish held several events, including a pancake breakfast and a chicken barbecue, to raise money to build a school for their community. The first event was a moderate success. The second brought folks from across St. Lawrence and Franklin counties, and by 6:00 p.m. the evening of the barbecue, several hundred people were lined up and down the lane of a Burke Amish farm, eager to dig into barbecued chicken and homemade baked goods. While Amish children played on a trampoline, their fathers cooked chicken and joked with their non-Amish neighbors. As smoke billowed from the grills, one waiting customer called out to one of the Amish cooks, "Holy smokes, Yoder, whatcha doing?" "Makin' chicken," the Amish man replied. "No eggs next week I guess."

Periodically rumors that food was running out spread through the waiting crowd, but there was an easy camaraderie between those in line and those doing the cooking. Guests paid admission at the door of the shed, a large building with a cement floor and corrugated siding. In return, they received a paper plate, plastic utensils, a napkin, and a plastic drinking glass and were invited to help themselves to barbecued chicken,

Figure 7.2. An Amish benefit supper. Even the toys on this Burke Amish farm reflect the group's willingness to accept more modernisms. These children, playing while their parents serve up a benefit supper, will be more at home with their non-Amish neighbors than will their Swartzentruber counterparts. Photo by author.

rolls, mashed potatoes, stuffing, gravy, macaroni salad, cole slaw, fresh peas and carrots, and a dessert. Gas freezers kept salads cold, while busy, white-aproned Amish women cooked vats of mashed potatoes over gas stoves. Dishes of pies and cakes were laid out on wide tables made of plywood sheets laid on wooden trestles. Waiting for his dinner, one man described the earlier fund-raiser: "They had a big breakfast a couple of weeks ago. There's a lot more [people at the dinner] than at the breakfast," to which his friend replied, "I'm gonna have to keep watching the [newspaper] for more of these."

Hosting a fund-raiser that brings large numbers of non-Amish participants onto Amish farms is not an unusual occurrence in more progressive Amish communities. In many communities, Amish schools have events such as bake sales or quilt auctions, to raise money for general operating expenses and to help keep the tuition costs down.[23] These events, at which the Amish interact casually with their non-Amish friends and neighbors, help to structure the relationship between the Amish and non-Amish worlds. In deciding where the Amish community ends and the world begins—not physically, but in the acceptable range of behaviors of church members—the church defines what Amish is and is not.

In their unwillingness to engage the world in the same way as their Burke counterparts, the Swartzentruber Amish have defined being Amish and being New Yorkers quite differently. The Swartzentrubers limit interaction with the outside world to carefully restricted arenas: isolated rural construction sites, the local grocery store or doctor's office, and small farm stands. Unlike the Burke Amish children jumping on a trampoline while their parents engaged in small talk with non-Amish neighbors, Swartzentruber children rarely encounter outsiders. Swartzentruber parents would not invite the non-Amish world to come in a crowd to their homes. Schools in the Swartzentruber community are built by Swartzentruber parents, from wood they have cut and sawed themselves, on land donated by a community member.

The Challenges of Amish Diversity

The presence within one geographic area of different kinds of Amish settlement challenges the surrounding non-Amish society to understand that simply because one Amish community accepts particular behaviors or restrictions does not mean all others will do so. For the Amish, being good citizens means passive obedience to local, state, and national laws, provided that these laws do not conflict with the Ordnung of one's church. Nevertheless, since each Ordnung is most basically a rejection of at least some of the norms of the dominant society, some conflict is inevitable. Moreover, since contemporary Ordnungs are the result of a long process of negotiation and shaped by each community's particular past, what might present a conflict will vary.

Consequently, those in the non-Amish world face the reality that there is no "one size fits all" means of integrating their Amish neighbors into everyday life. An agreement reached with one Amish community may not hold for the next, and each new technological advance or legal shift in the dominant society will have widely varying effects within the Amish world. For example, as a result of changes in banking rules mandated by the USA Patriot Act passed in the wake of September 11, 2001, banks must now ask customers to provide a Social Security number and identification. While members of some Amish churches routinely get

Social Security numbers and so can easily comply with this new regulation, many in more conservative groups, including the Swartzentruber Amish, do not get them, and so younger members of those communities—those just turning twenty-one and needing to establish their own accounts—have effectively been denied access to local banks.[24]

Understanding the diversity of the Amish world has been particularly important for health-care professionals, who face considerable variation in what constitutes appropriate health care and child rearing in Amish communities. In a 2006 guide prepared for New York State health-care workers, public health official K. R. Bobseine advised, "Many Amish people are un- or under-immunized and there have been several incidences of Vaccine Preventable Disease Outbreaks in Amish Communities [nationwide] in the past several years," including:

1979: Polio diagnosed in a total of 17 individuals, 14 of whom were Amish (82.4 percent).
1991: More than 400 cases of rubella reported in Amish communities in Michigan, New York, Ohio (278 cases), Tennessee and Pennsylvania.
1990: 171 cases of rubella reported in Minnesota, New York, and Ohio.
1999: Haemophilus influenza type b outbreak in Pennsylvania.
2004: Pertussis outbreak in Delaware.
2005: 4 cases of polio reported in Minnesota in Amish community; first cases of "wild" polio in the United States in 26 years.

More recently, outbreaks of measles have focused attention on the unwillingness of many parents, not just Amish, to vaccinate their children. Amish resistance to immunizing their children has varied considerably from one church to another. In 1991, a survey of *Budget* scribes by the Amish publication *Family Life* found that the vaccination rates in Amish communities varied from 0 to over 90 percent. One correspondent wrote simply, "We feel to trust in our heavenly father. Our forefathers didn't have the baby shots, so why should we?" Similarly, another wrote, "I feel we should put our trust in God rather than the technology of the world. I think God put these diseases here for a purpose to chasten us sometimes." On the other hand, another asserted, "We would not want to deny that there may have been cases where shots have caused adverse effects or even possibly death, but our feeling is that there would probably be many more sicknesses, paralysis and deaths if no one took them."

Writing from the Clymer-area settlement in western New York, where the vaccination rate is above 80 percent, the scribe was pragmatic: "They do not allow the school children on the bus if one child in a family is sick from 1 of the diseases. So if for no other reason than to keep peace with the public, it would be a good idea to take shots."[25]

The North Country Amish are similarly divided in their responses to vaccination. One Old Order Amish mother of four noted, for example, that her own mother insisted that her grandchildren be vaccinated, but her mother-in-law and, consequently, her husband were adamantly opposed. As a result, her first child had received all the recommended shots, her second had had only three, and the two youngest had not received any. A Swartzentruber mother of two said that vaccination had simply "never got started with our people," as if it were a fad that had not caught on. On the other hand, her bishop claimed that vaccination was an individual thing. He said that he doubted it was necessary, but it wasn't something the church had taken a stand on. The bishop's daughter asserted that her niece, who had a sickly child, had vaccinated the infant. The niece herself denied this, claiming that she had never vaccinated her children because to do so would be "against their religion," a position that was echoed by another Swartzentruber woman, who argued that vaccination was "just something we Amish wouldn't want to do." In an article written for the *New York Times*, Gardiner Harris quoted a Minnesota Amish father of seven, who, like the Swartzentruber bishop, claimed "nothing in Amish law forbids vaccinations." According to Harris, the man planned to vaccinate his children if he thought it necessary but that the Amish definition of "necessary" might not be that of the surrounding non-Amish society.[26]

Faced with different church standards and traditions, secular officials are often stymied, and non-Amish neighbors wonder what is "really Amish." Expecting members of one group to meet standards of behavior held by another can cause a number of problems. For example, while dental care in some Amish communities includes regular checkups and teeth cleaning, in others it involves having teeth pulled and being fitted for dentures before you are twenty-one years old. In a particularly worrisome instance, a nurse at a local hospital questioned whether Amish parents truly loved the small child they had brought to the emergency room since they did not "hug him" as non-Amish parents would likely have done.[27] Clearly, how these differences are interpreted can have potentially unpleasant consequences for the minority Amish culture.

The most difficult cultural clashes come over how to properly care for children. In 2008, a family court judge ruled that a Swartzentruber Amish couple from the Hopkinton settlement had neglected their young son because they had refused to allow him to have the open heart surgery doctors said was necessary for him to survive. The Swartzentruber Amish, however, will not accept open heart surgery because, as the bishop said in testimony, "it stops the heart." Similarly, the boy's father testified that " 'stopping the heart' is too close to taking chances of killing the boy" and added that he "also was concerned with the possibility that [his son] might need a pacemaker after the surgery (a risk of surgery) since that device is also against his religious beliefs." In the end, the judge gave the Department of Social Services supervision of the child and ordered the surgery.[28]

The difficulties caused by cultural and religious difference are often exacerbated by linguistic ones. The boy had been operated on shortly after birth, a procedure parents said they had not understood and would have stopped if they had. Several years later, in a similar case involving a Swartzentruber family in the Heuvelton area, court-appointed lawyers for the parents successfully argued to have an interpreter provided for the family and the community.[29]

The second case, like the first, involved a child who, in the eyes of medical practitioners, needed open heart surgery, although, unlike in the earlier case, the child was not in immediate danger. Instead doctors argued that the small hole in the child's heart would lead to hypertension, resulting in a shortened life span. For the Swartzentruber Amish, who believe firmly that a person's life span is in God's hands, this was not an argument for violating their beliefs about open heart surgery. In response to testimony that, without such surgery, a child will die or have a shorter life span, the response of many Swartzentruber Amish is that death comes to everyone. Talking of children who die young, many parents are comforted by their belief that the little ones are in heaven and will never suffer. As part of the proceedings, the father testified in the hope that his child would be spared surgery, quoting Matthew 19:14, "Let the little children come unto me and do not forbid them for of such is the kingdom of heaven."[30]

Later, talking about the motto, "In God We Trust," which was posted in large letters on the wall behind the judge's chair, a bishop noted, "You English don't really believe that, do you." In the end, the second child too was ordered to have the surgery.[31]

Other Amish do not understand the Swartzentrubers' views on open heart surgery. Even in the nearby conservative Swiss Amish community of Norfolk, a mother wondered why they were so unwilling to have this operation; she herself had an uncle with a pacemaker. Yet it is not only the Swartzentruber Amish who confound medical practitioners. In refusing some treatments, such as chemotherapy, and discouraging the use of life flight helicopters, even when getting someone to the hospital as quickly as possible seems of paramount concern, the Amish often perplex health care workers and other professionals.[32]

Still, there have been many cases in which the Amish have collaborated successfully with non-Amish authority.[33] In fact, the Amish prefer to find compromises in which compliance with the law does not violate their beliefs. Many Old Order Amish communities, including the one in Burke, now take part in the loosely organized National Amish Steering Committee, which, although formed in 1966 to negotiate changes to Selective Service policies dealing with Amish conscientious objectors, now attempts to work more broadly with secular authorities to address issues of general concern to the Amish churches.[34] An effective advocate, the Steering Committee has negotiated an exemption for the Amish on religious grounds from OSHA requirements that hard hats be worn at construction sites and mediated Amish participation (or nonparticipation) in a variety of programs, including Social Security.

This willingness to compromise is also evident in local relationships between the Swartzentruber Amish and officials in St. Lawrence County. In the early 1980s, for example, five Swartzentruber Amish men, jailed for their refusal to attach the orange slow-moving-vehicle triangle to the backs of their buggies, were released following a compromise worked out by church leaders and county officials. As part of the settlement, the Swartzentruber Amish agreed to put gray reflecting tape on their buggies in lieu of the orange triangle and to attach a lantern to one side.[35] The Swartzentruber Amish also agreed not to drive their buggies after dark unless absolutely necessary.[36]

Diversity and the Future

Today the Burke and Hopkinton Amish communities have been joined by two other nearby settlements, one established in 2009 in Bombay, about twenty miles northwest of Malone, and another established two years later in Ellenburg Center, in Clinton County, about twenty miles

Figure 7.3. Going fishing! With fishing in mind, a young Swartzentruber man tows his boat by the sign announcing the boundary of the Adirondack Park. Photo by Robert FitzRandolph.

east of Malone and just southeast of Burke. With one church district each, these new communities, daughter settlements of the large Fort Plain Byler Amish settlement, have established North Country ties while remaining linked to the Mohawk Valley region. Adding brown Byler Amish buggies to the black ones of the Burke and the Swartzentruber Amish, these new arrivals bring even more Amish diversity to the North Country.

Engaging the non-Amish world differently, the new Amish communities in St. Lawrence County, Franklin County and nearby Clinton County challenge their non-Amish neighbors to recognize that the Amish world is diverse and that what is true of one group will not necessarily be true of another. Increasingly, New Yorkers across the state will be similarly challenged as Amish settlers, drawn by the promise of affordable farm land, move to the northeast. In the five years between 2010 and 2015, more than twenty new settlements have been started in the state, each of them different from all of the others despite ties of family and fellowship. Each has brought to New York State a different way of being Amish.

The move to New York, and even to new regions within the state, will also challenge the Amish. In each new settlement, families confront geographical differences and new political and social realities. In Burke, Hopkinton, Bombay, Ellenburg Center, and other Amish settlements around New York State, newly established communities are engaging in an ongoing negotiation to find their place, remaining pilgrims even as they put down roots. The effort will undoubtedly change them, even as their commitment to their respective Ordnungs reinforces their faith in the actions of daily life.

8

Challenges to Amish Settlement

Maintaining Community and Identity

> I wonder how many people can say they've lived in three failed
> settlements.
>
> —An Amish woman in Fillmore, NY

Not all the Amish who come to New York are successful in their
attempt to settle here. At least six Amish settlements in New York State
alone have become extinct since 1950, namely the settlements in Sinclairville (Chautauqua County; 1950–1960), Clyde (Wayne County; 1979–
1999), Newport (Herkimer County; 1979–2003), Dundee (Yates County;
1981–1988), Albion (Orleans County; 1986–1996), and Poland (Herkimer
County; 2002–2007).[1]

Amish settlements are, for the most part, individual enterprises, un-
dertaken by families acting in concert rather than by groups organized
in advance. Nevertheless, moves are not random. Often several men will
visit a potential settlement location together to see whether there is sufficient farmland available for community expansion and good access to
markets. Amish churches do not formally oversee the move and do not
sanction it in any official way other than to remain in fellowship with
those who have left the parent community, provided they left while in
fellowship and remain obedient to the Ordnung. Whether the community survives or fails depends in part on how wisely the settlement site
has been chosen, how quickly and how well members of the new settlement establish themselves economically, and whether others see the
settlement as one likely to grow and prosper.[2]

Ultimately, however, the success or failure of a settlement is due to
circumstances that are peculiar to the group. Some, like the first Amish
to settle in New York State, in 1831, simply stop identifying as Amish.
Similarly, the Swiss Amish who remained in Pennsylvania when their
brethren moved to New York have since moved to Missouri; changed
their dress patterns, their rules regarding courtship, and elements of

Figure 8.1. Playing at the auction. These Amish children move between two worlds. Photo by Linda Ulrich-Hagner.

their church service; and begun to identify as Mennonite.[3] Most remarkably, these former Amish have changed their Ordnung to forbid the use of motors of any kind. Women use hand-crank washers, and men saw wood by hand. The group plans to build a schoolhouse that can also be used for church services, meaning that they will abandon the Amish practice of holding church services in private homes.

Other communities, like the first Amish settlement in Poland, New York, simply disappear when all the members of the community choose to move elsewhere. The same forces that lead Amish families to search for new homes in strange places challenge the continued health of a newly established Amish community. Some settlements die because personal conflicts tear neighbors apart or because disagreements arise over community practices.

And some communities just never seem to get started. One settler to the Clymer region recalled, "In Geauga, where we came from originally, land was too expensive, and so we moved to Carroll County [Ohio]."

He and his family had not planned to move again, but they ultimately were forced to, because there were not enough other settlers to Carroll County for the church to survive. "We liked it there and hoped more would move in, but they didn't and some moved out."

Like long-established communities, new settlements face environmental, personal, and economic forces external to the group that can put at risk the well-being of community members. There may not be a single reason why one settlement takes root and prospers and another, even in the same region, does not. In Clyde and Poland, new Amish settlements have replaced failed ones, hoping to avoid the problems of their predecessors.

Internal Challenges to Community Survival

The source of community failure may sometimes be found within the community itself. When the first Amish family arrived from Geauga County, Ohio, to start the Sinclairville settlement in Chautauqua County in early November 1950, the future seemed bright. The community grew quickly in the first year, and by February 1951, four more families had bought farms. Moreover, from the beginning, Sinclairville attracted a number of Amish visitors from the parent community since it was a mere 130 miles away and on the way to Niagara Falls, a popular tourist destination for Amish families from the Midwest. The settlement was also a destination for Amish who liked to hunt and fish. A steady flow of visitors came through the area, including ministers who delivered guest sermons.[4] Nevertheless, unlike the neighboring Conewango Valley settlement founded only a year earlier, the Sinclairville settlement never prospered. All told, only nine families joined the community, and all had moved away by the end of April 1960. The first settler to the community was the last to leave.

The Sinclairville settlement likely failed for a variety of reasons. For one thing, despite its location, it never attracted enough families to sustain it. John A. Hostetler has asserted that a settlement needs to have at least eleven families in order to succeed.[5] Eleven families would be a large enough settlement to show others that the community is stable, perhaps to allow for marriages to occur within the community.[6] The Sinclairville community never achieved this crucial number. Nor did Sinclairville have the leadership it needed. Small settlements are even more likely to fail if there is no ministry. There were no ministers among the first arrivals to Sinclairville, and the church relied on Geauga County for ministerial oversight until Bishop Dan J. F. Miller moved in with his daughter's family in 1951. Unfortunately for the community, Bishop Miller and his family left after only a year, and so the Sinclairville settlement remained dependent on Geauga County for the remainder of its existence.

The reason why Sinclairville failed to attract more families and a minister or two is probably that there were problems within the community. Members of the community need to share a sense of purpose and clear agreement on church rules if the church is to prosper.[7] Certainly difficulties that might be easily overcome in an established community may doom a new one. The founder and last resident of the Sinclairville settlement noted, "The crops were generally good and . . . the farmers had 'made a very good go of it.'" But, when asked why everyone had moved out, he blamed "church difficulties."[8] Good farmland is a reason for moving to a region. It is not enough, however, to keep the community afloat if its members cannot agree on the Ordnung or the behavior that defines community members as Amish.

Identifying the Threats

How to ensure families are able to thrive under the guidelines of the Ordnung; how to keep young folks under control and lead them to church membership; and how to direct change, including change to the Ordnung, and not be overtaken by it are key issues in the survival of communities, new and well established. For example, one man expressed his concern to readers of the *Diary* that the English language would make inroads in his community, replacing Pennsylvania Dutch. Writing from his community in Philadelphia, New York, he urged "to all who reads [*sic*], let's stay with our mutter sproch [mother tongue]; we the Amish are losing out fast."[9] In subsequent letters to the *Diary*, he has been unrelenting in his concern that the Amish not lose their language, counseling readers that "vir rolla unser glauba halta in deuitch [*sic*] nicht in English"—We should express our faith in [Pennsylvania] Dutch, not in English.[10] Later he wondered "why are so many spending their time reading the English Bible? It looks like some spend more time reading the English than the German. We were brought up with the German Bible, which we inherited from our forefathers," adding in Pennsylvania Dutch, that using the German Bible makes folks think they're German, but using the English Bible makes them think they're English.[11]

Losing language is about losing Amish identity, for language serves as a potent symbol of the separation of the Amish community from mainstream society. The *Diary* scribe is not alone in his concerns. A Prattsburgh father noted simply, "If children use too much English, we say "es genunk," [that's enough], and we remind them to speak German." When a number of young folk in the Norfolk community were asked whether it was important to use Pennsylvania Dutch, the majority said yes. Asked why, they responded much like a Swartzentruber mother who said simply, "It's just our way; that would be our way to speak." Another Swartzentruber mother acknowledged that her school-aged children sometimes spoke English among themselves, but, like the Prattsburg father, she made them stop if they did it too often. As an article in *Family Life* put it, "Useful as the English is to us, we have to keep English speaking in its proper place. That place is not in our homes nor in our church services."[12]

Others fear that young people are "losing out" because they do not know about their own history. Writing from Ava, New York, a *Diary* scribe expressed concern that many of his fellow Amish were not interested in the Amish past. "Perhaps we should start teaching Amish history in school."[13]

But perhaps the biggest challenges facing each community, especially as the settlement becomes larger and more established, are how to deal with a growing population, a lack of available farmland, and new technology. As always, the Amish response to these pressures has been shaped by community-specific patterns of decision making grounded in tradition, Ordnung, and the community's understanding of key Amish values. Amish who desire to maintain their low-tech agrarian lifestyle or hope to halt changes in the Ordnung that they think have gone too far have often chosen to move to regions where they can find cheap, available farmland. Others, however, determining that "the old patterns . . . [are] no longer viable"[14] have moved away from farming, permitted greater and more varied interaction with the non-Amish world, and adopted and adapted hundreds of state-of-the-art technologies.

In the mid-twentieth century, 90 percent of Amish families earned their living through farming. By the end of the century, however, the percentage of those farming was as low as 50 percent in Ashland, Ohio, the parent community of the Fultonville/Glen settlers; 12 percent in Delaware, the parent community of the Burke Amish; and 17 percent in Holmes County, homeland to the Swartzentruber Amish.[15] In New York, more progressive settlements may also have only a minority of families engaged full-time in farming, but generally the shift away from agriculture is not as striking as it is in the parent settlement. Only 7 percent of Geauga County households are dependent on farming for the family income, but the number is much higher in their daughter settlements of Clymer and Woodhull, where 20 percent and 25 percent, respectively, are farming.[16]

A Conservative Response

Moving is a conservative choice because it allows the Amish to maintain the low-technology lifestyle traditional on the small family farm or in the home-based shop. Not only can the family gather together for all meals, but the limited technology helps to reinforce the ideal of a family in which all work together and children learn from older siblings, parents, and grandparents. Because the technology doesn't change very much or very quickly, the wisdom of the elderly is never outdated. Further, family interactions can cut across gender. Wives, mothers, and sisters can be involved with the work of husbands, fathers, and brothers and vice versa. As one mother noted, "Boys have to fill in when there are no girls." Her first five children were boys, and so she laughed, "My oldest boy was good at cooking baking and cleaning. The floors were always washed when I came home."

Privileging the small family farm or home-based shop as the ideal Amish environment also means that the home, not the school, is where children learn to carry out the family and work traditions of their parents and grandparents, and in the most technologically conservative communities, the lessons of school are of limited importance. In turn, marginalizing school learning further distances the community from the mainstream world, making even the smallest technological innovation more obvious—and thus more easily controlled.

Finally, limiting technological innovation helps to ensure strong family and community networks of exchange and mutual aid. It requires that community members interact face to face in a variety of contexts, further reinforcing behaviors emphasized by the Ordnung: simplicity and dependence on God and the church community. Ultimately it strengthens the ties that bind the church community, clearly marking the boundaries between the community and the world, and making change that might lead to assimilation even more difficult.

In moving to New York to maintain a more traditional lifestyle, with limited technology and family-centered small farms and home-based

Figure 8.2. A cabin being built for a non-Amish customer foregrounds the home of its Swartzentruber Amish builder. While working with their parents to learn the skills they will need to lead an Amish life, children often come into contact with the dominant society. Photo by author.

shops, the Amish have emphasized the value of cultural capital over monetary capital—the exchange of labor, friendship, and community support rather than the exchange of cash. There may be less money for nonessential items and little leisure time. As letters to the *Diary*, *Budget*, and *Die Botschaft* testify, travel is usually to participate in church community events, such as weddings, funerals, and barn raisings, all of which provide further opportunity to share labor and reinforce community ties.

External Challenges to Community Survival

Even the most tightly knit group will reach a decision to move if it feels threatened by circumstances it cannot control.[17] For example, Anabaptist groups have generally moved rather than submit to mandatory service in the military. Indeed, the first Amish settlers to New York were fleeing conscription. As Arletha Zehr Bender put it, writing about her French Amish ancestors, "There were good reasons why they chose to emigrate. Only two alternatives confronted them. They could give up nonresistance or emigrate."[18] The Amish left in large numbers.

Similarly, after World War II, Amish settlers left the United States for Canada to avoid the draft. As Amish historian David Luthy explained, "The cheap land prices and the fact that their sons would not have to serve in the 1-W program of alternative service in large city hospitals appealed to the Amish," who established eight settlements in Ontario between 1953 and 1962.[19] Some of these settlers later returned to the United States in response to the enactment of legislation in Ontario requiring that all milk be cooled in bulk tanks. Shortly after their arrival in 1974, the first Swartzentruber settlers to St. Lawrence County found themselves facing rapidly escalating assessment costs. Interviewed for a local newspaper, a minister for the community asserted, "We are being forced off our land by these high rates. We purchase property that other people wouldn't buy and then we fix them up. We are being charged for improving our property. A modern farmer wouldn't be able to survive here. We do not believe in fighting, so we would have to leave if this doesn't get resolved." Another community member, interviewed for the same article, agreed, noting that "if one Amish family moves from the area, others would probably follow. . . . It's like a flock of sheep. . . . Right now, several of us are waiting to see what happens with our assessments, but [my neighbor] is serious about leaving and has put his farm up for sale."[20]

The new settlement in Somerville, on the border between St. Lawrence and Jefferson counties, is a result of conflict between Andy Weaver Swartzentruber settlers in Nicktown, Pennsylvania, and the Cambria County (PA) Sewage Enforcement Agency. The Nicktown settlement, founded in 1998 by Swartzentruber Amish from Ohio, with additional settlers from upstate New York, first encountered legal difficulties in 2006, when neighbors filed anonymous complaints about the outhouses at the two Amish schools. In violation of local sewage ordinances, waste from the school privies had been removed in plastic buckets and dumped on fields, leading authorities to padlock the schools and impose fines and, ultimately, jail sentences on community members. In a handwritten note to authorities, community members wrote, "We feel this sewage plan enforcement along with its standards is against our religious (beliefs). Our forefathers and the church are conscientiously opposed to install [*sic*] the sewage method accordingly to the world's standards." Added one of those charged, "I'd rather go to jail, and abide by our religion."[21] As the schools remained closed, the Pennsylvania Department of Education began an investigation into whether the Swartzentruber children were being educated. In the end, the Swartzentruber Amish simply sold their farms, bought new ones in New York, and left.[22]

Today the Clyde settlement is facing a different kind of challenge, for New York State has approved the siting of a 94,000 square foot casino in the heart of the Amish community. "Gambling goes against the teaching of the Bible," asserted Clyde bishop Daniel Schwartz, "and the fruits of gambling are all bad."[23] Schwartz lives directly across a two-lane road from the site where the casino will be built, and other Amish farms dot the region. It remains to be seen whether the new casino will spark an Amish exodus as many fear.[24] Contemplating whether to stay in the Norfolk community, one Amish woman mused, "If we want to move, we should just go to Clyde, but we can't afford the land," adding "and then there's the casino. I don't know how Clyde is going to make it."

The Other Old Orders

The majority of new Amish settlements in New York have been successful. And, as the Amish population continues to increase, more and more non-Amish are finding that they have new horse-and-buggy neighbors. Nevertheless, the Amish are not the only "Plain People" to make their home in the Empire State. Other modern-day Anabaptist settlers to New York include members of the New Order Amish, the Beachy Amish, the Wenger Mennonites, and the Horning Mennonites. Like their Old Order Amish counterparts, these different groups strive to live apart from the world and, as admonished in Romans 12:2, unconformed to it. While outsiders have considerable difficulty telling members of these different plain communities apart, each has realized the Anabaptist principles of the Schleitheim and Dordrecht confessions differently.

The Amish and the Mennonites began to arrive in North America at about the same time, but they generally did not travel together, and once in the New World, their communities evolved somewhat differently. While the Old Order Amish continue to worship in each other's homes, and each church district is distinct from all others, even from those with which it fellowships, the Old Order Mennonites worship in meetinghouses and have adopted a conference structure that unites the different churches under a central authority. Nevertheless, since their arrival in North America, the Mennonites have faced challenges similar to those of their Amish brethren. Like the Amish, the various Mennonite churches have differed in how they have confronted the vicissitudes of history, geography, internal conflict, and pressure from the dominant culture.

Old Order churches in North American differentiated as traditional Anabaptist groups struggled to deal with change in the broader society.[25] Like the Amish, the Mennonites were challenged by the religious and technological developments occurring in nineteenth-century North America. By the end of that century, most Mennonites had succumbed to the lure of these widespread changes and had embraced many of them.[26]

Not all Mennonites were willing to adopt new ways, however. In 1893, Bishop Jonas Martin, unhappy with changes in the Lancaster Conference of Mennonites, led similarly minded church members to form a new organization, the Weaverland Conference of Mennonites. In 1927, only thirty-four years later, the Weaverland Conference itself divided, again over innovations that some saw as worldly, particularly the decision to sanction automobile ownership. The more conservative faction called itself the Groffdale Conference, but became more commonly known as Wenger Mennonites after their leader at the time of the schism, Bishop Joseph Wenger. The more progressive faction continued to be called the Weaverland Conference but became popularly known as Horning Mennonites after their leader, Bishop Moses Horning.

Because the 1927 division was not over worship practices but rather over issues of daily life, both the Wenger and the Horning Mennonites consider themselves to be "Old Order." The Wenger Mennonites clearly fit the picture this phrase generally conjures; they are much like the Amish in dress, they drive buggies, and they use German at home and in church. But their Horning brethren are still very "plain" and have generally retained "the basic tenets of the Old Order Mennonite faith as upheld by . . . the original leaders of the late 1880s Old Order movement."[27] Although they have shifted to English for religious observances, the Horning Mennonites have continued to govern their member churches, conduct worship services, ordain ministers, and hold communion in much the same way as their Wenger counterparts.[28] Further, despite the Horning Mennonite adoption of automobiles and other technology, the majority of Horning children continue to finish formal schooling with the eighth grade, and the church continues to mandate plain dress and restrict the use of technology. Like other Old Order groups, the Horning Mennonites decline to proselytize and have continued to reject Sunday schools, which Old Order churches have historically associated with the practices of mainstream Protestantism.[29]

In New York State today there are Horning Mennonite churches in both Wayne and Seneca counties, and Wenger Mennonite churches in Yates and Ontario counties and in Malone, in Franklin County.[30] In 1999, another plain Mennonite group, the Stauffer Mennonites, started a settlement in Orleans County. More conservative than either the Wenger or the Horning Mennonites, the Stauffer Mennonites trace their roots to an 1845 schism in the Lancaster Mennonite Conference over whether and how to discipline a father and several sons who had involved the civil authorities in a family dispute. Minister Jacob Stauffer saw the punishment meted out by Bishop Christian Herr as lax, refused to accept the decision, and as a result was himself silenced. Ultimately, Stauffer and his supporters established a new congregation. Because they met at the Pike meetinghouse, the Stauffer Mennonites also became known as Pike Mennonites. Today there are several Stauffer divisions, all of which are more conservative than many Old Order Amish groups.

Because the Stauffer Mennonites also rely on horse-and-buggy transportation and, unlike either the Wenger or Horning communities, have not sanctioned the use of electricity in their homes, they are often mistaken for Old Order Amish. For example, a picture appearing on the front page of the July 15, 2000, Orleans County newspaper the *Daily News* showed a boy plowing with a team. The caption read "An Amish boy," but the youngster's clothing marks him as Stauffer Mennonite.[31] But it is not only those in the dominant society who have difficulty distinguishing the Stauffer Mennonites from the Amish. Speaking about the Stauffer Mennonites, an Old Order Amish woman in the Fultonville-Glen community commented, "They're a decent Mennonite. I thought they were a higher [more progressive] Amish, but they're Mennonite."

And there are indeed varieties of Amish in the state beyond the Old Order. Near the Stauffer Mennonite settlement in Orleans County, for example, is a New Order Amish church. Perhaps more properly considered a subgroup of the Old Order Amish,[32] important differences remain between the two groups. Some New Order groups have permitted tractors, and some have allowed electricity. Most important, however, the New Order Amish have articulated a belief in the assurance of salvation, the "strange belief" that divided some Swiss Amish communities, including those in New York, in the 1980s,[33] and they take measures to accommodate converts.

There are also four Beachy Amish congregations in New York. Resulting from a schism in the Somerset County, Pennsylvania, Old Order Amish church, the Beachy Amish Mennonites maintain plain dress, but, unlike their Old Order and New Order counterparts, they use English, have Sunday schools, and tolerate the use of electricity and the automobile. Finally, there are congregations that, like the Beachy Amish, have maintained plain dress and other markers of Anabaptist identity, and identify simply as "Amish Mennonite."[34]

Together with the Old Order Amish, these plain communities interact and cooperate with each other. Separate from the dominant society, pilgrims finding their way, theirs is a lived faith based in tradition and maintained in the yielding of individual will to church, family, and God. They are New Yorkers, contributing to the diversity, productivity, and vitality of the state.

9

Challenging the Non-Amish Neighbors

Uneasy Integration

We have much to be thankful for to live in a land of religious freedom.
—*1001 Questions and Answers on the Christian Life*

Although the majority of Amish settlers have been successful, integration into local life has not always been easy. When the Amish do not act like other newcomers, hurt feelings may result. According to one local newspaper article, the first Amish arrivals to the Heuvelton area were welcomed with open arms, but they didn't respond to this welcome as expected. A non-Amish resident quoted in the article recollected that "the first year, the Methodist Church had a covered dish supper to entertain them and not one of them came." The resident noted further, "I think some farmers with sons who want farmland resent them. They pay from $300–$800 an acre," she said, and "they don't buy many groceries, because they buy most things in bulk and split it up, and no gas. They buy some feed and some hardware items.'"[1] To this day, many persist in believing (wrongly) that the Amish do not pay taxes.

This perception that the Amish take from the local economy without giving back is not shared by all, however, and as the Amish settle in a region, they soon become economically integrated. Whether it is donating to auctions to support volunteer fire departments, working with dairy cooperatives, or operating roadside vegetable stands and selling storage barns to their neighbors, the Amish quickly become involved in maintaining the area's economic health.

Nevertheless, because of the many myths, half-truths, and imaginative fictions about the Amish, first encounters can be puzzling. One blogger, commenting on his experience passing an Amish buggy while on a cross-country biking trip, noted that the two women inside looked glum. A short time later, he passed an Amish man and a little boy who were "all

Figure 9.1. A Clymer-area, Amish-owned roofing company. When a new settlement is established, its Ordnung determines how it integrates socially and economically with its new neighbors. Photo by author.

smiles." The blogger went on to report: "I learned later that this is the way of the Amish, Amish women do not talk to or apparently even look at strange men. I also learned that an Amish woman is never allowed to conduct business of any kind and that an Amish man will not conduct business with a woman, period! I would have loved to learn more about these mysterious people."[2] Under the impression that Amish life is rigidly patriarchal, people may be surprised to learn that many Amish women, like Amish men, do operate businesses and play an active role in community activities.

Other stereotypes inspire irrational expectations on the part of the non-Amish community. For example, a local university administrator who proclaimed, "Who better [than the Amish] to go to for produce?" said she felt betrayed when a watermelon purchased at an Amish stand was tasteless. Assuming that real Amish shun all modern conveniences and lead wholesome lives removed from modern vices, non-Amish shoppers look askance at the Amish woman who puts cheese curls and soda in her shopping cart. The writer Sue Bender, searching for the "plain and simple life," was dismayed and disappointed to find that the first Amish family she visited used refined, white sugar; fortunately, she was able to find a "real"

Figure 9.2. Unlike his counterpart in Clymer (figure 9.1), this conservative Amish retailer does not have a Better Business rating, nor can he be found on Angie's List. Photo by Varick Chittenden.

Amish family, one that used honey and whole-wheat flour.[3] Tourists' expectations for Amish behavior may be far more rigorous than the rules by which most Amish live; one Old Order woman, "aware of what she aptly named a 'blown up' picture of the Amish," expressed the desire that someone "send us some of those Amishmen that they talk about. We could use some [to make their settlement a better community]."[4]

All stereotypes aside, the Amish are, most simply, a people who, as a result of their faith, make different choices than their non-Amish neighbors. Unfortunately, these different choices not only cause misunderstandings between neighbors, but they can also bring the Amish into more serious conflict with local secular authorities. The Amish point to Romans 13, in which Paul asserts that "the powers that be are ordained of God," and therefore believe that church members should respect government and other civil institutions. Article XIII of the Dordrecht Confession asserts, "We also believe and confess that God instituted civil government for the punishment of evil and the protection of the good as well as to govern the world and to provide good regulations and policies in cities and countries.

192

Therefore, we may not resist, despise, or condemn the state. We should recognize it as a minister of God." Whether the government is good or bad does not matter; it is still instituted by God, and so it must be obeyed.

Nevertheless, if that worldly authority asks an Amish church community to engage in behavior that it feels violates its Ordnung, the community's understanding of how scripture is to be realized in daily life, then the Amish feel they have no choice but to refuse. Article XIII of the Dordrecht Confession reminds church members that Christians must "honor and obey [civil government] and be ready to perform good works in its behalf" but *only* "insofar as it is not in conflict with God's law and commandment."

Whatever happens, God's laws must be followed above all else. Gelassenheit, the "giving up" of one's will to yield to the will of God, which is essential if one hopes to be worthy of salvation, requires that one follow the rules of the church, which are based on Christ's teachings. Gelassenheit also means that the Amish are prepared to suffer the consequences that follow from civil disobedience. Initially, tied financially and personally to their community, the Amish will generally try to compromise. Ultimately, as we have seen, they will move. Yet as Paton Yoder has noted,

> The Amish . . . have been involved in too many clashes with the government for them to be considered docile. If laws that clash with God's higher law must be broken, even then they are stubbornly passive. In the words of one Amishman, "We are taught to mind our own business and obey the government, but when the chips are down and the government interferes with our way of living, we can balk like a stubborn mule!"[5]

When the Amish are fined for an infraction incurred for behavior mandated by the Ordnung, for instance, they generally refuse to pay, believing that to do so is to admit guilt and, by extension, that their position is wrong. Since they have based their position on God's law, and God's law cannot be wrong, they cannot pay the fine. Found guilty of violating local sewage ordinances, for example, the members of the Swartzentruber settlement in Nicktown, Pennsylvania, declined to pay fines or perform community service because to do so would go against their religion. In the end, they moved away, choosing to start again elsewhere rather than go against their religious beliefs.

The Law and the Amish

Putting the Ordnung and the church first has resulted in conflict with legal authorities over a variety of issues.[6] In 2005, for example, a member of the Old Order Amish community in Poland, New York, reported in the *Diary*

193

that food inspectors had prevented her from selling her own canned goods because her kitchen had not been inspected. Later she was also prevented from selling canned goods produced by Amish canners in Pennsylvania. She explained that the inspectors had required them to empty the jars of food and then pour bleach over the contents so that it could not be used to feed chickens. It was not, she reported, "a pleasant experience in throwing away 150 jars of good food, thinking of hungry people and I pleaded with them to just use it for my own family but they insisted and if we would have refused to do so they would have issued a hearing."[7]

In a number of different states, the Amish have come into conflict with local, state, and federal authorities over issues as diverse as puppy mills [breeding puppies for sale to commercial enterprises], child labor, home-cooked meals for the tourist trade, and the requirement that homes be built with sewer systems.[8] In 2003, a New York State building code went into effect, requiring that windows in new residential dwellings be at least 5.7 square feet to allow for easy access and egress in emergencies. Measuring the windows in an existing Amish house, the code enforcement officer in Chautauqua County found that they did not meet the state requirement, and the officer denied permits to Amish residents who had hoped to use the same plans to begin construction on new homes. A reporter for the *New York Times* wrote that "to the outsider, the solution is obvious: enlarge the windows by a smidgen."[9] But in Amish churches, where life is regulated by Ordnungs that encode generations of faith, religious belief, and tradition, change is never simple. "'It sounds easy to someone who isn't Amish, but if you're Old Order Amish it's not easy,' said . . . the bishop of one of the two Amish districts in Chautauqua, clad in the traditional male uniform of a navy denim jacket fastened by hooks and eyes. 'If you break a tradition, where's the tradition? You're not a faithful member.'"[10]

In their apparent intransigence, the Amish often cite the constitution and challenge mainstream society to live up to its promise of religious freedom. While many argue that it is unfair to exempt the Amish from laws others must obey, whether officially or through lack of enforcement, others insist that laws must be written in such a way that they respect the religious rights of all. The Religious Freedom Restoration Act (RFRA) requires that the government meet stringent standards in formulating laws that would affect religious practice. Overturning the 1990 U.S. Supreme Court ruling in *Employment Division v. Smith* that Government could restrict religious practice as long as the restrictions were not aimed at a particular religious group,[11] RFRA requires that such legislation serve a compelling governmental interest and do so in the least restrictive way possible.[12]

This is often easier said than done, for clashes between the Amish and secular governments may be described as "fundamental clashes between diverse social orders."[13] This is evident in the most serious conflicts—those involving family relationships, which pit non-Amish notions of individualism, public welfare, and child rearing against Amish notions of parental responsibility, church, Ordnung, and Gelassenheit. For example, attempts by civil authorities to protect children by regulating how, when, and where they can be employed seem to many Amish parents to imperil their children's education in the Amish way of life. Traditionally, Amish children have joined their parents to do household chores and farmwork. This sort of labor has rarely excited interference from authorities. But as more Amish parents engage in nonfarming livelihoods, many running sawmills or doing construction, their children have followed them into those workplaces, too. This movement of children off the farm and into potentially dangerous environments (as if the farm were not, itself, potentially dangerous) has concerned many non-Amish, who worry that work in sawmills, harness shops, or other home-based manufacturing sites puts them at risk of injury and death.

In 1996, three Amish sawmill operators were fined for violating the Fair Labor Standards Act, which forbids the employment of children under the age of fourteen in a manufacturing facility. Other Amish businesses have since come under scrutiny, frustrating many Amish parents who worry about what their children will do with their time between finishing eighth grade at age fourteen and beginning work at age sixteen.[14] As Christ K. Blank, chairman of the Old Order Amish Steering Committee, told Congress, "We believe forced idleness in this age to be detrimental to our long-standing Amish way of raising our children and teaching them to become good productive citizens."[15]

In a conflict such as this, the Amish church can become the battleground on which the culture wars are fought. For some, the Amish represent the nation's pioneer past, a group that has managed to hold on to strong family values, a work ethic, and Christian beliefs that are in danger of disappearing in modern twenty-first-century America. In 2003, Congressman Joseph R. Pitts, a conservative Republican representing Pennsylvania's Sixteenth District, which includes Lancaster County, cosponsored legislation that would permit Amish teenagers ages fourteen to sixteen to work in Amish sawmills.[16] In congressional hearings, Pitts expressed doubt that it would be "more dangerous to work in a sawmill than to have a federal bureaucrat destroy the ability for a Christian community to teach their children in a way that is culturally appropriate."[17] As he noted on another occasion, implicitly pitting life in the rural heartland against that of the big city, "These are little family businesses trying to keep their kids in their way of life. These are not sweatshops in New York City. If the Labor Department wants to find some real violations, they should find some sweatshops."[18] Writing in the *Wall Street Journal*, the columnist Hannah Lapp agreed, arguing that, instead of requiring the Amish to obey child labor laws, the Labor Department "would do better to study Amish child-labor practices as a guide to solving problems in child-spoiling mainstream society."[19]

Opponents of the legislation, which was ultimately signed into law by President George W. Bush on January 23, 2004, asserted that the exemption favored one religious group over others and put children at risk. In a letter to the *Washington Times*, Bernard E. Anderson, the assistant secretary of labor in the Clinton administration, wrote,

> Our nation's child labor laws reflect the public interest in having safe and healthy workplaces for young people, regardless of the size of the enterprise, the relationship of the worker to the employer or the sector of the economy in which the enterprise operates. . . . The U.S. Labor Department has deep respect for the Amish faith and its strong family traditions. But Amish children are American children. The children and youths of all families and all faiths have the right to be protected from hazardous and life-threatening conditions in the world of work.[20]

Similarly, Nicholas Clark, a labor expert with the United Food and Commercial Workers Union, argued that "the bill would deny Amish children the very real benefits of government health and safety protection that are afforded Catholic, Baptist, Jewish or any other children of non-Amish faith."[21]

Opponents of the legislation also maintained that it was backward-looking and inappropriate for a changing world. Quoted in a 2003 article in the *New York Times*, the former head of the Labor Department's Wage and Hour Division in the Clinton administration, John R. Fraser, said, "We should certainly respect and tolerate religious and cultural beliefs that date from centuries ago, but it would be irresponsible and dangerous to begin to tolerate seventeenth- and eighteenth-century practices with respect to child labor."[22]

With their right to employ their children in sawmills and home businesses now protected by federal law, the Amish continue to educate them for Amish labor. Whether they will be able to do so in the future is hard to guess. In discussing the aftermath of *Wisconsin v. Yoder et al.*, the 1972 Supreme Court case that allowed Amish parents to stop sending their children to high school, Shawn F. Peters suggests that times may be changing. Quoting Chief Justice Warren Burger, he writes, "To maintain an organized society of faiths requires that some religious practices yield to the common good."[23]

Indeed, in recent years, several articles and notes in law school reviews have argued that Yoder should be overturned because children today are recognized to hold substantive constitutional rights separately from their parents, including the right to an "open future."[24] In other words, as David Cheng put it, an Amish child "must be exposed to competing ideas [i.e., through attendance at high school] before he can make any meaningful decision about whether to follow the Amish way of life or a secular lifestyle."[25] Cheng asserted further that, in deciding on behalf of the Amish in *Wisconsin v. Yoder*, the government became complicit in violating the rights of Amish children because it allowed parents to isolate their children from the secular world and so deny them the opportunity to make intelligent, informed choices as adults. The state, he wrote, must assure that children receive an education that will make it possible for them to enjoy personal and political freedom.[26]

Whether the Supreme Court will ever revisit *Wisconsin v. Yoder* to ensure that Amish children have access to an education that exposes them to ideas their parents find threatening remains to be seen. Were the Court to do so, however, it would find a very different Amish world than existed in 1972. Arguably, the importance of the Yoder decision lies in its empowerment of Amish communities and, in easing the way for hundreds of one-room schoolhouses, its encouragement of Amish diversity.[27] As Ordnungs have changed, permitting a greater range of occupations, so too have the behaviors that characterize Amish life. And as Amish communities become more diverse, they will challenge secular authority in different ways.

Facing Conflict and Adversity

When clashes occur within the Amish community or between the Amish and the "world," the Amish do not seek legal help. As

Hostetler has noted, "The Amish . . . are admonished to suffer injustices rather than instigate legal suits or defend themselves in the courts."[28] Yet, as the battle in Congress over the issue of child labor demonstrates, they have benefited from the willingness of others to act on their behalf. Arguing for the Amish in the 1972 *Yoder* case, attorney William B. Ball was retained by the National Committee for Amish Religious Freedom, an organization formed in the mid-1960s by a Lutheran minister, the Reverend William Lindholm.[29] Nearly forty years later, the Becket Fund for Religious Liberty took on the case of Swartzentruber Amish and filed suit against the Town of Morristown on their behalf. The Becket Fund had been alerted to the situation by Public Defender Steve Ballan; it was assisted by the large New York City law firm of Proskauer & Rose, which worked pro bono on behalf of their Amish clients.[30]

For the Amish, conflicts with secular authorities and non-Amish neighbors reinforce a worldview that casts the Amish as "strangers and pilgrims" (1 Peter 2:11), transients passing through the earthly kingdom on their way to Christ's. Moving to escape difficulties, either internal church problems or conflicts encountered in a particular regional setting, only strengthens the Amish belief that they are just passing through on the way to eternal life. The Amish see their sojourn in the physical world as "short and very purposeful, for nothing less than eternal salvation lies beyond the horizon."[31]

Further, attempts by secular governments to enforce codes that the Amish see as counter to God's law reinforce the Amish belief that God's people will suffer persecution in the physical world. Today's Amish still read *The Martyrs' Mirror* and find consolation in it for the persecution they have faced in the English world for their resistance to mandatory schooling, military service, child labor restrictions, use of the orange SMV triangle, or building codes.[32] What the Amish identify as persecution proves to them that they are, in fact, serving God, for as Christ suffered for his faith, so too must his followers. While this passivity can be exasperating to secular authorities, it also means that the Amish will be inspirational to many.

When a local man went to the West Nickel Mines school in Lancaster County in October 2006 and shot ten little Amish girls, killing five, the non-Amish world was astonished by the immediate expression of forgiveness and compassion from the families of the murdered children to the family of the murderer. As Ann Taylor Fleming commented on the PBS show *News Hour*,

> The modern media world descended en masse into this rural enclave, as if dropped back through time, poking and prodding the grief of the families and the community as a whole. And what they found and what we heard from that community was not revenge or anger, but a gentle, heartstricken insistence on forgiveness. . . . In a world gone mad with revenge killings and sectarian violence, chunks of the globe, self-immolating with hatred, this was something to behold, this insistence on forgiveness. It was so strange, so elemental, so otherworldly.[33]

A Swartzentruber Amish man commented after the shooting that a neighbor, "this English lady," had said she was worried that "we Amish wouldn't have anything more to do with English people." Recounting his conversation with the woman, the Swartzentruber man expressed surprise at her concern, noting first that "she hadn't done anything." Then, he added, "I told her that I didn't hope any Amish person would ever do something like this, but we're people too and there's good ones and bad ones." It was, he asserted, necessary to forgive. Similarly, asked what he would like his non-Amish neighbors to know about the Amish, a member of the Clymer-area community said that "a good thing came out of Nickel Mines. The people understand us better, [and they understand] that we want to be a forgiving people."

The forgiveness that has so astonished mainstream society is fundamental to the Amish understanding of Christian behavior and so is incorporated formally and informally into the fabric of their daily lives. The gospel of Matthew plays a central role in the Amish understanding of forgiveness.[34] Read prior to the fall and spring communion services, Matthew 18:21–35 tells of a servant who is forgiven of his debts by the king. In turn, however, the servant does not forgive the much smaller debt owed him by another. When the king hears of his servant's lack of forgiveness, he grows angry and demands that the servant pay him back after all, leading to the moral of the story, given in Matthew 18:35, "So likewise shall my heavenly Father do also unto you, if ye from your hearts forgive not everyone his brother their trespasses."

In other words, the Amish understand forgiving and being forgiven as two sides of the same act. In daily recitations of the Lord's Prayer, the Amish beg forgiveness as they forgive others.[35] Forgiveness is key in "giving up," the Gelassenheit that marks one's willingness to yield to the will of God. In forgiving, one sets aside individual anger and sense of vengeance, thus strengthening the church and reinforcing a sense of belonging and commitment. Further, in forgiving—in following Christ's example—one has hope of being forgiven and, ultimately, of being saved.

In 2014 New Yorkers were able to see forgiveness and compassion at work in another Amish community. In August, two Swartzentruber sisters, ages six and twelve, were kidnapped from their family's farm stand. Only days later, following the return of the girls and the arrest of their captors, the girls' father expressed how "sorry" he felt for the suspects. "It's sad," he said. "They must have ruined their whole life [sic]."[36]

Events like the kidnapping reveal and strengthen the ties between communities with very different ways of life. The non-Amish residents of New York's North Country were surprised at the compassion expressed by the Swartzentruber father and later by the generous gathering of Amish to build a garage for local residents Jeffrey and Pamela Stinson in gratitude to the couple, who drove the girls home to their parents after the kidnappers had released them.

At the same time, the Amish were surprised at the outpouring of non-Amish concern and willingness to help find the children. One Amish man called it "miraculous" and noted that that the girls came home just as a church in Heuvelton was holding a prayer vigil. He also expressed amazement at the number of police and other English folks involved in the search. Said an Amish minister, commenting on the way many non-Amish North Country residents had helped look for the girls, "It brings the community together—not just the English but the Amish too."

The Amish Need Us

But the Amish and non-Amish communities have always been intertwined, a fact noted by reporters who covered the kidnapping. For example, *New York Times* reporter Kirk Semple interviewed one local farmer who noted that he liked to help out his English neighbors because "you never know when you're going to need help."[37]

No Amish group is self-sufficient. The Amish rely on their non-Amish neighbors for a variety of small favors, from access to a freezer or use of a phone to a ride to a local hospital in an emergency. Amish people shop in non-Amish stores and welcome non-Amish tourists to farm stands. They use non-Amish banks, patronize non-Amish restaurants, buy medicines from local pharmacies, and sell craft products to tourists. In more progressive communities, the Amish work for non-Amish employers. In short, the Amish rely on the non-Amish world for their economic well-being.

But there is a more profound link between the Amish and their non-Amish neighbors, for even as the plain people interact with the secular world, they reject it, and, in doing so, define themselves.

A key step in creating a new social movement is crafting an ideology sharply different from the old.[38] The first Anabaptists took heart in their belief that, by being different from the mainstream churches, by following the letter of the scripture and establishing a true believers' church, they had returned to the straight and narrow way. The Schleitheim Confession argued explicitly that "all Catholic and Protestant works and church services, meetings and church attendance . . . which are highly regarded by the world and yet are carried on in flat contradiction to the command of God" were to be avoided, for "all those who have fellowship with the dead works of darkness have no part in the light."[39] To become a church member was to make an active choice to be different, for, as the Schleitheim Confession put it, "All creatures are in but two classes, good and bad, believing and unbelieving . . . and none can have part with the other."[40] Persecution by a fallen and wicked world only confirmed their faith that the path they had chosen was the right one.

Similarly, those who chose to follow Jacob Ammann nearly two hundred years later needed to distinguish themselves from the main body of Mennonites whom they were rejecting. While the majority of Mennonites viewed Ammann's insistence on strong Meidung as "a new, idolatrous doctrine,"[41] Ammann and his followers characterized the Mennonites as spiritually arrogant and argued that they "did not remain in the teachings of Christ." Writing to Mennonite church leaders in the Palatinate to defend his own actions, Ammann quoted the Apostle Paul: "You cannot drink the Lord's cup at the same time as the devil's cup." Ammann added, quoting the book of James, "Do you not know that friendship with the world is enmity with God? Whoever wants to be a friend of the world will be an enemy of God."[42]

For the Amish, who believe fervently that they must remain separate from the world,[43] being different or "unconformed" is a sign of faith. And being different in a fallen world, the Amish expect that they will be persecuted, just like their Anabaptist ancestors. When they must appear in court because, having followed the Ordnung, they have violated different statutes and laws, they do so firm in their belief that they are suffering for their faith. Worldly society establishes the norms to which Amish society cannot conform and, thus, helps to shape Amish life.

This need to remain separate and different from worldly society has influenced how the Amish and other Anabaptist groups view change, both within the community and outside it. For the Amish and other Anabaptist groups, as Mennonite author J. Craig Haas has pointed out, "The teachings of Christ stand firm, but the world is ever changing." Thus, he wondered, "If Christians change with the times, is the cause of that change found in the world, or in Christ? In what ways may disciples of Jesus accept change?"[44]

For the Old Order Amish, the answer is relatively simple. If God's truth is unchanging, then God's church must also resist change. After reading a copy of an Ordnung from the nineteenth century, one Swartzentruber bishop expressed his relief that so many of the practices of his church had stayed the same. Yet there have been some changes. The Amish walk a tightrope, evaluating every innovation to ensure that it does not represent a threat to the church or that it is not a sign of the drift that would blur the lines between the church and the world. As one Amish writer argued, "The will of God remains constant; but society changes. . . . The church, by prayerful study of the Word of God and by the leading of the Holy Spirit, needs to take a position on such issues and require a standard of conduct accordingly for its members."[45]

Just as it divided Ammann's followers from other Mennonites, the need to be separate also divides each Amish church community from those with which it has ceased to fellowship, for belief is expressed in everyday actions and divisions marked in the way one dresses, furnishes one's home, or builds one's buggy. One bishop warned how difficult it was to determine a path through the obstacles presented by the modern world, noting "newer methods are sometimes to the good and sometimes not." Even as the Amish become more entangled in the mainstream economy, they are likely to highlight cultural and religious difference by drawing an ever-sharper line between church practices and worldly ones.[46] Assertion of a particular Old Order identity is both a rejection of worldly norms and, at the same time, a rejection of other possible ways of being Old Order Amish.

But We Need the Amish Too

But while the Amish define themselves by their insistence on being different from "the world," their worldly neighbors often envy the Amish for their "simple" lifestyle. Without cars, telephones, television, and other trappings of modern civilization, the Amish seem somehow more "real" and honest to their non-Amish neighbors.[47] As a result, the Old Order Amish have, ironically, become part of modern American popular culture, the stuff of fiction by writers as diverse as Carolyn Keene, P. L. Gaus, Beverly Lewis, and Jodi Picoult. Science fiction grandmaster Arthur C. Clark reportedly told his friends Amish jokes, while some suggest that Isaac Asimov modeled a key community in his *Foundation* series on the plain way of life.[48] The director Peter Weir contrasted the darkness of big-city life with the peace of the Lancaster County Amish community in his Oscar-winning film, *Witness*. Weird Al Yankovic sings of "living in an Amish paradise," and Amish-themed romances have become one of the fastest growing fictional subgenres. While the Amish were once seen as a backward sect, many people now praise them as guardians of America's pioneer values. As J. A. Hostetler noted, "Today they are featured in national magazines as hearty Americans . . . models of how modern people may choose to survive—physically, culturally, and spiritually."[49]

Similarly, in her exploration of Amish-themed romance fiction, Valerie Weaver-Zercher suggests that readers are changed by time spent in a fictional Amish world and are, perhaps, better able, after considering the dilemmas of fictional Amish life, to deal with the dilemmas of their own lives.[50]

At the same time, popular perception of the Amish has too frequently been influenced by non-Amish imaginings of the Amish world. Television producers send Amish teenagers to New York City or Los Angeles, so that the TV-viewing public can watch as they encounter "big city life" for the first time in a "Rumspringa" adventure unlike that known by Amish young folks. A bizarre Amish mafia led by "Lebanon Luke" supposedly keeps the peace in Lancaster County—watched by thousands of viewers on the Discovery Channel.[51] Why are shows such as these so popular? Daniel Laikind of Stick Finger Productions, the company behind such programs as "Amish in the City" and "Amish: Out of Order," says it's "the A word." According to Laikind,

> The public appears to have a never-ending fascination with the Amish . . . simply because they are different. . . . They live among us, but they don't live like us. How do they do it? How is it possible that they know about all the cool stuff that we have and yet they willingly choose

not to use it? There is something about a culture that is able to remain so separate, that keeps itself at an arms length from the things that we strive, for that is enticing.

In many ways the Amish represent a way of life we wish we could live. It is a type of fantasy."[52]

Clearly, as this exploration of Amish life in New York has shown, worldly acceptance of the Amish is complicated. The Amish fit a variety of cultural stereotypes important in American society: they are pioneers, individualists, spiritual gurus, and back-to-the-land environmentalists; but they are also Luddites, scofflaws, and religious extremists. Rejection of social norms is, after all, rejection of those who establish them and the laws that perpetuate them.

The Old Order Amish have rejected the dominant society, but that society cannot reject the Amish. They are fellow citizens, whether they like it or not, and so must be acknowledged and accounted for in the dominant society even as they try to avoid it. The Old Order Amish and other plain groups have come to represent a commitment to religious freedom, free speech, cultural diversity, and even religious values, and as the mainstream society embraces those values, it must accommodate the Amish. Just as the Old Order churches need mainstream society to set the worldly norms they reject, non–Old Order society needs the Old Orders to be fellow citizens, for they reinforce our notions of ourselves and our legal and cultural commitment to religious liberty, freedom, and the right to be different.

Moreover, the Old Orders challenge mainstream Americans to come to terms with the boundaries many of them have drawn between their own religious beliefs and their secular lives. To what extent will the citizens of New York allow faith-based initiatives to replace secular institutions? How will they accommodate change that threatens religiously defined values of family, childhood, life, and death? If one holds dearly particular beliefs, can one perform the duties of citizenship that would cause one to violate those beliefs? Can one hold public office and pledge to uphold laws that one's religious beliefs say are wrong? Pacifists facing the draft can opt to become conscientious objectors, but what about judges whose job requires them to marry two people that they feel personally should not be allowed to marry?

The Old Orders thrive in a nation that guarantees religious freedom, but they find that freedom to be a double-edged sword, for in maintaining a commitment to religious belief, they inevitably come into conflict with some of the nation's other ideals and laws. They benefit from citizenship in the national polity, yet reject many of the demands of citizenship, demands that, in effect, challenge their notions of religious belief. In all these ways, the Old Order Amish challenge their neighbors to question whether a nation in which many citizens claim religious identity can indeed separate church from state.

10

The Future of New York's Amish

Two Worlds, Side by Side

> How can it be, that 'time' so swiftly passes by?
> —Scribe from Clymer, New York, in *Die Botschaft*, 2009

Perhaps one of the most important consequences of the U.S. Supreme Court's decision in *Wisconsin v. Yoder et al.* is that it empowered Amish communities and, by making it easier for them to operate their own one-room schoolhouses, encouraged Amish diversity. As Ordnungs have changed, permitting a greater range of occupations, so too have the behaviors that characterize Amish life. And as Amish communities become more diverse, they will challenge secular authority in different ways.

This is certainly true in New York State, where nearly two centuries after the first Amish arrived in New York State, New York Amish church communities continue to grow in both size and number. By 2011, New York State had the fifth largest—and the fastest growing—Amish population.[1] The Young Center's 2015 Amish Profile estimates the number of New York church districts at 128 in 52 settlements.[2] A count only a year later shows 136 church districts.[3] With an increase of 19 settlements, and 47 church districts since the first edition of *New York Amish* appeared, there is little reason to believe that the State's Amish population won't continue to expand and become more diverse, challenging both Amish and non-Amish residents to accept new neighbors who look and act differently.

Two Worlds

Although New York's Amish communities may not be as well-known as those in Lancaster County, Pennsylvania, or the Holmes County region of Ohio, which attract millions of visitors each year, they're increasingly on the radar of visitors to the state. Writing to *Trip*

Advisor, for example, one tourist asked fellow travelers about New York's "Amish Trail." "I saw while researching Niagara Falls, there is a[n] Amish Community in Western NY," he noted, "I was wondering if this is close enough to Niagara Falls to be able to visit as a day trip?? I can't find anything on Google Map. One of the towns mentioned was Cattaragus [*sic*]."[4]

Most New York Amish are content to stay off the beaten tourist path, but they are hardly isolated. Instead, as non-Amish New Yorkers living in close proximity to Amish neighbors know, Amish homes are interspersed with English ones, and Amish New Yorkers shop in English stores, visit English doctors, sell their goods to English customers, and take an active role in the economies of their regions.

Nevertheless, while they interact daily with their non-Amish neighbors, all Amish remain committed to a lifestyle of religiously mandated non-conformity nonconformity. The result is two worlds, integrated in some ways perhaps, but always separate. As a separate community within the dominant society, today's twenty-first-century Amish are

Figure 10.1. Church benches stacked outside an Amish home. The Amish find strength in their faith. Photo by author.

always aware of the threat "worldliness" poses to their way of life, and even the most conservative face the pressures it exerts.

Some Amish parents worry that the technology of the non-Amish world will attract their children and threaten their church community. For example, told by an English neighbor that several young Swartzentruber boys had been observed charging phones at a local gas station, one Swartzentruber mother immediately asked if her son had been among them. Many worry about other worldly temptations as well. In 2009 the Associated Press reported that two young men from the Troyer settlement in the Conewango Valley had been ticketed for having beer in their buggy. One, just seventeen years old, was charged with underage possession of alcohol, and his friend, at twenty-two, was charged with providing beer to a minor.[5] More recently a young Amish man from the Norfolk community was charged with having taken a friend's truck without permission, operating it without a license, and endangering an underage passenger.[6]

New York's Amish exist with, depend on, and sometimes even get in trouble with their non-Amish neighbors. Most interactions are the stuff of interesting letters to the Amish newspapers. One Lowville scribe wrote, for example, how one of the local drivers for the community arrived with a letter addressed to the scribe's sister in the Path Valley, "but the town and state were Lowville, NY. No return address." According to the scribe, the driver "said they were discussing it at the post office and he said give it to me, I'll get the address. So we put it on and he went his way . . . I call that service."[7] A *Botschaft* scribe from Fort Plain described the arrival of fire trucks to get a cat out of a tree, noting "I would think if a cat found its way up it would find its way down too."[8]

The Amish hope that all interaction will be so benign. Unfortunately, as the English world changes, Amish farmers and business owners will find it more and more difficult to deal with a society that is increasingly technological and relies less and less on face-to-face interaction and personal relationships.

The difficulties are already apparent in daily economic exchanges. As noted in chapter 7, for example, the need for social security numbers and photo IDs has already hampered the most conservative Amish as they attempt such simple transactions as opening a new checking account. More recently, one local official noted that "we're seeing some of the Amish looking for commercial loans, but because of the new federal regulations, banks aren't allowed to loan money [to folks] without social security numbers or photo IDs." Before, locally owned banks or credit unions knew the community members with whom they were interacting and could make loans on the basis of personal acquaintance; now lending institutions can be fined for not requiring the proper identification and credit history.

Further, as the mainstream world increasingly relies on digital communication, the Amish are cut off from both business and government, and their access to important information is limited. Healthcare workers at the Cancer Services Program of St. Lawrence County have worried, for example, about how to get information about cancer screening clinics to the County's Amish population. Betsy Hodge of Cornell Cooperative Extension noted that the organization's newsletter was going online and worried because she "knows from visiting farms that the Amish read the newsletter." "If I could email them, it would be great," she added, "but getting them in the loop is tough."

In 2011, the New York State Department of Taxation and Finance made electronic filing of sales-tax returns obligatory, affecting all of the state's Amish communities. As an Amish man quoted in the *Watertown Daily Times* put it, "They want to do everything electronic."[9] For the Amish, who don't have electricity, much less computers, the problems were clear. Although a spokesperson for the Department of Taxation and Finance allowed that the state would be "judicious" in leveling fines against the Amish, she also said that the department assumed that anyone with concerns about the new process "would call the Taxpayer Contact Center," another thing that, of course, the Amish could not easily do. Lamented a representative of State Senator Patricia A. Ritchie,[10] "After the State insisted on e-filing of taxes, these poor [Amish] families would get past due notices—and would want to pay—and get a computer generated message telling them to call the phone hotline. When we would try to talk to [state tax officials], they wouldn't believe it."

State tax officials aren't the only ones who don't get it when it comes to their Amish neighbors. Some of the challenges the Amish face come as they interact with "newly rural" New Yorkers, as well as with longtime residents whose families are increasingly distant from the farms of New York's past. Arriving to take advantage of less urban surroundings, many transplanted residents are eager to enjoy New York's natural beauty but are unwilling to endure the sights and smells of traditional agriculture. A *Diary* scribe from the relatively new settlement in Holland Patent, New York, commented on community life, noting,

This community was started in 2011. We don't have much to complain about as far as not being accepted by the locals. Most people, especially the older people and the farmers, are quite friendly and easy to get along with. However, there are some here and there who seem to resent our presence (and/or the horse manure on the road). The local authorities say they get quite a few complaints on it, but even though there is a law on manure or mud or other foreign objects on the road, they are not going to enforce it. Then they would also have to enforce it on the farmer who spills a little manure or such minor thing on the road. They say that the number one industry here in Oneida County, NY is farming, so they are lenient on such things.[11]

Talking about St. Lawrence County to the north of Holland Patent, one local official acknowledged that, "being rural, we already had regulations in place allowing the right to farm. Some of the issues facing the Amish were settled with earlier non-Amish farms."[12] The problem, he asserted, is that "people without an agricultural background are moving into rural areas and discovering that cows poop and go 'that has to stop.'"

Intervention by State Senator Ritchie's office has solved the tax-filing problem for the time being, and right-to-farm legislation protects the activities of various Amish groups around the state. Unfortunately, there are sure to be other issues affecting Amish-English relationships. As St. Lawrence County Public Defender Steve Ballan, who represented the Swartzentruber Amish charged with building code violations in Morristown, New York, noted, "Where their way of life intersects with ours, it will become more and more challenging. Things like building codes are continually being amended and they're not building in any exceptions. The laws [are] changing and bringing them into conflict." Sounding a cautionary note, Herman Bontrager, a member of the National Committee for Amish Religious Freedom, suggests that permit disputes with the Amish are most common in areas where they are relative newcomers.[13]

As new communities are established in areas that have never before seen Amish settlement, there may also be a deeper, more human issue to overcome. According to Harvey M. Jacobs, a professor in the urban and regional planning department at the University of Wisconsin, Madison, whose research focuses on land use and public policy, Amish neighbors can be unsettling to English communities. Talking specifically about a community in Loyal, Wisconsin, site of a new Swartzentruber Amish settlement, he suggested that many in the non-Amish community might feel "a sense of alienation, a confusion and anger" about "these people [who] live amongst us and yet don't live with us." As one New York State official put it, "It's a lot easier to have perceptions and opinions about people you don't know." St. Lawrence County Public Defender Ballan noted, somewhat sadly, "The differences [between Amish and English] are becoming greater and greater, and people are becoming less and less tolerant of things that are different."[14]

Only time will tell whether and how the diverse Amish and English communities will continue to coexist. The goal, said one official, is "to get people talking to each other and local governments talking to constituents. . . . The best way to break down barriers is to get them talking to each other."[15]

Going Forward

The future holds other challenges. Asked how life had changed in the last fifty years, many New York Amish noted that it has become more expensive and that farms are getting harder to come by. Talking about the Clyde settlement in the Finger Lakes, one woman noted that, while the older families were all involved in vegetable farming, younger community members were mostly "working out," that is, working for others at carpentry or other jobs. "They have to in order to make a go of it," she said. A Swartzentruber bishop expressed concern about young couples just starting out who might have to take out expensive mortgages to buy farms. "I don't want them to get saddled with such debt," he worried. Cornell Cooperative Extension resource educator Betsy Hodge noted that she had

> met with some [Amish] farmers just over the border into Franklin County . . . and they were all talking about how valuable farmland has become. The farm we were meeting at is surrounded by Amish farms. We are wondering how the Amish will be able to find land for their offspring to settle in the area at the prices per acre for farmland. Perhaps they will do trades or have other businesses. There aren't many places with cheaper farmland or as much available farmland, but it is way more expensive than it was 5 years ago.[16]

While one Swartzentruber housewife commented on Amish settlers from Pennsylvania, who seemed to have more money to spend on farms and were "always looking," another noted simply—and sadly—that the land is getting "too crowded."

The Amish express reliance on God and faith that God will provide. Many of their non-Amish neighbors acknowledge the challenges but continue to see in Amish settlement a spark of hope, particularly for life in rural New York. As resource educator Hodge, put it, "They can teach us a lot of the skills we've lost." Stephen Knight, president of SPARX, a for-profit corporation founded in New York's North Country by United Helpers,[17] argues that "the Amish have a locally-centered, robust economy, and a locally-owned business generates three to five times the income of an absent-owned one [when the owner is not a resident of the community]." Moreover, he argued, "absent-owned businesses send all profits out of area, starving the community of capital."[18] According to Knight, SPARX hopes to work with the Amish and other local farmers and distributors to create a local food hub. "It's a new paradigm," he says, "to invest locally rather than supporting large corporate entities that send money out of the community." Knight notes that he has had conversations with a number of Amish farmers, who just say "tell us what to grow."[19]

Others have expressed the hope that the Amish will keep small family farms alive. "We feel like they'll take over a lot of these [unproductive or abandoned] farms, and we'll see what they'll do with them," asserts resource educator Hodge, who characterizes her many Amish clients as "innovative and interested in trying things." She adds, "I throw out ideas, and they say 'what about this and what about that.' They do some innovative things. And they have a good sense of humor."[20]

Innovation and good humor were both in evidence in a report from a scribe in Conewango, New York, who excitedly described "a different-looking manure spreader" he was in the process of making. He had made one twelve years earlier that his son was now using. The frame of the new one, he said, "is mostly stainless steel, the widespread beater has serrated teeth and does the job of middle beater and widespread. The top cylinder is rolled SS with spikes welded on, once welder was here. There are no cast parts on the cylinder or widespread, still a few wrinkles to iron out."[21] In this innovative design, the inventor both kept within the Ordnung of his church community and relied on the help of a welder from the outside. Quintessentially Amish, he has blended old and new to create a device that will better serve his fellow farmers as they attempt to earn a living in the traditional way. And he has done it with the help of an outsider.

Figure 10.2. An Amish boy draws his world. The Amish dream is that their children will grow up to live like their parents: contributing church members, separate from the world.

Whatever the future brings to New York's Amish communities, they will surely be living in a world that continues to change, and they will change too, in the ongoing interaction between groups with different lifestyles, priorities, and goals. The diversity of the Amish world is a testament to the issues and concerns that drive the Amish to resist or adopt new technologies and different patterns of interaction with neighbors, businesses, and government agencies. Each church feels this pressure to adapt to the outer world while maintaining their commitment to Old Order ways. Each church simultaneously confronts pressures from within as church members grapple with their own responses to these new developments, temptations, and challenges. The challenge for the

Amish is always how to control that change to preserve the church community. For their non-Amish neighbors, the challenge will be to understand the Amish diversity that results.

For the foreseeable future, Amish families will continue to migrate to the Empire State. As long as there is farmland to be had at prices they can afford, the Amish and their other plain counterparts will come here to find respite from internal and external difficulties and a safe and productive neighborhood in which to raise their children. They will continue to establish new settlements, work with non–Old Order neighbors to create thriving businesses, wrestle with legal and social questions that challenge both the church and secular society, and confront the demands of history, geography, and social context.

In so doing, the Amish will continue to fascinate, anger, exasperate, and inspire their fellow New Yorkers. Ideally, their fellow New Yorkers will in turn come to appreciate the diversity of their Old Order neighbors. As one Swartzentruber man said, "You live your way, we live our way, and it's a free country," he said. "And we hope it continues."[22]

214

Acknowledgments

I am not Amish, nor do I come from an Amish background. Thus I speak as an outsider, albeit one who has had the privilege of being invited into Amish homes in a number of different settlements. I feel blessed by the willingness of Amish friends and acquaintances to share with me their thoughts and advice. I have learned much from them, and my life is made richer by knowing them. Given the Amish preference for anonymity, I will not list the different Amish individuals who, over the years, have spoken with me, helped me, taught me, and become my friends. But I wish to show my gratitude to them nevertheless. This book could not have been written without their help and support.

I am also grateful to David Luthy and his wife, Mary, for welcoming me to work in the Heritage Historical Library. I owe a special debt to Donald B. Kraybill for his friendship, mentoring, encouragement, and advice, and to my friend and research colleague, Steven M. Nolt, whose work has guided me in many ways. The Young Center for Anabaptist and Pietist Studies has been an invaluable resource for me. I am particularly grateful for the work of Stephen E. Scott, who taught me much about Amish population and affiliation; to Edsel Burdge Jr., who has helped to keep me up to date on population changes; to Jeff and Ann Bach, for their good humor, friendship, and support. I also owe special thanks to Carol Cady, the GIS specialist at the Launders Science Library at St. Lawrence University for the maps she prepared for both the first and the revised edition of this work. Finally, I am grateful to my colleagues for their support. In the course of my research I have come to know two remarkable women, Linda Ulrich-Hagner and Linda Esposito. Without their help, my research of the Amish in New York would have been far more difficult to accomplish.

I am also grateful to the readers who offered advice on the manuscript. Their comments improved it greatly. I accept full responsibility for the faults that remain.

This work could not have been completed without financial support from the National Endowment for the Humanities as part of a collaborative research grant on "Amish Diversity and Identity in the Twentieth Century" and from the Research and Creative Endeavors Program at SUNY Potsdam.

Finally, thank you, Bruce, for your love, patience, and support. This is for you, Seth, and Miriam, and Sam.

Appendix A

*Existing Old Order Amish Settlements
in New York (as of December 2015)*

The following information is drawn from the work of David Luthy at the Heritage Historical Library; Joseph Donnermeyer, professor, Rural Sociology Program, Ohio State University; and Edsel Burdge Jr., research associate at the Young Center for Anabaptist and Pietist Studies. Dates in the left column indicate the year in which each community was founded. Slashes indicate alternative names for the settlement. The names are those under which news of the settlement appears in the *Budget*, *Die Botschaft*, and the *Diary*.

1949	Conewango Valley, Cattaraugus County	1988	Fillmore, Allegany County
1974	Norfolk, St. Lawrence County	1990	Addison, Steuben County
1975	Heuvelton, St. Lawrence County	1997	Clyde, Wayne County
1976	Dewittville/Mayville, Chautauqua County Clymer/Sherman/ Panama, Chautauqua County	1999	Lowville, Lewis County
		2000	Richfield Springs, Otsego County
		2002	Malone/Burke, Franklin County South Columbia/ Otsego County
1979	Prattsburgh, Steuben County		
1981	Romulus/Ovid, Seneca County	2003	Locke/Summerhill, Cayuga County
1982	Friendship/Belfast, Allegany County	2003	Little Falls, Herkimer County
1983	Woodhull/Jasper, Steuben County		Hopkinton/Nicholville, St. Lawrence County
1986	Fort Plain, Montgomery County	2005	Fultonville-Glen, Montgomery County

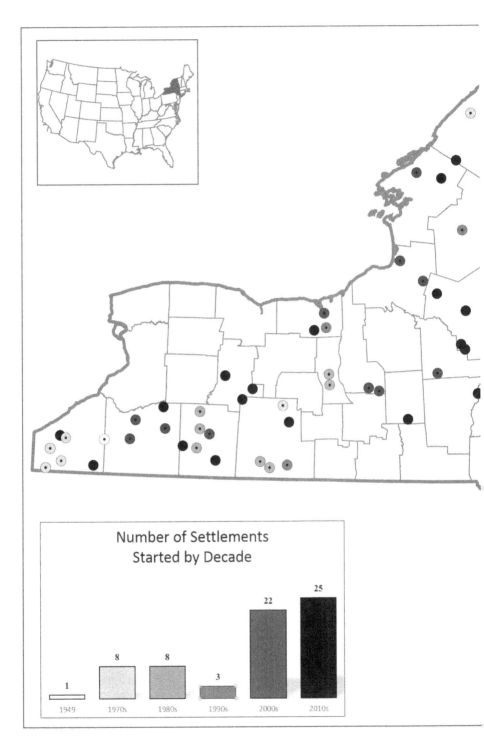

Appendix A Map. Amish settlements in New York State.

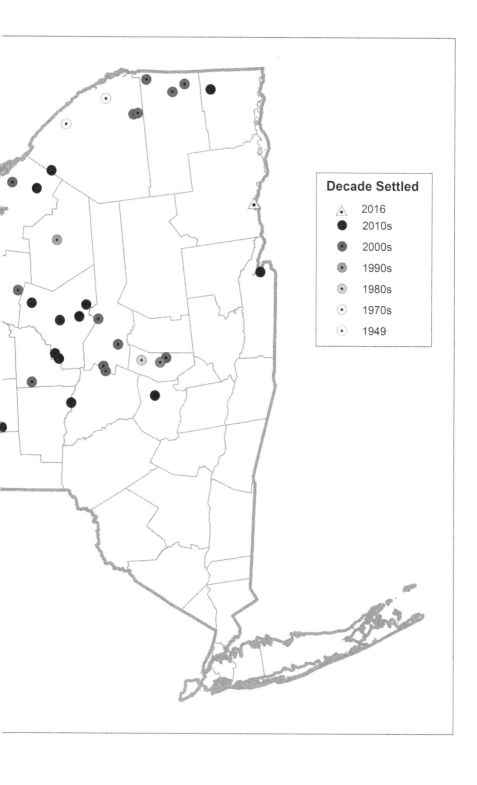

Decade Settled	
△	2016
●	2010s
●	2000s
●	1990s
●	1980s
⊙	1970s
⊙	1949

2005	LaFargeville, Jefferson County	2011	Mayville, Chautauqua County
2006	Williamstown/Pulaski, Oswego County		Ellenburg Center, Clinton County
	Georgetown, Madison County		Remsen/Rome/ Holland Patent, Oneida County
	Mohawk Valley, Montgomery County		Springwater/ Dansville, Livingston County
	Little Valley/East Otto, Cattaraugus County		Delevan, Cattaraugus County
2007	Poland, Herkimer County		Frewsburg, Chautauqua County
2009	Angelica, Allegany County	2012	Philadelphia, Jefferson County
	Bombay, Franklin County		Ava/Lee Center, Oneida County
	Franklinville/Cuba, Cattaraugus County		Hammondsport, Steuben County
	North Rose, Wayne County	2013	Wellsville, Allegany County
2010	Marathon, Cortland County		Somerville, St. Lawrence County
	Orinskany Falls/ Augusta, Oneida County		Whitehall, Washington County
	Mount Morris, Livingston County		Lyons, Wayne County
	New Berlin, Chenango County	2014	Cobleskill, Schoharie County
	Camden, Oneida County		Augusta, Madison County

Appendix B

Extinct Old Order Amish Settlements in New York

This information was compiled by David Luthy at the Heritage Historical Library, in Aylmer, Ontario, July 2007. See D. Luthy, *The Amish in America: Settlements That Failed, 1840–1960*, and D. Luthy, *Why Some Amish Communities Fail: Extinct Settlements, 1961–2000*. Additional information comes from J. Donnermeyer and D. Luthy, "Amish Settlements across America."

1831–1910	Croghan, Lewis County. As noted in chapter 1, this community is still extant, but it now identifies as Mennonite. The 1910 date is an arbitrary ending point, used because it marks the date the community joined six other independent Amish congregations to form the new Conservative Amish Mennonite Conference.
1950–1960	Sinclairville, Chautauqua County
1979–1999	Clyde, Wayne County
1979–	Newport, Herkimer County. One family lingers.
1981–1988	Dundee, Yates County
1986–1996	Albion, Orleans County
2002–2007	Poland, Herkimer County
2010–2012	Tyrone, Schuyler County

Appendix C

Amish Migration and Population in New York State, 1983–2013

Table C1. Amish migration to and from New York (number of households)

	1983–2007		1998–2007	
	To NY	From NY	To NY	From NY
DE	31	0	28	0
IA	2	2	2	1
IL	0	3	0	2
IN	13	14	12	5
KY	36	53	34	22
MD	37	0	20	1
ME	1	3	1	3
MI	28	35	27	5
MN	6	9	0	3
MO	0	5	3	4
MT	0	2	0	2
NC	0	1	0	0
OH	229	109	203	20
OK	0	1	0	1
ON	15	3	2	0
PA	343	156	190	45
TN	6	3	1	0
VA	2	2	2	2
WI	13	26	9	5
WV	1	1	1	1
Total	763	428	535	122
	Within NY—120		Within NY—63	

Source: Data compiled by Stephen Scott, Young Center for Anabaptist and Pietist Studies, Elizabethtown College, Elizabethtown, Pennsylvania.

Table C2. Amish population change in New York State, 2008–2013[1]

Settlements			Districts			Estimated population		
2008	2013	#change	%change	2008	2013	#change	%change	2008	2013	#change	%change
29	49	20	69%	75	118	43	57%	10,125	15,930	5,805	57%

Source: "Amish Population Change 2008–2013," Young Center for Anabaptist and Pietist Studies, Elizabethtown College, http://www2.etown.edu/amishstudies/PDF/Statistics/Population_Change_2008_2013.pdf.

Appendix D

Amish Divisions

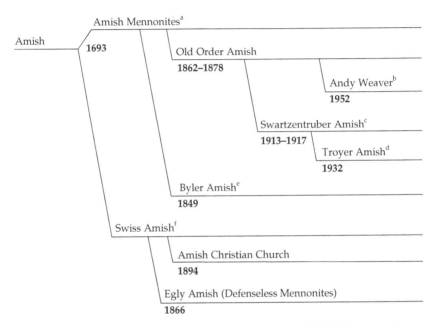

[a] Following the Diener-Versammlungen or ministers' meetings (1862–1878), more change-minded Amish congregations formed regional conferences. Some churches remained independent until the 20th century. The conservative groups remained committed to their traditional practices and became known as the Old Order Amish. (See chapter 1.)

[b] The Andy Weaver Amish date officially to 1952. The group takes its name from Bishop Andrew J. Weaver, a conservative-minded bishop in Holmes County, Ohio, who disagreed with the Old Order churches over enforcement of the Bann. (See chapter 5.)

[c] The Swartzentruber Amish had ceased to fellowship with the Old Order Amish in Ohio by 1917. There have been several schisms in the Swartzentruber churches since then, and now, in addition to the Troyer Amish, a separate group, there are several distinct factions that identify as Swartzentruber Amish. (See chapter 3.)

[d] The Troyer Amish originated in a schism within the Swartzentruber Amish. (See chapter 2)

[e] The Byler Amish originated in Mifflin County, Pennsylvania, in 1849 following a schism with the larger Amish church. The Byler Amish remain more conservative than many of their Old Order brethren. (See chapter 2.)

[f] The Swiss Amish did not take part in the Diener-Versammlungen. Schisms within Swiss Amish churches resulted in the formation of the Egly Amish Church (also called the Defenseless Mennonites, known today as the Fellowship of Evangelical Churches) and the Amish Christian Church. (See chapter 6.)

Notes

Preface

1. As Enninger noted succinctly, "In this culture, the choice the field worker has is to work on the basis of the obtainable data or to gain no insights at all." See W. Enninger, "On the Organization of Sign-Processes in an Old Order Amish (OOA) Parochial School," 149–150.

1. Who Are the Amish?

1. "New Yorkers Are Neurotic and Unfriendly, Says Cambridge University 'Personality Map,'" Telegraph.co.uk, September 11, 2008, http://www.telegraph.co.uk/news/worldnews/northamerica/usa/2779683/New-Yorkers-are-neurotic-and-unfriendly-says-Cambridge-University-personality-map.html.

2. Infoplease, U.S. Population by State, 1790–2008, http://www.infoplease.com/ipa/A0004986.html.

3. U.S. Census Bureau, Population Distribution and change: 2000–2010, 2010 Census Briefs, http://www.census.gov/prod/cen2010/briefs/c2010br-01.pdf. See also http://labor.ny.gov/stats/nys/statewide-population-data.shtm.

4. "Amish Population Growth 1992–2008 Highlights," Young Center for Anabaptist and Pietist Studies, Elizabethtown College, http://www2.etown.edu/amishstudies/Population_Trends_1992_2008. "Amish Population by State (2015)," Young Center for Anabaptist and Pietist Studies, Elizabethtown College, http://groups.etown.edu/amishstudies/statistics/population-by-state/. See also "Amish Population Change 1992–2013, Top Ten States, Young Center for Anabaptist and Pietist Studies, Elizabethtown College, https://groups.etown.edu/amishstudies/files/2015/08/Population_Change_1992-2013.pdf.

5. A. Yousey, *Strangers and Pilgrims*, 33.

6. A number of sources provide information about this early settlement. See A. Yousey, *Strangers and Pilgrims*; D. Luthy, *Settlements That Failed*; J. Houpert, *Les Lorrains en Amérique du Nord*.

7. As the historian Arletha Zehr Bender noted, her pacifist French Amish ancestors could either give up their commitment to pacifism and nonresistance—a defining characteristic of Anabaptism—or they could leave. See Bender, "From Alsace to Adirondacks," 18–19.

8. The reference to "hook and eye," cited in R. J. Lyndaker's self-published *The History and Genealogy of an Amish-Mennonite Family from New York*, strongly suggests that Kiefer

was Amish. Other sources call Kiefer a Mennonite or a "fellow Amish Mennonite." See A. Yousey, *Strangers and Pilgrims*, 32; Bender, *A History of the Mennonites in Croghan and Lowville*. As for Kiefer's roots in Metz, Hough notes that this was where Kiefer was from in his 1860 work *A History of Lewis County*. The French historian J. Houpert, in his work *Les Lorrains en Amérique du Nord*, accepts Hough's claim that Kiefer came from Lorraine, maintaining that Hough could well have been acquainted with Kiefer. Houpert also notes that most of the immigrants to the Lewis County region came from the area around Metz, and that their immigration documents and prayer books were issued or printed in Metz.

9. Kiefer himself may have been influenced by a land agent to leave France. In the *Gazetteer and Business Directory of Lewis County, NY for 1872–73*, H. Child writes that P. Somerville Steward, who settled in Belfort, near Croghan in Lewis County, in 1830, "was, as the agent of Le Ray, instrumental in bringing settlers to this locality. Under his exertions, many immigrants from Europe were attracted here. The first of these was John Keifer [*sic*]" (82).

10. In *Plain Diversity*, their study of the Amish of Indiana, S. Nolt and T. Meyers suggest that Amish affiliations are best understood as products of an ongoing "cultural conversation" within the church and between the church and non-Amish society.

11. The Croghan Naumberg congregation in Lewis County is the oldest of this affiliation in the United States. Benedict Weyeneth was sent by the founder of the movement, Samuel Froehlich, a former Reformed Church minister who was influenced by Anabaptist doctrine. Yet while the Amish and Mennonites baptized by pouring water on the individual, Froehlich asserted that baptism required immersion. Further Froehlich said that baptism could take place only after a conversion experience and a confession of faith, and that the conversion experience had to involve some visible emotional sign that would serve to demonstrate true repentance. Moreover, in contrast to the Amish, whose understanding of nonresistance and pacifism made any connection with the military unacceptable, Froehlich preached that church members might fulfill noncombat roles within the military. Finally, Froehlich and his followers taught that theirs was the one true Christian church. According to the Apostolic Christian Church website, Froehlich's influence in North America dates to an invitation "from a group in another denomination in upstate New York . . . asking for help in settling some spiritual disputes." Froehlich responded by sending Benedict Weyeneth (http://www.apostolicchristian.org/page.cfm?p=559). Other sources say that the man who invited Froehlich to send a representative was none other than Joseph Virkler, the son of the settlement's bishop, Rudolph Virkler (see Luthy, *Settlements That Failed*, 289). Like those in modern-day Anabaptist congregations, members of the Apostolic Christian Church strive to live lives unconformed to the world. (See the Statement of Beliefs on the church website: http://www.apostolicchristian.org/page.cfm?p=554.)

12. As Hostetler put it, "The Amish are often perceived by other Americans to be relics of the past who live an austere, inflexible life dedicated to inconvenient and archaic customs." Hostetler, *Amish Society*, 3.

13. L.H. Zuck, in "Anabaptism: Abortive Counter-revolt within the Reformation," called it a "counter-revolt" and defined the early Anabaptists as "those of a religious motivation, either non-resistant or violent, who attempted unsuccessfully to reform the leading Reformers" (212).

14. Martin Luther, "Address to the Christian Nobility of the German Nation" (1520). In J.H. Robinson, ed. *Readings in European History*, 2.

15. At this time, Switzerland was more a loose confederation of thirteen cantons, or autonomous regions, than a unified country. While some cantons joined the reform movement, others remained loyal to the Catholic Church.

16. An account of that first rebaptism can be found in the *Grosses Geschictes-Buch*, or *Chronicle of the Hutterian Brethren*.

17. In "The Anabaptist Vision," H.S. Bender noted that both Luther and Zwingli had considered forming a believers' church, but that each rejected the idea. As he wrote, "Both

leaders decided that it was better to include the masses within the fold of the church than to form a fellowship of true Christians only. Both certainly expected the preaching of the Word and the ministration of the sacraments to bear fruit in an earnest Christian life, at least among some, but they reckoned with a permanent and largely indifferent mass. In taking this course, said the Anabaptists, the reformers surrendered their original purpose, and abandoned the divine intention. Others may say that they were wise and statesmanlike leaders" (12).

18. Although the term was a pejorative one in the beginning (and rejected by the Swiss Brethren), it stuck and is today widely used to describe collectively the various churches that trace their roots to that first rebaptism, including the Amish, the Mennonites, the Brethren, and the Hutterites.

19. With his execution, Felix Manz became the first martyr of the Anabaptist movement. Swiss authorities called the execution of Anabaptists by drowning "the third baptism."

20. Both men and women faced torture, exile, and martyrdom, and women played an active role in spreading Anabaptist teachings. In the Introduction to their 1996 *Profiles of Anabaptist Women*, C. A. Snyder and L. A. Huebert Hecht note, "The early phase of Anabaptist development opened up many more possibilities of direct participation and leadership for women than was the social norm in the sixteenth century, or than would become the norm in later Anabaptism.... Women exercised remarkable 'informal' leadership in proselytization, Bible reading (in some cases), in 'unofficial' teaching and preaching, in hymn-writing, and (in the early movement) in prophetic utterance" (11).

21. The Schleitheim Confession, *Mennonite Confession of Faith*, 24.

22. Ibid., 21.

23. Ibid., 22.

24. All quotes are from the King James Version.

25. Compiled by Thieleman J. van Braght, the complete title is *The Bloody Theater, or Martyrs' Mirror of the Defenseless Christians Who Baptized only Upon Confession of Faith, and Who Suffered and Died for the Testimony of Jesus, From the Time of Christ to the Year A.D. 1660.* This book collects the tales of those who were willing to die for their Christian faith, beginning with the Apostles. In particular, it tells the stories of European Anabaptists who were martyred between 1524 and 1660.

26. According to H.S. Bender in "The Anabaptist Vision," after executing 350 Anabaptists in the Palatinate, the Count of Alzey "was heard to exclaim, 'What shall I do, the more I kill, the greater becomes their number!'"

27. In their article, "Alsace (France)," C. Neff and E. H. Correll note that the Anabaptists met "in the forests at Eckbolsheim, Lingolsheim, St. Oswald, and in the region of Schnakenloch. This is the origin of the expression, "the forest church of the Anabaptists."

28. A. Yousey, *Strangers and Pilgrims*, 25.

29. Menno Simons, "Excommunication, Ban or Separation." See *Menno Simons.net Life, Writings, Doctrine, Images, and Links*, http://www.mennosimons.net/ft067-excommunication.html.

30. Menno Simons, "Explanation of the True Apostolic Separation or Excommunication," *Menno Simons.net Life, Writings, Doctrine, Images, and Links*, http://www.mennosimons.net/ft052-explanation.html.

31. Menno Simons, "An Admonition or Instruction from the Word of God, How a Christian Should Be Disposed; and Concerning the Shunning and Separation of the Unfaithful Brethren and Sisters, Either Deceived by Heretical Doctrine, or Leading a Carnal, Shameful Life," *Menno Simons.net Life, Writings, Doctrine, Images, and Links*, http://www.mennosimons.net/ft153-kindadmonition.html.

32. "Admonition or Instruction." See *Menno Simons.net Life, Writings, Doctrine, Images, and Links*, http://www.mennosimons.net/ft153-kindadmonition.html.

33. There are thirty-eight articles in the Dordrecht Confession, but only seven in the Schleitheim Confession.

34. The Dordrecht Confession, *Mennonite Confession of Faith*. See article XI, "The Washing of the Saints' Feet," 64–66, and article XVII, "The Shunning of Those Who Are Expelled," 79–82. Article XVII states that those expelled must be "shunned and avoided by all the members of the church . . . whether it be in eating or drinking, or other such like social matters."

35. Although the Alsatian congregations had largely accepted the Dordrecht Confession, it was not until 1660, nearly a generation later, that a number of Alsatian ministers actually signed it, perhaps in the mistaken belief that their counterparts in Switzerland were doing so as well.

36. Even today excommunication (Bann) and shunning (Meidung) are not the same for all Amish and Mennonite congregations. Generally, however, excommunication means that one is no longer a member of the congregation and is excluded from discussions of the Ordnung and from communion. Shunning means that members of the congregation will limit their social interaction with the excommunicated individual. In some congregations this means that baptized church members will not eat at the same table with someone who is excommunicated. In others, church members will avoid all interaction with the excommunicated individual, even refusing to write to that person, to invite them into their homes, or to do business with them. This latter observance of shunning is called *streng Meidung*.

37. Hostetler, *Amish Society*, 40.

38. J. Guth, "The Danger of Peace," in *Readings from Mennonite Writings, New and Old*, ed. H. C. Haas, 387–388.

39. For further information on the schism that divided the Amish branch of the Anabaptist movement from the Mennonite, see S. Nolt, *A History of the Amish*, and J. A. Hostetler, *Amish Society*. J. Roth, *Letters of the Amish Division: A Sourcebook*, provides translations of letters between parties involved in the schism, including Jacob Ammann.

40. In their study of French Anabaptist immigration, *Recherches historiques sur les Anabaptistes de l'ancienne principauté de Montbeliard, d'Alsace et du territoire de Belfort*, Mathiot and Boigeol suggest that most of the immigrant Amish Mennonite settlers who established churches between western Pennsylvania and Iowa were from France, and they highlight the settlements in Stark and Wayne counties (1830) in Ohio, founded by Alsatian Amish, and the settlement in Fulton, Ohio, founded by Amish from Alsace and Montbéliard (262–263). In "Old Order Amish Settlement: Diffusion and Growth," Crowley concurs, commenting that between 1817 and 1861, a period he refers to as the second wave of Amish immigration to North America, the overwhelming majority of Amish immigrants came from Alsace and Lorraine. The immigration from France greatly depleted the French Amish population. The last independent Amish congregation, the Ixheim Amish church near Zweibrücken in the Palatinate, merged with the neighboring Ernsweiler Mennonite church in 1937.

41. See W. K. Crowley, "Old Order Amish Settlement: Diffusion and Growth." See also Hostetler, *Amish Society*, 65; S. Nolt, *A History of the Amish*, chap. 6.

42. Graber, "Gleanings from Yesterday," 17.

43. In his study *Mennonites of the Ohio and Eastern Conference from the Colonial Period in Pennsylvania to 1968*, G. M. Stoltzfus notes that forty of the seventy-two participants at the 1862 meeting were from Ohio (158). There is little on record to suggest that the Lewis County Amish were much involved in these meetings, however.

44. S. Nolt, *A History of the Amish*, 175.

45. For a discussion of the different meanings of Ordnung and the Diener-Versammlungen, see J. Gingerich, "Ordinance or Ordering."

46. Terms such as *conservative* and *progressive* indicate the degree to which a church district has chosen to be separate from the non-Amish society that surrounds it. The more conservative a church is, the less its reliance on modern technology and the more limited its interaction with the non-Amish world. The Amish themselves will sometimes use the term *high* to refer to more progressive groups, and *low* to describe those that are more conservative. Or, more likely, members of one group will say about those in another more progressive or more conservative group simply that "they're not like us."

47. For more on the Diener-Versammlungen and the Amish divisions of the nineteenth century, see P. Yoder's *Tradition and Transition: Amish Mennonites and Old Order Amish, 1800–1900*. See also J. A. Hostetler's "Amish Problems at the Diener-Versammlungen" and his later work, *Amish Society*, as well as B. Hostetler's "The Formation of the Old Orders," and S. Nolt's *A History of the Amish*.

48. In *The Riddle of Amish Culture*, D. B. Kraybill has noted that the Lancaster Old Order churches made the decision to reject the telephone about the time the Peachey church was formed, adding, however, that although the Old Order forbid the installation of telephones in private homes, it never rejected the use of the telephone. In many Amish communities, telephones may be installed in small booths at the end of the lane, in schoolhouses, or even in shops on private property (190–191). As Kraybill has pointed out, "The Amish have readily used a neighbor's phone for emergencies and have borrowed phones in nearby garages or shops for many years." For an in-depth discussion of the telephone in Old Order culture, see Zimmerman Umble, *Holding the Line*.

49. See Nolt, *A History of the Amish*. There is variation among New Order communities, with those in Lancaster County permitting somewhat more technological innovation than those in Ohio, for example.

50. J. A. Hostetler, *Amish Society*, 225.

51. In his book *Compulsory Education and the Amish*, A. N. Keim quotes Bishop David O. Treyer of Ohio, who, writing in 1870, argued "all Christian churches must be fenced-in (um zäunt) with rules and regulations which are based and grounded on God's Word. For without such a spiritual fence no church can long survive. Where no Christian 'Ordnung' exists, God cannot be served" (10).

52. The term *affiliation* is used to describe a grouping of two or more Amish church districts or congregations that share at least twenty years of history (Kraybill, Johnson-Weiner, Nolt, *The Amish*, 138). If congregations are affiliated, then their Ordnungs, and consequently their lifestyles, are similar. Affiliations, which may have subgroups, are generally recognized by others in the Amish world. There are some forty different Amish affiliations. In New York State, we can see at least twelve, including the Troyer, Byler, Nebraska, and Swartzentruber Amish.

53. See Kraybill, Johnson-Weiner, and Nolt, *The Amish*, especially chap. 15, for a discussion of the move away from farming in many Amish communities.

54. Pathway Publishers, *1001 Questions and Answers on the Christian Life*, 139.

55. That the Amish are coming to New York State in order to maintain an agricultural lifestyle will be expanded on throughout this work.

56. The Old Order churches have historically associated Sunday Schools with the practices of mainstream Protestantism. Moreover, since Sunday School classes have often been taught by women, they challenge the traditional understanding of gender roles in Old Order communities. See Kraybill and Bowman, *On the Backroad to Heaven*; see also the discussion of gender roles and teaching in Johnson-Weiner, *Train Up a Child*, especially 156–158.

57. Translations of German titles are from Hostetler, *Amish Society*, 106.

58. For more on Amish dress, see S. Scott, *Why Do They Dress That Way?*

59. As R. Stevick puts it in *Growing Up Amish*, "The Amish regard parenting as a profound calling from God, to whom they are accountable. Virtually all of them believe that parents carry a heavy responsibility for the outcome of their children" (90).

60. Mrs. J. D. Byler, "To Have Them Seek Jesus," reprinted in *The Challenge of the Child: Selections from "The Blackboard Bulletin" 1957–1966*, ed. Stoll, 28–29.

61. See S. Cronk, "Gelassenheit."

62. Members will donate land to the congregation as needed, whether for a cemetery or school. Generally, the location chosen will be that most convenient to the community, but land for a cemetery may be donated by the family that needs it first.

63. For further information on the *Ausbund*, see J. S. Umble, "The Old Order Amish, Their Hymns and Hymn Tunes," and B. S. Blank, *The Amazing Story of the Ausbund*.

Interestingly, hymn tunes may also divide the Amish, for the more progressive groups sing the hymns at a faster tempo.

64. *Ernsthafte Christenpflicht* (complete title: *Die Ernsthaffte Christenpflicht, Darinnen Schöne Geistreiche Gebäter, Darmit sich fromme Christen-Herzen zu allen Zeiten und in allen Nöthen trösten können. Gedruckt im jar 1739, Abu finden in Kayserslautern bei dem Buchbinder*) contains thirty-six prayers for daily devotions and special needs. First published in the early eighteenth century, it continues in regular use in most Amish households. See Friedmann, "Ernsthafte Christenpflicht."

65. For further information on Old Order publications, see D. Zimmerman Umble and D. Weaver-Zercher, *The Amish and the Media.*

66. In his 1993 article "The National Amish Steering Committee," Olshan refers to this as the "National Amish Steering Committee." "Old Order Amish Steering Committee" is the term used by A.S. Kinsinger, its first chair, in his 1997 work *A Little History of Our Parochial Schools and Steering Committee From 1956–1994.*

67. The Amish population currently numbers approximately 300,000 nationwide, more than double the Amish population in 1990. See "Amish Population Profile 2015," Young Center for Anabaptist and Pietist Studies, Elizabethtown College, http://groups.etown. edu/amishstudies/statistics/amish-population-profile-2015. In 1992, the estimated Amish population was 128,145. See "Amish Population Change 1992–2013," Young Center for Anabaptist and Pietist Studies, Elizabethtown College, http://www2.etown.edu/ amishstudies/PDF/Statistics/Population_Change_1992_2013.pdf.

68. In *Riddles*, Kraybill has noted that approximately 10 percent of young people defect from the church in the Lancaster County settlement (117). In *Plain Diversity*, their study of the Amish in Indiana, Nolt and Meyers found that approximately 30 percent of young people in progressive church districts defect but only about 7 percent in the most conservative (83). In his 1994 study of Amish defection, "The Old Order Amish: To Remain in the Faith or to Leave," Thomas Meyers suggests defection rates vary considerably depending on such factors as sibling position, marital status, and gender. He presents figures showing defection rates of up to 37 percent. See also Kraybill, Johnson-Weiner, and Nolt, *The Amish*, 162–168.

69. Hostetler, *Amish Society*, 399.

2. Cattaraugus and Chautauqua Counties

1. The letter was signed by Enos J. Miller. He was a preacher and had arrived with his family from Wayne County, Ohio.

2. Conewango Valley, NY, *Budget*, March 17, 1976.

3. Conewango Valley, NY, *Diary*, January 1999.

4. *1001 Questions and Answers on the Christian Life*, 139.

5. See M. Olshan, *The Old Order Amish in New York State*. Olshan uses pseudonyms to refer to the different Amish settlements he discusses. Nevertheless, it is fairly easy to identify the groups with the descriptions he provides. For example, "Oldtown" is identified as "the oldest existing Amish community in New York" (17). Further, a chart gives February 1949 as the date of the first Amish land purchase and identifies Holmes County, Ohio, and Enon Valley, Pennsylvania, as the settlements of origin. See also R. Farmanfarmaian, "Autumn in Amish Country," who has suggested that the migrants to western New York have "grown uncomfortable with Ohio's expanding population."

6. See Hostetler, *Amish Society*, 370–371.

7. Yoder's group came to be known as Swartzentruber Amish when, after Yoder's death, both of the group's bishops happened to be named "Swartzentruber." I deal with the Swartzentruber schism in greater detail in chapter 3.

8. See chapter 1 for a discussion of Bann, Meidung, and strong Meidung.

9. Undated note by D. Luthy referring to a 1998 conversation in Norwich, Ontario. Heritage Historical Library, Aylmer, Ontario.

10. Letter dated July 1, 1998 from D. Stutzman to D. Luthy, Heritage Historical Library.

11. In *The Riddle of Amish Culture*, 54–55, Kraybill notes that "the symbols of Gelassenheit articulate surrender, bond the community together, and mark off boundaries with the larger society."

12. All quotations are from my field research (participant-observation) conducted in New York Amish communities since 1985. Individuals are unnamed to respect their wishes and their privacy.

13. See Olshan, *The Old Order Amish in New York State*, 18. As the Amish man tells the story, "The Amish were among the only can shippers. They went to the [Ontario] milk board, said that religious convictions prevented them from using the bulk tanks, and asked if the board could designate one plant to take can milk. The board came up with all sorts of reasons why it couldn't take the Amish suggestions, and then finally told the truth, and all the Amish stopped shipping milk."

14. Conewango Valley, New York, is roughly two hours (175 miles) from Enon Valley, Pennsylvania, and approximately three hours from Berlin, Ohio, in Holmes County.

15. Conewango Valley, NY, *Budget*, January 23, 2008.

16. See Hewner, "Fertility, Migration, and Mortality in an Old Order Amish Community."

17. http://enchantedmountains.com/files/downloads/map/2015-amish-trail-brochure-small.pdf. This interactive digital trail map and brochure provide evidence that Amish tourism has become more important in the region since the first edition of *New York Amish*. Only a few years ago, tourists had to content themselves with a photocopied map from the Valley View Cheese Company. The interactive map, which covers several settlements in the area, lists a variety of Amish-owned businesses (color coded by product offered), as well as a number of new non-Amish-owned businesses, including the Amish Cottage B & B and Mystic Hill Olde Barn Country Gift Shop, that are capitalizing on the Amish presence.

18. S. Galet, "Stepping Back."

19. C. Smyczynski, "Exploring Western New York's Amish Community."

20. See Amish Trail Brochure and Map, http://amishtrail.com/amish-trail-brochure-and-map.

21. The title translation was supplied by a Troyer Amish man in the Conewango Valley. *Hiwwe wie Driwwe* was founded in 1997 by Dr. Michael Werner, a scholar of Pennsylvania German, and is written entirely in the Pennsylvania German dialect. Approximately 2,400 copies are published twice a year, and there are subscribers in the United States, Canada, and Europe.

22. In the first edition of New York Amish, this settlement was called simply Mayville. Today, however, there is another settlement in the region called "Mayville" and, like the Amish, I am using the "Dewittville" to distinguish the two.

23. L. Foderaro, "No Wiggle Room in This Window War."

24. Amish from the New Wilmington, Pennsylvania, area have also established settlements in Friendship and Fort Plain, New York, and individual families have moved to join existing settlements.

25. Olshan, *The Old Order Amish in New York State*, 14.

26. Anon., "The Migration of Amish to Geauga County," report in *Der Gemeinde Brief*, July 29, 1992.

27. Today, the percentage of heads of households in Geauga County, Ohio, whose primary occupation is farming may be as low as 7 percent. See Kraybill, Johnson-Weiner, Nolt, *The Amish*, 282.

28. The failed settlement in Sinclairville, in Chautauqua County, which also had its roots in Geauga County, Ohio, is discussed in chapter 8.

29. See Stephen Scott's *Why Do They Dress That Way?* for a good overview of dress patterns in Amish communities.

30. Readily available to tourists visiting Chautauqua County, the photocopied maps "Amish Map for Northern Chautauqua County" and "Amish Map for Western Chautauqua County" show both Amish and non-Amish businesses and gives tourist tips. They note, for example, that "going to the Amish community is an adventure unlike your normal shopping experience," caution tourists not to take photos of the Amish, and warn that Amish businesses will be closed on Sundays. Online versions of these maps are available through www.tourchautauqua.com.

31. Teacher salaries in this community average between $350 and $400 a month, depending on the teacher's age and experience. Teachers in conservative communities, such as Mayville or the Conewango Valley, generally earn less. For more on Old Order schools and teachers, see Johnson-Weiner, *Train Up a Child.*

32. Clymer, NY, *Die Botschaft*, March 2, 2015.

33. For this anecdote, I am grateful to L. Ulrich-Hagner, whose ongoing friendship with members of the Clymer-area settlement has offered me further insights.

34. See chapter 1.

35. Conewango Valley, NY, *Diary*, July 2006.

36. Ibid., February 2007.

37. Frewsburg, NY; Little Valley/East Otto, NY, *Diary*, November 2014.

38. Cuba, NY, *Diary*, February, 2016.

39. There are two settlements in the Richfield Springs, New York, region. The Clymer group is "back and forth," meaning that they exchange ministers, with the settlement that has its origins in Geauga County, Ohio, which identifies itself as "South Columbia." The other Richfield Springs settlement was started by Amish from Lancaster County, Pennsylvania. See chapter 5 for more on the Mohawk Valley area settlements.

40. Black Creek, NY, *Budget*, October 27, 1982.

41. Friendship, NY, *Diary*, January 2005.

42. Black Creek, NY, *Diary*, January 2014. (Despite a different mailing address, this is still the Friendship community.)

43. Black Creek, NY, *Diary*, January 2016.

44. Fillmore, NY, *Budget*, January 29, 1992.

45. Ibid., February 2000.

46. Wellsville, NY, *Diary*, January, 2013.

47. The Nebraska Amish, the result of a schism in 1881 in the Amish church in Mifflin County, Pennsylvania, have no connection to the state of Nebraska. They are called "Nebraska Amish" because in the early days of the division the new church community received help from a bishop from that state.

48. Dansville, NY, *Diary*, November, 2015.

3. St. Lawrence County's Swartzentruber Amish

1. Letter from D.L.S. to T., November 19, 1974. Heritage Historical Library, Aylmer, Ontario.

2. In her chapter "Rising Land Prices Bring Changes," Amelia T. Reiheld writes, "As Holmes County land prices continue to rise, those who move away from the area to continue farming find themselves cut off from the close-knit family and community support of their childhood" (in J. Kinney, ed., *The Amish of Holmes County*, 160). This has not been a problem for the Swartzentruber Amish, who have tended to move in groups, often several siblings and their families moving together.

3. Quoted by M. Ellen, "DePeyster Townsfolk See Amish as Reason for Population Surge."

4. For an excellent study of the Holmes County, Ohio, Amish settlement, the homeland of the Swartzentruber Amish, see C. E. Hurst and D. L. McConnell's 2010 work, *An Amish Paradox. Diversity and Change in the World's Largest Amish Community*.

5. Since 1974, the Swartzentruber Amish have founded six new settlements in New York State, and at least three families in the Heuvelton area have bought land in Essex County to start a seventh. As one Swartzentruber woman commented with some amazement, "They're starting so many [new communities]."

6. D. Luthy, "The Origin and Growth of the Swartzentruber Amish."

7. See R. Weaver, "Amish Ministers' Meetings of 1865 and 1917." In his article "Glimpses of the Amish Church in Holmes County, Ohio, 1917–1922, and Report of a Ministers' Meeting in 1922," Weaver has asserted that Sam Yoder "discouraged his ministers from communing with the main group."

8. Weaver, "Glimpses of the Amish Church in Holmes County, Ohio." A translation of the original report of the meeting, which is reprinted in this article, noted, "There were 53 bishops and ministers present from Ohio, Illinois, Indiana, and Pennsylvania. Sam Yoder and his ministers were also invited but did not want to have anything to do with the meeting" (9).

9. The report of the meeting stated that "many consider Sam Yoder's outward visible standard to be praiseworthy" and left open the opportunity for reconciliation. See Weaver, "Glimpses of the Amish Church in Holmes County, Ohio." Hurst and McConnell, *An Amish Paradox*, also discusses the origin and evolution of the Swartzentruber Amish. See 35–43.

10. See Luthy, "The Origin and Growth of the Swartzentruber Amish," chap. 2.

11. Ibid. Schlabach's statement is in the files of the Heritage Historical Library, Aylmer, Ontario.

12. According to a letter written by a member of the Jeck Jecky group, "When talking about our group here [in Tennessee] we are referred to as Knox *leut* [*leut* means "people"]. Or Jeck Jecky leut, yes some still call us Swartzentruber leut we don't mind. Yes our group here in Knox and Minn. dien with Nebraska leut, Holmes-Wayne Co. Swartzentruber group has no connection with the Nebraska leut anymore since they helped Jeck Jecky group in Minn and here." This man notes further that "there are 2 groups in Big Valley known as Nebraska leut that don't dien with each other, but they have special arrangements with the young folks. They aren't supposed to attend each other's singings. If a young person's magnetic field gets too strong and draws a young person from the other group, then the couple decides which group they want to be at home with. Then the ministers of that group will perform the Wedd[ing] Ceremony. Sam L. Hostetler is the Bishop that has been helping our group, they have 4 districts in Big Valley, 1 in Penns Valley, another district or settlement that just started at Andover, Ohio where the Geauga Amish moved out of they bought some of those farms [and have] 7 families. We have 2 districts here in Knox Co., 4 in Minn [and] 1 district just started near LaCrosse Wisc." Letter from E.S. to D.L., May 29, 1992, Heritage Historical Library, Aylmer, Ontario. A subsequent schism in the Jeck Jecky faction has led to the Perry Glick group, which has one church district in Wisconsin.

13. R. Stevick, *Growing Up Amish*.

14. As one Amish man put it, "This min[ister] . . . was . . . sure it was the first boy that did it, so they didn't baptize the one nor take the other out of the Bann as some figured they were both telling an [*sic*] lie." Letter from D.S. to D.L., July 27, 1993, Heritage Historical Library, Aylmer, Ontario. See Stevick, *Growing Up Amish*, 100.

15. According to one Amish observer, "It was only a small handful who stuck up for this [minister], but enough to stall the works. The Holmes Co[unty] bishops came together to try and solve the problem and didn't get any where [*sic*] so they called together the out of state bishops also." Letter from D.S. to D.L., July 27, 1993. Heritage Historical Library, Aylmer, Ontario.

16. The Amish letter writer D.S. noted in a letter written several months later: "Yes, Lodi is going through a split right now. You know that Bish. Eli Hershberger and Bish. Mose M.

Miller have split away from the others in Holmes and Wayne Co. I don't know if that split is done yet there, but it is in the process in Lodi. The way it looks now, Bish. Isaac Keim and . . . maybe . . . Bish. Andy Weaver are going with the Mose Miller group and about ¾ of the Lodi people are going with them. So . . . it's too bad." Letter from D.S. to D.L., April 15, 1994, Heritage Historical Library, Aylmer, Ontario.

17. The "Joe Troyer church" or "Joe church" is not the same as the Troyer church, which resulted from the 1931 schism.

18. By "English shoes," she means those that, like sneakers and other forbidden footwear, make no separation between the heel and the rest of the sole.

19. There are also two Andy Weaver Swartzentruber church districts in Lafargeville in Jefferson County, one in Hammond, on the border between St. Lawrence and Jefferson counties, two in Brier Hill, an extension of the Heuvelton settlement, and one in Sommerville, also in St. Lawrence County. In spring 2016, there were seven Andy Weaver Swartzentruber bishops, all in the Heuvelton area, who had "oversight" for these thirteen districts, as well as the one Andy Weaver Swartzentruber district in Sherman, Maine.

20. At the time of a schism, church members have great freedom to choose their affiliation. In this case, half of the community sided with their bishop in joining the Yoder/Keim faction, while the other half decided to join in with the Joe Troyer districts. There are no Hershberger/Miller districts in this community.

21. Of course, change can be in a more conservative direction as well. Talking about the Perry Glick church, a group in Veroqua, Wisconsin, that schismed from the Jeck Jecky faction in the early 1990s, one woman noted, "That's a real nice church there." Asked why the group had ceased to fellowship with the Jeck Jecky churches, she said, "I guess they wanted more tools for the men outdoors. But he [Perry Glick] went backwards quite a bit. They're pretty much like us now. You'd never see a difference."

22. This same informant commented that members of the Jeck Jecky group in Minnesota also "dress like we do and drive the same buggies."

23. In the Holmes County region of Ohio, members of the Joe Troyer and Isaac Keim faction use two lanterns (See Hurst & McConnell, *An Amish Paradox*, 43), but this is not the case in New York.

24. *Young Companion, Family Life*, and a third magazine, the *Blackboard Bulletin*, are published by Pathway Publishers, which also produces a series of school readers and accompanying workbooks, storybooks for children, and books on Anabaptist history. Pathway publications often discuss Old Order values, history, and Old Order life, and the exploration of religious topics may make it difficult for even some of the more progressive groups to adopt Pathway publications. The editors at Pathway acknowledge that members of more conservative groups are not likely to subscribe to Pathway publications.

25. For an in-depth discussion of Swartzentruber Amish schools, see Johnson-Weiner, *Train Up a Child*, chap. 3.

26. Schnitz pies are turnovers with a filling made from dried apples, or "schnitz." They are served at frolics and at church.

27. Victor E. Stoltzfus, "Amish Agriculture," 196–206. For further discussion of the way in which these relationships are changing as some Amish communities adopt more technology and move away from an agrarian lifestyle, see Johnson-Weiner, "Technological Diversity and Cultural Change."

28. In recent years some Amish mothers, including Swartzentruber mothers, have taken advantage of the services of a local midwife, a member of a Mennonite community, where the delivery is in a homelike setting. There may also be several visits to the midwife before the birth to ensure that all is going smoothly. When the time comes, the father will drop any older children at a neighbor's house and get a driver.

29. Although this period in a young Amish person's life is well-known in mainstream society as "Rumspringa," literally, "running around," the Swartzentruber Amish, like many other Amish groups, tend to say their teenagers are "by the youngie."

30. Families with one or more daughters in the young folk will move younger children to ensure that each of the older girls has a bedroom to herself.

31. Stevick, *Growing Up Amish*, 229.

32. Unlike more progressive Amish (e.g., those in the Clymer area), who may purchase clothing ready made, the Swartzentruber Amish sew their own clothing at home. As a result, a young girl's courting dress may be something she has sewn herself or it may have been made by her mother or an older female relative. In any case, it has passed her mother's scrutiny!

33. See Stevick, *Growing Up Amish*, 229–238. A 2004 study by J. Donnermeyer and E. Cooksey found that the rate of infants born less than nine months after the parents' wedding (an indication of premarital sexual activity) varied considerably from one Amish group to another. The study analyzed Amish directories, however, so does not include the Swartzentruber Amish, who do not contribute to directory compilation.

34. Letter to the author, March 13, 2008.

35. These activities all take place under supervision of the oldest couple in the church district who are not family members.

36. The role of women in businesses varies considerably from one Amish community to another. Kraybill, *The Riddle of Amish Culture* (84, 261) has estimated that between 15 percent and 17 percent of the Amish-owned businesses in the Lancaster County Amish settlement, one of the most liberal, are owned by women, some of whom employ their husbands.

37. Allowing bulk tank dumping stations means that each Swartzentruber farmer who wishes to ship milk is assigned a bulk tank in a central station. Each farmer will bring his cans of milk and "dump" them into his assigned bulk tank, where it will be tested before it is collected and shipped to the dairy for processing. With this system, Swartzentruber farmers can ship grade A milk. Thus the bulk tank dumping stations allow the Swartzentruber Amish to continue dairy farming, which would have been impossible had they been dependent on a local cheese factory to purchase the milk shipped in cans. A bishop with the Andy Weaver faction notes that bulk tank dumping stations will be allowed only in communities in which there is no local cheese factory, meaning that this change will affect the Swartzentruber churches in the Heuvelton area, but it will not affect those in Holmes County, Ohio.

38. Commenting on the stability afforded the Amish by the new dumping stations, reporter Amy Halloran noted that "the Amish in the area are now flourishing. They never got paid much for their milk because of Grade B pricing, and often they went two to three months without pay. Cost of production on these small farms is less than other dairies, so the difference is significant. The biggest station has eight bulk tanks and the smallest has just one; most have four." Amy Halloran, "Milk Cooperative Joins with Amish to Open New Markets," *Lancaster Farming*, June 15, 2013, http://www.lancasterfarming.com/ Milk-Cooperative-Joins-With-Amish-to-Open-New-Markets.

39. Asked about the electrical lines that would feed into a building on an Amish farm, one man replied that the electricity would go to the building and not to the land. Because the dairy cooperative, Agri-Mark, owned the building, he asserted, this would not be an issue. Another Amish man agreed, noting that, in addition to having electrical power, the small dumping stations were not built to Swartzentruber specifications. Among the differences in construction he cited were factory-built trusses. He also noted that the commercial lumber used to build the stations had more knots in it than the Swartzentruber Amish considered acceptable, that the wood was pine and not the hardwood Amish carpenters like to use, and that the commercial 2x4 boards were not quite 2 inches by 4 inches, as they would have been if sawn in a Swartzentruber mill. Commenting on the Agri-Mark arrangement, a *Watertown Daily Times* article noted that "the cooperative built community milk houses for the Amish and deducts the cost of electricity, which is in Agri-Mark's name, from their milk checks." See "Artisanal Cheese Makers Growing Amid Big Producers," *Watertown Daily Times*, March 16, 2014; reprinted by the Northeast Agribusiness & Feed Alliance, http://

cqrcengage.com/northeastalliance/app/document/1859976;jsessionid=4ZRlppAzk7rVK
L0k1lhWVhYF.undefined.

40. M. Ellen, "DePeyster Townsfolk See Amish as Reason for Population Surge."

41. *Budget*, October 31, 2007.

42. Conversation with MJM, April 2014.

43. In 2009, the Becket Fund for Religious Liberty filed a lawsuit in the U.S. District Court for the Northern District of New York on behalf of fourteen Amish men, alleging that the Town of Morristown had violated the Amish men's rights under the First and Fourteenth amendments of the U.S. Constitution, Article 1 of the New York State Constitution, the Fair Housing Act, and the Religious Land Use Act. This case, which was settled in 2012, will be discussed further in chapter 4.

4. From Lancaster County to Lowville

1. Lowville, NY, *Diary*, February, 2016.

2. In 1972, the U.S. Supreme Court decided in the case of *Wisconsin v. Yoder et al.* that "enforcement of the State's requirement of compulsory formal education after the eighth grade would gravely endanger if not destroy the free exercise of . . . [Amish] religious beliefs" (A. N. Keim, *Compulsory Education and the Amish*, 98). Since then, most Old Order communities have established their own schools and/or worked out compromises with the state authorities.

3. For a discussion of Old Order schooling, see Johnson-Weiner, *Train Up a Child*, and Dewalt, *Amish Education in the United States and Canada*. For a contemporary look at the issues surrounding *Wisconsin v. Yoder et al.*, see A. N. Keim, *Compulsory Education and the Amish*. S. F. Peters, *The Yoder Case*, explores the impact of the Supreme Court's decision. Johnson-Weiner, "Old Order Amish Education," explores the Yoder decision and its relevance for today's Amish.

4. E. M. Shirk, *Report of Committee of Plain People*, 86.

5. J. F. Esh, *The Amish Moving to Maryland, 1940*, 2; see also Shirk, *Report of Committee of Plain People*; C. Lapp, *Pennsylvania School History*; D. B. Kraybill, *The Riddle of Amish Culture*.

6. "New Amish School Strike Looms in Pennsylvania," *New York Times*, September 5, 1938.

7. "Amish Lose Fight for Old Schools," *New York Times*, June 28, 1938.

8. J. F. Esh, *The Amish Moving to Maryland*, 4. Given that this move would be the first in a series of moves that would ultimately lead to a second Amish settlement in Lewis County, it is an interesting coincidence that the name of the land agent was "Keefer," a variant of the surname of the land agent instrumental in persuading the first Amish settlers in New York to come to the same region.

9. Wagler, "Education, A Grave Responsibility," 66.

10. Quoted in Kraybill, *The Riddle of Amish Culture*, 174. Kraybill attributes this quote to Aaron E. Beiler.

11. Esh, *The Amish Moving to Maryland*, 25–27.

12. Ibid., 29.

13. P. Kennedy, "Summary of Raw Milk Statutes and Administrative Codes," http://www.realmilk.com/milk-laws-1.html.

14. Dairylea merged with Dairy Farmers of America in 2014.

15. D. Kraybill, *The Riddle of Amish Culture*, 238.

16. According to Kraybill, Johnson-Weiner, and Nolt, *The Amish*, 36 percent of Lancaster County Amish have farming as their primary occupation (282).

17. R. Rhodes, "No Longer Living Off the Land," 1, 7.

18. See Kraybill, Johnson-Weiner, and Nolt, *The Amish*, chapter 17, for a discussion of technological change in Amish society.

19. When the ground is frozen, it is easier to drag lumber out of the wood lot. Wood can be cut in any season, and there are no religious prohibitions on cutting lumber in summertime, but the soft ground makes it difficult to pull the logs out of the woods. Moreover, there are other chores to do in other seasons.

20. Johnson-Weiner, *Train Up a Child*. In Old Order Amish communities, the language used for speaking and interacting with others in the group is Pennsylvania German. English, learned in school, is generally used for reading, letter writing, and talking to outsiders. Still, the pattern of German-English interaction varies across communities. While some insist that English be spoken at school, even during recess, so that the children become fluent, others are less demanding.

21. According to one woman, "Everyone tries to get Social Security numbers at birth. There's a midwife who helps with home births, but she won't give her name so it's hard to get the Social Security."

22. D. Zimmerman Umble, *Holding the Line*, 119. This work is an in-depth look at the Amish rejection of telephones.

23. D. Kraybill, *The Riddle of Amish Culture*, 195. See also Kraybill, Johnson-Weiner, and Nolt, *The Amish*, 323–324.

24. D. Morse, "Still Called by Faith to the Booth."

25. Among the settlers in Lowville is a grandchild of Stephen Stoltzfus, who helped to found the Maryland settlement. There are also members of the community who have moved to the area from the Byler Amish settlement in Mayville/Dewittville, which is a daughter settlement of the New Wilmington, Pennsylvania, church community. As noted in chapter 2, the Byler Amish from New Wilmington, Pennsylvania, are known as a more conservative group. Currently there are also New Wilmington daughter settlements elsewhere in New York, including Frewsburg, Franklinville, Friendship, and Fort Plain. See chapter 2 for a description of Byler Amish settlement.

26. See chapter 2 for a description of the Byler Amish community in Mayville/Dewittville.

27. The Locke (also called Summerhill) settlement was started in 2003. Writing to the *Diary* in September of that year, one of the newcomers introduced herself and announced, "We are starting a new settlement up here. Have just 4 families so far. We moved up in March from Pa. and welcomed the 4th family a couple weeks ago" (*Diary*, September 2003).

28. Lowville, NY, *Diary*, May, 2015.

29. Ibid., February, 2015. The Ava/Lee Center community was founded in Oneida County in 2012 by settlers from Mercer and Atlantic, Pennsylvania. A more conservative community, it had one church district and 23 families by January 2015. Bombay, in Franklin County, is a Byler Amish settlement founded in 2009 by settlers from the large Ft. Plain settlement in the Mohawk Valley. See chapter 5 for more about the Ft. Plain community.

30. Stoltzfus noted, in the December 2013 *Diary*, that there were "2 church districts, 13 boys, 11 girls, young folks. Around 65 school children in 3 schools. A few produce growers. 1 sawmill the rest are farmers. 1 carpenter."

31. Writing in the *Watertown Daily Times*, Steve Virkler noted that the first thing seminar organizers learned was that the Lowville Amish hold their weddings on Tuesdays and Thursdays in the fall and that the seminar, originally planned for a Thursday, had to be rescheduled. S. Virkler, "Amish to Be Topic of Seminar."

32. "Tug Hill Speaker: Creating, Capitalizing on an Identity Is Key," *Watertown Daily Times*, April 1, 2005.

33. "Lowville Will Waive Fee for Amish Schoolhouse," *Watertown Daily Times*, June 23, 2007.

34. Letter to the *Watertown Daily Times*, December 30, 2005.

35. "Quilt Show Gives Insight on Amish," *Watertown Daily Times*, March 19, 2006. An earlier article on the event ("Quilt Event Showcases the Amish," *Watertown Daily Times*, March 18, 2006) suggested: "[For] anyone who wants an introduction to Amish culture,

Sackets Harbor may be a good stop this weekend. The Seaway Trail Discovery Center will showcase Amish-made quilts and offer lectures on Northern New York Amish communities." Sackets Harbor is a town about an hour northwest of Lowville (not far as distances in the North Country are measured).

36. S. Virkler, "Lowville Supervisor Retiring After 20 Years."

37. These events are covered in a number of articles appearing in the *Syracuse Post-Standard*. See, for example, D. Tobin, "No Serenity in Summerhill. Amish Make a Home in Cayuga County . . . But Are They Welcome?" *The Post-Standard*, Sunday, November 25, 2007. Interestingly, this article points out that the town has no legal basis for its insistence that contractors provide proof of insurance and reports that some people, including the Amish, see this as discriminatory.

38. A. Sorenson, "Alleged Amish Discrimination on Madison County Lakes."

39. M. Ellen, "Defender Wants Charges against Amish Dropped."

40. Ultimately, while the Swartzentruber Amish made some concessions, agreeing, for example, to ensure windows met code requirements, the town also acknowledged that a number of Swartzentruber building practices already met the code. On the key issue of smoke detectors, the result was a draw. The Town of Morristown agreed to remove mention of smoke detectors from the permit application, thus allowing the Amish to purchase building permits without promising to install the detectors, which would violate their religious beliefs. In certifying a building for occupancy, the code enforcement officer now arrives with as many smoke detectors as are needed and a single nail for each to hang it up. After the enforcement officer leaves, the Amish family, like any other homeowner, is free to remove and discard all smoke detectors.

41. D. Weaver-Zercher, *The Amish in the American Imagination.*

42. Cf. R. Buck, "Bloodless Theatre"; also M. Louden, "The Image of the Old Order Amish," esp. 113–116.

43. "Onondaga County Has Open Arms for Amish." Letter from M. Kinne to the *Syracuse Post-Standard*, November 27, 2007.

44. "Amish Struggle. Manipulation of Power Hurts a Respected Community." Letter from T. Herman to the *Syracuse Post-Standard*, November 28, 2007.

45. "Good Amish Neighbors Deserve Same Treatment." Letter from S. Taylor to the *Syracuse Post-Standard*, December 1, 2007.

46. D. Tobin, "No Serenity in Summerhill."

47. "There Are Good Reasons Why Contractors Have Rules." Letter to the *Syracuse Post-Standard*, December 6, 2007. This debate plays out wherever the Amish have settled. In a particularly striking example, one response to an online posting about a murder-suicide that occurred in an Amish family in Ohio, some readers posted comments urging others to pray for the family. Others, however, castigated their Amish neighbors. Wrote one reader, "People, wake up. . . . The Amish are not as innocent as they are portrayed to be." Another agreed, writing, "I heard Amish are exempt from going to war, filing taxes an[d] other stuff, and why don't they have to have seat belts in their buggies and car seats and booster seats[?] I am a U.S. citizen the same as the Amish. If I have to follow government rules why don't they?" Posted responses to "Amish Family Dead after Apparent Murder-Suicide," http://www.cantonrep.com/article/20090225/news/302259738.

48. "Contractor Liability Makes Insurance a Must." Letter to the *Syracuse Post-Standard*, December 6, 2007.

49. "Buggies Are a Hazard." Letter to the *Watertown Daily Times*, January 31, 2006.

50. "Amish Buggies Should Have Safety Equipment." Letter to the *Watertown Daily Times*, February 5, 2006. At this writing, some have been urging the St. Lawrence County legislature to revisit the SMV orange triangle issue. Since reaching an agreement with local authorities in 1984, the Swartzentruber Amish in New York have followed the practice established in Ohio of marking their buggies with gray reflecting tape rather than with the orange triangle. See also chapter 7.

238

51. Readers' comments to D. Tobin's 2012 article in the *Syracuse Post-Standard*, "Cortland County Town of Marathon Split over Amish Community's Demand for Separate School Buses." The readers' forum included a variety of negative comments on the Amish themselves, ranging from the perceived special treatment they receive to the manure left on the roads by their horses. Ultimately, in June 2012, after the Amish registered their two schools with the State Education Department, the Marathon Board of Education voted 6–0 to provide the busing the Amish had requested.

52. "Another Embarrassment for Gouv." Posted in the Gouverneur Forum. http://www.topix.com/forum/city/gouverneur-ny/TGQUI2JFV5QRAA3A4/p2. This issue is not unique to New York State. See, for example, Alexei Barrionuevo, "Amish May Be Good Neighbors, but Not Their Horses." *New York Times*, October 18, 2005, http://www.nytimes.com/2005/10/18/us/amish-may-be-good-neighbors-but-not-their-horses.html?_r=0; Joe Corcoran, "Amish vs. Auburn over Horse Manure," WKU (Kentucky) Public Radio, June 16, 2015, http://wkyufm.org/post/amish-vs-auburn-over-horse-manure#stream/0. Moreover, Gouverneur is not the only town in St. Lawrence County to deal with the issue. See L. Robinson, "Amish Horse Manure Causing Stink in Village of Heuvelton," http://www.ogd.com/article/20140814/OGD/140819374.

53. A. Yousey, interview with author, July 25, 2006.

54. Lowville, New York, *Diary*, September 2014.

55. Lowville, New York, Budget, December 2006.

56. Lowville, New York. The Diary, February, 2014.

57. Letter to the author, August 2007.

58. A fence frolic is likely a gathering to build or repair fences around farmland. Lowville, NY. *Diary*, May 2014.

59. See E. T. Hall, *Beyond Culture.*

5. The Mohawk Valley Amish

1. G. Goth, "Old Order Finds New Life Upstate."
2. There was still only a single bishop at this time.
3. Fonda, NY, *Diary*, February 2006.
4. Fort Plain, NY, *Diary*, January 2013.
5. Goth, "Old Order Finds New Life Upstate."
6. Ibid.
7. E. Spencer, interviewed by J. Shepard, "Amish Resurrect a County."
8. "Palatine Cheese Quietly Fills Niche Market for Flavored Cheddar that 'the Big Guys' Can't," *Cheese Reporter*, March 2, 2007, http://www.cheesereporter.com/Company%20Profiles/Palentine.pdf.
9. "Dairylea's Partnership with Local Amish Community Continues to Grow," Press release, Dairylea Cooperative, June 29, 2005, http://www.dairylea.com/News_and_Publications/PressReleases/AmishPartnershipwithDairylea_000.htm. In 2014, Dairylea merged with Dairy Farmers of America (DFA).
10. "Christiana, PA. Wm. Run Road." *Die Botschaft*, May 7, 1997.
11. *Know This Place: Welcome to Otsego County, NY*, 12, http://knowthisplace.com/ny/otsego-ny-bk. The city of Oneonta is the region's only incorporated urban community.
12. Quoted in M. Von Dobeneck, "Neighbors to North Cast Lure for Amish."
13. Quoted in E. Klimuska, "Farmer Seeks Amish 'Home Run.'"
14. Richfield Springs, NY, *Diary*, January 2002.
15. Richfield Springs, NY, *Budget*, June 19, 2002.
16. This would be important to him because he would not want others to confuse his settlement with the newer one or to think that the two settlements were in fellowship if they were not.

17. Middlefield, OH, *Budget*, October 8, 2003.

18. Richfield Springs, NY, *Diary*, January 2007.

19. Ibid. January, 2015.

20. Hostetler, *Amish Society*, 373.

21. Ashland, OH, *Die Botschaft*, December 22, 2004.

22. Letter from D.L.S. to D.L., February 8, 2005, Heritage Historical Library.

23. Letter from D.L.S. to D.L., September 21, 1998, Heritage Historical Library.

24. Hostetler, *Amish Society*, 369, cites concerns over "youth standards" as one of the primary reasons the Amish form new settlements.

25. This is not the same church as the Swartzentruber Andy Weaver faction.

26. In *A History of the Amish*, Nolt has placed the date of the schism between 1955 and 1957, although he notes that it was preceded by discussions about shunning.

27. This position on strong shunning is similar to that of the ultraconservative Swartzentruber churches.

28. Letter to the author, December 8, 2007.

29. This has led Kraybill, in "Plotting Social Change across Four Affiliations," 56–57, to characterize the Andy Weaver church as "midway between the Swartzentrubers and the Old Orders" in terms of its traditionalism, classifying the "traditionalism" of the Swartzentruber Amish as "extreme," that of the Old Order Amish as "moderate," and that of the Andy Weaver Church as "high."

30. Letter to the author, February 2007. The writer goes on to note that the Georgetown community has "8 families (mostly from Jasper, N.Y.) and many more boys than girls with the youngie. Here it is opposite, so for some reason there was an attraction to go there."

31. According to one Fultonville resident, "There's no bed courtship—that was a cause of the earlier Swartzentruber split." He was grateful for this, noting that "once there's a practice like that in the church, it's hard to change."

32. A member of one of the Swartzentruber churches agreed. Acknowledging that some of the more progressive groups looked down on the Swartzentruber Amish for their continued sanctioning of bed courtship, he asserted that a girl could just as easily get into trouble in a chair.

33. Unlike men in other Mohawk Valley settlements, who wear suspenders over their shirts, the men in the Fort Plain (Byler Amish) settlement wear only one suspender, which is attached through a slit in the side of the shirt, with the shirt covering the suspender. In fact, many don't wear suspenders at all. There are other clothing differences as well. A woman from the Lowville settlement noted that Fort Plain (Byler Amish) women wear brown bonnets, and instead of a cape over their coats, they wear "mandli," coats with an attached shoulder cape. Further, she added, they don't use buggy robes to cover themselves on cold days. "They think they're tough."

34. Richfield Springs, NY, *Diary*, December 2003.

35. It is not simply that the drawings cost a lot of money, for the Amish will pay what is necessary if, in their eyes, the expense is warranted. But because Amish homes tend to be very similar (especially in more conservative settlements), and Amish carpenters have grown up building these homes, the Amish see architectural drawings as unnecessary. The cost of such drawings thus adds unnecessarily to the cost of the home—turning a simple dwelling into an overly expensive "mansion." It is, simply put, wasteful, and, therefore, counter to their beliefs about how a Christian should live. The failure of the Amish to provide architectural drawings was also part of the conflict over building permits in the Town of Morristown, New York (see chapters 3 and 4). As part of the settlement, a local architect provided architectural drawings of a typical Swartzentruber home without charge. For the Amish, it was important that these drawings represent how they build all of their homes rather than a particular building that they were about to build.

36. Goth, "Old Order Finds New Life Upstate."

37. Fultonville-Glen, NY, *Budget*, August 31, 2005.

38. Ibid.
39. "Dairylea's Partnership with Local Amish Community Continues to Grow."
40. Letter to the author, February 2007.
41. Kraybill, *The Riddle of Amish Culture*, 297.
42. This couple was clearly concerned that those moving in from other settlements might be unwilling to adopt the practices of their new church. This could, the couple feared, cause the Fultonville-Glen settlement to accept some of the practices the newcomers brought with them, thus changing the church.
43. Letter from N. H. to D. L., April 23, 2003, Heritage Historical Library.
44. Richfield Springs, NY, *Diary*, September 2005.
45. Gordonville, PA, *Diary*, December 2006.
46. Ibid.
47. Dolgeville, NY, *Diary*, February 2007.
48. Letter from C.J.S. to D.L., January 2006, Heritage Historical Library.
49. Mohawk Valley, NY, *Diary*, January 2013; January 2014; January 2016.
50. In *Plain Diversity*, Nolt and Meyers noted that the Lancaster Amish have "remained remarkably settled, self-contained, and self-sustaining" (129). Descendants of Amish who arrived in the first wave of Anabaptist immigration, the Lancaster Amish have stayed relatively settled in their corner of southeastern Pennsylvania. They provide a sharp contrast to the descendants of later arrivals who share a history of regional migration and intermarriage. Although there has been some movement out of the Lancaster region in the past, such as the move by some to Maryland noted in chapter 4, the establishment of two communities in Indiana in the 1980s, and the founding of the New York settlements, for the most part the Lancaster Amish have dealt with the lack of farmland by starting numerous family businesses.
51. Orinsky Falls, NY, *Diary*, January 2016.
52. Ava, NY, *Diary*, February, 2016.
53. Fultonville, NY, *Budget*, July 2010.
54. North Lawrence, NY, *Diary*, October 2010.
55. Letter to D.L. from J.B., Atlantic, PA, July 15, 2012. Heritage Historical Library Archives.
56. Baling hay rather than putting it into storage loose is a sign of a progressive Amish community. In *The Riddle of Amish Culture*, Kraybill suggests that the development of hay balers was directly related to expanding dairy herds and greater dependency on commercial fertilizer and that the use of these new machines marked the first widespread use of gasoline engines in Amish fields (229).
57. Ava, NY, *Diary*, August 2014. See chapter 4 for a brief account of taking down the barn to move it to the Philadelphia area.

6. In Search of Consensus and Fellowship

1. I have followed Nolt and Meyers in using the term *Swiss*, to refer to this faction of immigrants. However, since initially not all those arriving in the German stream during the second wave of Amish immigration from Europe had a connection with Pennsylvania, I have chosen to refer to these other Amish arrivals as simply "German" rather than "Pennsylvania German" for clarity and simplicity.
2. See Johnson-Weiner, "Keeping Dutch"; "Group Identity and Language Maintenance"; and "Community Identity and Language Change in North American Anabaptist Communities." Even today, despite Hostetler's assertion that Shwitsa "poses no real barrier to interaction with other Amish," non-Swiss, Pennsylvania German–speaking Amish often use English to talk to their Swiss Amish neighbors. As one Pennsylvania German–speaking farmer put it, they "don't talk like we do. We can't hardly understand them. When they come out here, we speak English to them." See Hostetler, *Amish Society*, 242.

3. W.K. Crowley, "Old Order Amish Settlement: Diffusion and Growth." The nineteenth-century Croghan settlement, which identified as Amish into the twentieth century, is an example of a Swiss Amish settlement that has now ceased to identify as Amish.

4. Nolt and Meyers, *Plain Diversity*, 109.

5. See chapter 1, especially endnote 11, for a discussion of the Apostolic Christian Church, its teachings, and its impact on the Croghan Amish community.

6. Like other immigrant names, this one has different spellings. Hostetler, *Amish Society*, renders the name as "Egli" and gives 1866 as the date for the founding of the Egly Amish movement. In *Plain Diversity*, Nolt and Meyers use "Egly" and say "after 1865," while in their article "Evangelical Mennonite Church," Rupp and Nussbaum also use the "Egli" spelling but say that the church was conceived "about 1864" and organized in 1866.

7. While initially the Defenseless Mennonite Church, more popularly known as the Egly Amish, was very strict with regard to its discipline and dress standards, the church eventually adopted a number of practices of more progressive Anabaptist groups. Sunday Schools started in the 1870s and missionary work in the 1890s. The Defenseless Mennonites became known as the Evangelical Mennonite Church and, after 2003, as the Fellowship of Evangelical Churches (see Rupp and Nussbaum, "Evangelical Mennonite Church"). In *The Amish Christian Church*, Schrock also provides an account of the schism.

8. Schrock, *The Amish Christian Church*, 50. From *Katechismus*, published in Berne, Indiana, in 1925. It appears in English for the first time in Schrock's account of the Amish Christian Church.

9. Nolt and Meyers, *Plain Diversity*, have claimed that the exclusivity of the Amish Christian Church led non-Amish to regard the group as a cult.

10. See M. Gingerich, "Reformed Amish Christian Church." Schrock, in *The Amish Christian Church*, offers an in-depth discussion of its origin and evolution.

11. See the discussion of salvation in chapter 1.

12. Dean, "North Amish Community Expands to Five Families."

13. "Settlement of Amish in Town of Norfolk, One of 1974 Highlights," *Massena Observer*, March 4, 1975.

14. See Olshan, *The Old Order Amish in New York State*. Again, Olshan uses pseudonyms when referring to the different Amish communities he is discussing. The Norfolk settlement appears as "Mapletown."

15. R.D. Lyons, "New York a Magnet for Religious Groups."

16. J.T. Mulder, "The Non-Conformists."

17. Olshan, *The Old Order Amish in New York State*, 16.

18. Quoted in ibid., 16.

19. D.K. Shipler, "A Family of Plain People Seeking Still Plainer Life."

20. D.K. Shipler, "Onlookers Greet Amish Travelers."

21. The Stauffer, or "Pike," Mennonites are an ultraconservative group that originated in a schism with the Lancaster Mennonite church in 1845. The group is, in many respects, more conservative than many Old Order Amish churches. See Scott, *An Introduction to Old Order and Conservative Mennonite Groups;* Kraybill and Bowman, *On the Backroad to Heaven*.

22. The "Hoover group," more properly known as the "Noah Hoover group," evolved from the Titus Hoover church and traces its origins to the Stauffer Mennonite Church (see above). This group has taken an extremely conservative position on technology. See Scott, *An Introduction to Old Order and Conservative Mennonite Groups*, for more information. See also Schrock, *The Amish Christian Church*, for an in-depth study of the Amish Christian Church.

23. A number of families moved from Snyder County to Somerset, Ohio, in 1990, where they established an Old Order Amish community. In 2005, the Somerset community disbanded, with more than half the families moving to Richards, Missouri, where they finally began to fellowship with the nearby Hoover congregation in Rich Hill.

24. Letter from H.T. to D.S. April 7, 1983, Heritage Historical Library, Aylmer, Ontario. A typewritten comment on the letter notes that it "is a good example of how hard up a new settlement gets when it changes regulations to attract families and to continue its existence."

25. A former Old Order Amish bishop who left the Amish to start a new community argued that the Old Order "are too much a cultural church"—that is, a church that relies on tradition and man-made rules instead of scripture. He urged those in the Amish community to unite in a "Fellowship of Faith." E. Stoll, "The Nature of the Church," n.d. This essay was part of a packet of unpublished letters by Stoll that circulated in Amish communities. I was asked to copy the packet for an elderly Amish woman, who gave me a set in thanks.

26. *Mt. Pleasant Mills* (PA) *Budget*, April 17, 1985.

27. Joseph Stoll (unpublished note), "A Visit to Snyder County, Penna. Oct. 23–25, 1984," Heritage Historical Library.

28. Ibid.

29. Letter from S.J.B. to J.S. December, 15, 1984, Heritage Historical Library.

30. Letter from V.D. and F.D. to E.S. December 15, 1985, Heritage Historical Library.

31. Letter from J.S. to E.S. February 15, 1986, Heritage Historical Library.

32. A.J. Lamme III, and D.B. McDonald, "Recent Amish Settlement in the North Country."

33. Some of these communities (e.g., Quincy) are Swiss, but others are not.

34. Prattsburgh, NY, *Diary*, May 1996.

35. Ibid., January 2005.

36. Prattsburgh, NY, *Die Botschaft*, January 16, 2006.

37. Prattsburgh, NY, *Diary*, January 2014.

38. Letter from J.A.W. to D.L., June 15, 1997, Heritage Historical Library. The internal quarrels played out partly in the community schoolhouse, when some parents became particularly concerned that the children were using texts that had an unacceptable doctrinal slant. In 1993, for example, all but the first graders were using Pathway Readers, which are published by the Old Order Amish Pathway Publishing Company in Aylmer, Ontario, an Amish community that is more progressive than the Norfolk church. By 1996, fifth and eighth graders were using texts from the *Dick and Jane* series and the *Road to Safety* series, respectively, and there were attempts to remove the rest of the Pathway books because some parents feared they were too moralistic and had too much religious content. The departure of some families for other settlements helped to resolve the issues and, by the start of the 2001–2002 school year and at the teacher's request, all grades had the Pathway Readers. See Johnson-Weiner, *Train Up a Child*, chap. 4, for a discussion of the Norfolk Amish school.

39. R. Wengerd, "The Move We Made." There was an earlier Amish settlement in the Clyde area. Established in 1979 by families who moved in from the Wayne County, Ohio, region, it did not survive. The one family left at the time the settlers from Norfolk were moving in soon departed and so never played a role in the new Swiss settlement.

40. Norfolk, NY, *Diary*, January 2011.

41. There remain problems. At this writing, there is again talk of families moving out. Nevertheless, the *Diary* scribe from Norfolk reported "18 families, 13 young folk (nine boys, 4 girls)" in January 2016.

42. Seymour, Missouri, has been experiencing internal dissension for several years, and the Swiss communities have divided in their support for the different factions.

43. Unlike other Amish farmers in the region, the Norfolk Amish do not have milk "dumping stations" connected to the grid (see chapter 3). Instead each farmer cools milk with a tank connected to a reefer unit, such as those used to provide cold storage for refrigerated trucks.

44. Norfolk, NY, *Budget*, October 5, 2006.

45. There are two Swartzentruber settlements near the Norfolk community, one in the Heuvelton area approximately forty miles away, and the other west of Potsdam, approximately twenty-five miles from Norfolk. See chapter 3 for more about the Swartzentruber Amish.

46. Personal correspondence, September 2014.

47. Luthy cites a conversation with the late sociologist J. A. Hostetler, who "remarked that for a settlement to succeed it must obtain at least eleven families." According to Luthy, "There is nothing magic about the number 'eleven'; what [Hostetler] meant is if a settlement stays too small too long, prospective settlers will wonder why it is not growing and will shy away from it." See Luthy, *Why Some Amish Communities Fail: Extinct Settlements, 1961–2003*, 1, 19.

48. See Lamme and McDonald, "The 'North Country' Amish Homeland." As noted in chapter 1, it is typical for a church district to have one bishop, two to three ministers, and a deacon.

49. As one former member of the community put it, "The boys are very loyal to their father [the bishop]." Letter to author, February 2008.

50. Olshan, *The Old Order Amish in New York State*, 21.

51. Ibid., 22.

52. Clyde, NY, *Diary*, January 1999.

53. Ibid., February 2007.

54. Lamme and McDonald, "The 'North Country' Amish Homeland."

55. Clyde, NY, *Diary*, June 2006.

56. Mt. Morris, NY, *Diary*, February, 2015.

7. On Franklin County's Western Border

1. As noted in chapter 3, endnote 4, Hurst and McConnell's 2010 work, *An Amish Paradox*, is an excellent resource for anyone wishing to know more about the diverse Holmes County, Ohio, settlement.

2. Waterloo, NY–Clyde, NY area, *Budget*, February 20, 2002.

3. Marion, KY, *Budget*, January 23, 2002.

4. Clare, MI, *Budget*, June 4, 2003.

5. Olshan, *The Old Order Amish in New York State*, 23.

6. Ibid., 23.

7. Burke, NY, *Diary*, February, 2015.

8. *1001 Questions and Answers on the Christian Life*, 139.

9. One woman said she wouldn't wear "yellow, pink, or deep plum."

10. See chapter 3, especially endnote 17.

11. The Andy Weaver Swartzentruber settlement in Somerville, New York, started when members of a settlement in Nicktown, Pennsylvania, including several originally from the Heuvelton settlement, sold their farms in response to conflicts with local authorities. See chapter 8 for more details about the Somerville settlement.

12. Homerville, OH, *Die Botschaft*, September 25, 2002.

13. These numbers were accurate as of 2015. For more demographic data, see the website of the Amish Studies Project, an initiative of the Young Center for Anabaptist and Pietist Studies at Elizabethtown College, Elizabethtown, PA, "Amish Population by State/Province, 2015," Young Center for Anabaptist and Pietist Studies, Elizabethtown College, http://groups.etown.edu/amishstudies/statistics/population-by-state/. See also "Ohio Amish," http://amishamerica.com/ohio-amish/.

14. J. Kendle, "Not All Amish Are the Same." In *The Amish of Holmes County*, ed. J. Kinney, 37. See also Hurst and McConnell, *An Amish Paradox*.

15. "Ohio Amish Country: Hand-crafted, Heart-felt," Holmes County, OH, Chamber of Commerce, http://www.visitamishcountry.com.

16. This includes the settlements of South Columbia, Richfield Springs, and Clymer. The settlements have historic connections. The South Columbia and Clymer settlements both trace their roots to Geauga County, Ohio, but the South Columbia settlement is a result of movement from Geauga County to Kentucky.

17. Nolt and Meyers, *Plain Diversity*, 191.

18. *1001 Questions and Answers on the Christian Life*, 138. The text suggests further that city life is also harmful to other creatures, noting "even among wild or domesticated animals, we find that overcrowding produces vicious and undesirable behavior."

19. Ibid., 138–139.

20. To support this hierarchical ordering within the church, the Amish (like many other Christian churches) point to 1 Corinthians 11:3, which reads, "But I would have you know, that the head of every man is Christ; and the head of the woman is the man; and the head of Christ is God." Similarly, the Amish cite 1 Peter 3:1, which reads, in part, "Likewise, ye wives, be in subjection to your own husbands." Galatians 3:28 reads, "There is neither Jew nor Greek, there is neither bond nor free, there is neither male nor female: for ye are all one in Christ Jesus." For a more in-depth discussion, see Johnson-Weiner, "The Role of Women in Old Order Amish, Beachy Amish, and Fellowship Churches."

21. In *Amish Society*, 256–257, Hostetler has noted that "although holding public office or any position of worldly power is forbidden, voting in local elections is not." He adds, "In some Pennsylvania Townships up to 40 percent of the Amish have voted." Amish participation in elections varies widely. See also Kraybill, Johnson-Weiner, Nolt, *The Amish*, 361–362.

22. Kraybill, *The Riddle of Amish Culture*, 157.

23. Bake sales are not always successful. A board member at one Indiana Amish school noted, for example, that, at his local school, "We're not sale people here. We used to have bake sales at the flea market but haven't for the last two years. The ladies decided it was time for the men to do some work and nothing happened."

24. According to a Department of the Treasury Fact Sheet (dated September 18, 2003), "On October 26, 2001, President Bush signed into law the USA PATRIOT Act, important legislation providing a wide range of new tools to combat money laundering and the financing of terrorists. In July of 2002, Treasury announced a proposed rule implementing Section 326 of the PATRIOT Act. [which] requires that financial institutions develop a Customer Identification Program (CIP) that implements reasonable procedures to 1) Collect identifying information about customers opening an account; 2) Verify that the customers are who they say they are; 3) Maintain records of the information used to verify their identity; 4) Determine whether the customer appears on any list of suspected terrorists or terrorist organizations." The fact sheet goes on to add that "as part of a Customer Identification Program (CIP), financial institutions will be required to develop procedures to collect relevant identifying information including a customer's name, address, date of birth, and a taxpayer identification number—for individuals, this will likely be a Social Security number." There does seem to be an out for the Amish who refuse to obtain Social Security numbers or other government identification. According to the fact sheet, "the final rule recognizes that in some instances institutions cannot readily verify identity through more traditional means, and allows them the flexibility to utilize alternate methods to effectively verify the identity of customers." A number of Amish have found, however, that financial institutions are not always willing to accept alternative forms of identification, particularly since, given that the most conservative Amish will not have their pictures taken, these do not have photos. Interestingly, one credit union has opted to require a written description of the person hoping to start an account—initialed by the individual's bishop. See Department of the Treasury Fact Sheet (www.treasury.gov/press-center/press-releases/

Documents/js7432.doc). See also the Press Release issued April 30, 2003, http://www.federalreserve.gov/boarddocs/press/bcreg/2003/200304302/default.htm.

25. Quotes are taken from responses to Vaccination Questionnaires sent in 1991 by David Wagler to the *Budget* correspondents before a two-part article on vaccination, "The Choice Is Yours," appeared in *Family Life* in November and December 1992. The questionnaires are in the archives of the Heritage Historical Library, Aylmer, Ontario.

26. See G. Harris, "5 Cases of Polio in Amish Group Raise New Fears."

27. I was asked this question after I gave a talk at a local hospital. It appeared from the discussion that followed that many of those encountering Swartzentruber Amish parents in emergency room situations were put off by the apparent "coldness" of these parents towards their offspring, unaware that what they were in fact witnessing were cultural differences in interpersonal interaction.

28. Quotes are from the transcript of the decision. St. Lawrence County Family Court, file #21043.

29. The judge asked the parents if they could speak English. Told by both that they had learned it in school, the judge asserted that there didn't seem to be a language problem. Only after an appeal to Albany was an interpreter, Dr. Mark Louden, professor of German at the University of Wisconsin, Madison, brought in. At first the court attempted to have Dr. Louden interpret via a two-way video conference call, in which the Amish parents would also be on camera and so visible to Dr. Louden. Citing their religious beliefs, the Amish refused to participate in this way. In the end, Dr. Louden was flown in for the proceedings, and many in the Swartzentruber community expressed their gratitude for his assistance.

30. St. Lawrence County Family Court, file #21043.

31. Some years after the first trial, one of the lawyers asked me if the parents hadn't been secretly pleased that their child had been ordered to have surgery. In fact, as soon as the year of court-ordered supervision by the Department of Social Services was over, the family left the area, thus ceasing contact with authorities and medical practitioners who knew about his condition. Others in the community expressed the fear that the child would have a more difficult life. For the Amish, heaven is real and life on earth a temporary, difficult passage that one can only hope will end with eternity in Paradise. Adults endeavor to be worthy, to life their faith, and follow Christ's teachings and example. Innocent children who die young are believed to have escaped the trials of earthly life and are considered fortunate to be with God.

32. See The Cleveland Clinic, *Treating the Amish and Addressing their Health Care Concerns: A Practical Guide for Health Care Providers*, http://www.health-share.org/health-info/docs/1700/1783.asp?index=3971.

33. See K. Bobseine's *Working with Amish Communities in New York State: Tips for Health Professionals*, 2006, which includes several examples of ways in which health-care professionals have worked cooperatively with Amish communities. *Serving the Amish*, by psychologist Dr. James Cates, provides a guide for professionals who work with Amish populations.

34. As Olshan noted in his 1993 article, "The National Amish Steering Committee," the Swartzentruber communities have opted out of formal participation in the Steering Committee. Olshan quotes a Swartzentruber bishop who commented, "We don't join groups."

35. The compromise was based in part on an agreement worked out previously in Ohio. See Cory Anderson, "Horse and Buggy Crash Study II."

36. This was, perhaps, an easy concession for the Swartzentruber Amish, for, as one man asked, why else would they go out? "Is it true," he inquired, "that you English [non-Amish] just drive around for fun?" At this writing, however, the orange triangle issue is again in the news, for a subcommittee of the St. Lawrence County legislature voted to require the symbol on all buggies. After several meetings with county legislators, the bishops have begun working to ensure that church members follow the requirements of the agreement by regularly replacing the reflecting tape and ensuring that the lanterns are clean and operating effectively.

8. Challenges to Amish Settlement

1. Luthy, *Why Some Amish Communities Fail: Extinct Settlements, 1961–2003.* In some cases, new Amish settlements have been established in areas vacated by earlier communities that have failed.

2. In a 1990 paper presented at the annual conference of the American Anthropology Association, sociologist Marc A. Olshan wrote that "the decision to move to New York, or any other location, is not coordinated or approved by any central authority. Families from an array of communities and affiliations initiate the move because they are feeling a little more restless, or crowed, or disenchanted with the current church rules, than their neighbors." This is still the case.

3. See chapter 6.

4. Luthy, *The Amish in America.*

5. This appears to contradict David Luthy's definition of a settlement as three families or a minister, his family, and one other (see chap. 6, esp. note 47). However, Hostetler is not defining "settlement" but rather indicating the minimum number of families a settlement must have in order to be viable. See Luthy, *Why Some Amish Communities Fail,* 19.

6. Hostetler, *Amish Society,* 395.

7. Ibid., 370; 394.

8. Luthy, *The Amish in America,* 293.

9. Philadelphia, NY, *Diary,* January 2013. Pennsylvania Dutch is also known as Pennsylvania German, or, among the Amish, variously "German," "Dutch," or "Deitsch." See Mark Louden's 2016 work, *Pennsylvania Dutch: The Story of an American Language.*

10. Philadelphia, NY, *Diary,* February 2014.

11. "Wann wir uns ueba in der Deutche [*sic*] Bibel denken wir Deutsch. Wann wir uns ueben in der Englischen, denken wir Englisch. It looks like we're losing out an der alt Deutsche Glauben, in die so-genannte Christlichen Gemeine." Philadelphia, NY, *Diary,* February, 2015.

12. For a more in depth look at the importance of English for Amish identity, see Johnson-Weiner, "Community Identity and Language Change in North American Anabaptist Communities." For more about Pennsylvania Dutch, see Mark Louden, *Pennsylvania Dutch.* See also Simon J. Bronner and Joshua R. Brown, *Pennsylvania German Encyclopedia.*

13. Ava, NY, *Diary,* March 2014.

14. Marc A. Olshan, "Amish Cottage Industries as Trojan Horse," 145–146.

15. Kraybill, Johnson-Weiner, Nolt, *The Amish,* 282.

16. Ibid., 282. Olshan, "Affinities and Antipathies," notes that Clymer grew almost entirely from the migration of families from Geauga County, while the Woodhull settlement consists of families that left Geauga County in 1972 to start a community in Troutville, Pennsylvania, and then moved from Troutville to New York beginning in 1983. Both groups were motivated to leave by changes in the Ordnung of the Geauga settlement, including the extent to which community members were leaving farming and other traditional occupations to take up factory work.

17. See Landing, "The Old Order Amish: Problem Solving through Migration."

18. A. Z. Bender, "From Alsace to Adirondacks."

19. Luthy, *Amish in America.*

20. D. Skolnick, "Amish Complain of Rising Taxes."

21. As quoted in "Citing Religious Beliefs, Amish Balk at Pa. Outhouse Regulations," First Amendment Center, Thursday, May 29, 2008, http://www.firstamendmentcenter.org/citing-religious-beliefs-amish-balk-at-pa-outhouse-regulations.

22. Interestingly, a number of Amish from the Woodhull, New York, community—much more progressive than their Swartzentruber brethren—have begun buying farms in the Nicktown area.

23. J. McKinley, "Casino Plan Frays Ties Between Amish and Neighbors," *New York Times,* October 4, 2014, http://www.nytimes.com/2014/10/06/nyregion/upstate-new-york-casino-plan-divides-amish-and-neighbors.html?_r=0.

24. J. Nittler and G. Cotterill, "Lawyer Expects Amish-Mennonite Exodus if Casino Comes to Town of Tyre," http://fingerlakesdailynews.com/news/details.cfm?id=120910#.Vx1XC9Lmpjo.

25. Kraybill and Bowman, *On the Backroad to Heaven*.

26. S. Scott, *An Introduction to Old Order and Conservative Mennonite Groups*, 13.

27. Ibid., 70. See also Johnson-Weiner, "The Weaverland Mennonite Schools." "Old Order" is a somewhat contested identity. Scott includes the Horning Mennonites, as well as the Markham-Waterloo (Ontario) Conference and the Ohio-Indiana Conference (Indiana Order), under the rubric "Automobile Old Orders" (70). Kraybill and Bowman, *On the Backroad to Heaven*, on the other hand, do not include the Weaverland Conference (Horning Mennonites) in their discussion of Old Order Mennonite groups because the Horning Mennonites have sanctioned the automobile for use by church members and the Horning churches have shifted to English in religious contexts.

28. S. Scott, *An Introduction to Old Order and Conservative Mennonite Groups*, 77. See Johnson-Weiner, "Community Identity and Language Change in North American Anabaptist Communities," for a discussion of the shift to English in the Weaverland Conference.

29. In Old Order eyes, Sunday Schools also threatened to undermine the role of the family in the religious upbringing of their children and, since Sunday School classes have often been taught by women, challenged traditional gender roles. See Kraybill and Bowman, *On the Backroad to Heaven*, 64–65.

30. In a 2012 entry to the *Global Anabaptist Mennonite Encyclopedia Online* (GAMEO), Jonathan Martin noted that the Groffdale Conference or Wenger Mennonite settlement in the Malone area, in Franklin County, was started by families from the original Yates-Ontario counties settlement (which itself started in 1974). GAMEO reports that by 2011 there were thirteen families in the community but no ordained ministers or church house.

31. The picture was filed in the Heritage Historical Library, in Aylmer Ontario. Author and librarian D. Luthy had noted on the page, "This is not an Amish boy, but Old Order Stauffer Mennonite. . . . There were only 2 Stauffer church families living in New York [at] the time this picture was taken."

32. See chapter 1.

33. See chapter 6.

34. Cory Anderson's 2012 book, *The Amish-Mennonites of North America: A Portrait of Our People*, provides a good introduction to the various conservative plain-but-not-Old Order Anabaptist groups (including the Beachy Amish churches and Amish-Mennonites). Anderson includes five congregations in New York State.

9. Challenging the Non-Amish Neighbors

1. All quotations are from M. Ellen, "DePeyster Townsfolk See Amish as Reason for Population Surge."

2. "Gary's 2005 Cross Country Bicycle Adventure: Maine to North Dakota," http://www.rollingroads.com/gary/newyork.shtml.

3. S. Bender, *Plain and Simple*.

4. R. Buck, "Bloodless Theatre: Images of the Old Order Amish in Tourism Literature," 10.

5. P. Yoder, "The Amish View of the State," 30.

6. For a good overview of the Amish and the law, see *The Amish and the State*, edited by D. B. Kraybill.

7. Poland, NY, *Diary*, October 2005. This community is now extinct.

8. The archives of the *New York Times* is a treasure trove of articles related to conflicts between the Amish world and the dominant society.

9. L. W. Foderero, "No Wiggle Room in This Window War."

10. Ibid.

11. *Employment Division, Department of Human Resources of Oregon v. Smith* had itself overturned the long-standing principle that government must demonstrate a "compelling state interest" in order to restrict religious practice. See "Employment Division v. Smith," Legal Information Institute, Cornell University Law School, https://www.law. cornell.edu/supremecourt/text/494/872. See also Peter Steinfels, "Clinton Signs Law Protecting Religious Practices," *New York Times*, November 17, 1993, http://www.nytimes. com/1993/11/17/us/clinton-signs-law-protecting-religious-practices.html.

12. "U.S. Code § 2000bb-1—Free Exercise of Religion Protected," Legal Information Institute, Cornell University Law School, https://www.law.cornell.edu/uscode/text/42/ 2000bb%E2%80%931.

13. Kraybill, ed., *The Amish and the State*, 17: "Anchored on opposing values and differing social structures, these duels are essentially face-offs between the Goliath of modernity and shepherds from traditional pastures. These conflicts of conviction, ostensibly religious in nature, mark a collision of cultures—an encounter between the forces of modernity and the sentiments of tradition."

14. J. Bone, "Amish Fight to Keep Child Labour." Bone writes of an Amish man who complained "that he was fined about $12,000 because his 13-year-old daughter was working at the cash register in his shop."

15. As quoted in the *Washington Times*, "Child-Labor Laws Clash with Amish," December 5, 1998.

16. Pitts cosponsored this legislation with the late Senator Arlen Specter.

17. J.R. Pitts, Testimony before the House Committee on Education and the Workforce, Subcommittee on Workforce Protections, October 8, 2003. H.R. 1943, To amend the Fair Labor Standards Act of 1938 to permit certain youth to perform certain work with wood products, and for other purposes, http://www.house.gov/pitts/press/speeches/031008s-amishhearing. htm.

18. As quoted by S. Greenhouse in "Foes of Idle Hands, Amish Seek an Exemption from a Child Labor Law."

19. H.B. Lapp, "Labor Department vs. Amish Ways."

20. B.E. Anderson, "The U.S. Department of Labor Wants to Protect All Children."

21. As quoted by D. Usborne, "Amish Fight for the Right to Put Their Children to Work."

22. As quoted by S. Greenhouse, "Foes of Idle Hands."

23. S.F. Peters, *The Yoder Case: Religious Freedom, Education, and Parental Rights*, 175. Peters is quoting from Burger's majority opinion in *United States v. Lee*, a 1982 decision in which Old Order Amishman Edwin Lee was ordered to pay Social Security taxes for non-Amish employees even though, he claimed, paying the taxes violated his First Amendment rights. Peters cites a number of other cases to argue that in recent years the Supreme Court justices have "chipped away at the interpretive framework they had used to shield the religious liberty of the New Glarus Amish [in *Wisconsin v. Yoder et al.*]" (175).

24. See K. Johnson-Weiner, ""Old Order Amish Education: The Yoder Decision in the 21st Century." Rights of "open future," proposed first by J. Feinberg in a 1980 article, "A Child's Right to an Open Future," are defined by D. Archard as "the rights given to the child in the person of the adult she will become." (See Archard, "Children's Rights.") In reference to the decision in *Wisconsin v. Yoder*, for example, Feinberg argued that "the case against the exemption for the Amish must rest entirely on the rights of Amish *children*, which the state as *parens patriae* is sworn to protect. An education that renders a child fit for only one way of life forecloses irrevocably his other options. . . . Critical life-decisions will have been made irreversibly for a person well before he reaches the age of *full* discretion when he should be expected, in a free society, to make them himself" (as cited by D. Davis, "The Child's Right to an Open Future: Yoder and Beyond," 95).

25. See D. Gan-wing Cheng's 2010 article, "Wisconsin v. Yoder: Respecting Children's Rights and Why Yoder Would Soon Be Overturned," http://papers.ssrn.com/sol3/papers.cfm?abstract_id=1636503.

26. In her article, "The Child's Right to an Open Future: Yoder and Beyond," Davis points out that an education that exposes Amish children to a wide variety of ideas might make it impossible for them to remain Amish. As she notes, "Even if [the Amish child] envies the peace, warmth, and security that a life of tradition offers, she may find it impossible to turn her back on 'the world,' and return to her lost innocence" (96).

27. As noted in chapter 4, before the Yoder case the overwhelming majority of Amish school children attended public schools (and many now still do); now, in each new settlement, the community establishes schools that prepare children to live Amish lives according to the Ordnung of the community. Today the diversity of these communities is reflected in very different ways communities build their schools, educate their children, earn their livelihood, and define their separation from the world. For in-depth studies of Old Order education, see Dewalt, *Amish Education in the United States and Canada*, and Johnson-Weiner, *Train Up a Child*.

28. Hostetler, *Amish Society*, 256.

29. The National Committee for Amish Religious Freedom has since provided legal help and advice to the Amish in a number of different cases, involving zoning, driver's license photos, and the slow-moving-vehicle emblem. According to W. Lindholm, "The National Committee for Amish Religious Freedom," in D. Kraybill, *The Amish and the State*: "In protecting the Amish from the infringement of the state, the committee has fortified the precious tradition of religious liberty in the United States and in so doing has helped to preserve the freedom for all religious minorities to practice their religious faith" (23).

30. See chapter 3, especially endnote 43; see also chapter 4, especially endnote 40. In Wisconsin, the National Committee for Amish Religious Freedom worked with the Amish community in Eau Claire County, Wisconsin, in their battle against building codes, a conflict similar to that waged in Morristown. In an editorial submitted to a local newspaper, National Committee representative David P. Mortimer characterized the case as a modern David vs. Goliath battle, writing, "It's clear the UDC [Uniform Dwelling Code] is harming Amish communities, and many wonder how a law with so many flaws could ever have been enacted in the first place. The answer: pressure from politically connected special interests like the Wisconsin Builders Association. With 6,000 members, five lobbyists, social networking tools, and a million dollar political action committee (PAC) and foundation, the Builders Association powerfully represents its interests to the legislature. The Amish, by contrast, have no lobbyists, no PAC, do not vote, and their religion actually prohibits them from running for public office or bringing a case to court. Since they have no electricity or email, the extent of their social networking is a handwritten letter to a legislator." Yet the Amish prevailed. In August, 2015, the Wisconsin legislature passed a budget that included a provision allowing the Amish to sign a waiver that would exempt them from the parts of the Uniform Dwelling Code that they feel violate their religious beliefs. According to Mortimer, "The threat of fines, the threat of court-ordered eviction from their homes, the risk of arrest, all of that goes away because of this form," adding his hope that waiver would serve as a model for other states. See R. Kremer, "New Waiver Exempts Wisconsin Amish from Some Building Code Requirements," *Wisconsin Public Radio*, http://www.wpr.org/new-waiver-exempts-wisconsin-amish-some-building-code-requirements.

31. J. Landing, "The Old Order Amish: Problem Solving through Migration," 46.

32. See chapter 1 for a discussion of *The Martyrs' Mirror*.

33. Quoted by the Mennonite minister and author, J.L. Ruth, in *Forgiveness*, 43. Ruth called Fleming's "the most eloquent and representative of the positive reactions," 43. See http://www.pbs.org/newshour/bb/social_issues-july-dec06-forgiveness_10-06/.

34. See Kraybill, Nolt, and Weaver-Zercher, *Amish Grace*.

35. In many Amish families, the silent prayer offered up before meals is the Lord's Prayer. It also features in daily devotions and in the church service.

36. S. Mende, "Amish Father: Compassion." Residents of the North Country, Amish and non-Amish alike, worked together to search for the two girls, a task made more difficult because there were no photographs of them, although the family was persuaded to work with a sketch artist to draw an image of the older child. Ultimately the girls were released by their captors, and they made their way to the home of the Jeffrey and Pamela Stinson, who drove them home.

37. K. Semple, "Abduction Case Tests Limits of Amish Ties to Modern World," *New York Times*, August 21, 2014, http://www.nytimes.com/2014/08/22/nyregion/after-abductions-new-york-amish-community-gets-attention-it-tries-to-avoid.html.

38. As Hostetler put it, "A sectarian movement must establish an ideology different from that of the parent group in order to break off relations with it. Emergent beliefs tend to be selected on the basis of their difference from the parental group." *Amish Society*, 48.

39. *Mennonite Confession of Faith*, 22, 24.

40. Ibid., 23.

41. J. D. Roth, *Letters of the Amish Division: A Sourcebook*, 75.

42. 1 Corinthians 10:21; James 4:4. All quotes are from Roth, *Letters*, 39.

43. The Amish editors of *1001 Questions and Answers on the Christian Life* noted simply that "the people of God should be entirely separate from the world" (121).

44. J. Craig Haas, *Readings from Mennonite Writings, New and Old*, 23.

45. *1001 Questions and Answers on the Christian Life*, 34.

46. See Kraybill, *The Riddle of Amish Culture*, especially chapter 11.

47. See W. Kephart, *Extraordinary Groups: An Examination of Unconventional Lifestyles* (New York: St. Martin's Press, 1987).

48. According to the website Amish Science Fiction, which is posted by Adherents.com at http://www.adherents.com/lit/sf_amish.html: "It may surprise many to learn that among popular science fiction novels, one of the books with the most extensive references to the Amish is Asimov's Foundation's Edge. They are called 'Hamish' in the novel, but are clearly based on the Amish. They are an agricultural society that emerges from the ruins of the galactic capitol world. There are many Hamish characters in the novel, and the group is very important in the storyline."

49. J. A. Hostetler, *Amish Society*, 397.

50. See Valerie Weaver-Zercher, *Thrill of the Chaste*.

51. Television portrayals of the Amish and Amish life in such shows as *Breaking Amish* and *Amish Mafia* (to name just two), are scripted and generally inaccurate glimpses into Amish society. In a 2013 essay for the *Huffington Post*, entitled "Fake Amish and the Real Ones," for example, the leading authority on Amish life, Donald B. Kraybill asserted that "the Amish Mafia of reality TV fame is a fabrication of the producers. Some of the actors were raised in the Amish community but never joined it. Their knowledge of Amish practices enables them to help stage what appear to be authentic scenarios." In anticipation of an Los Angeles version of *Breaking Amish*, he lamented, "If the LA version is anything like the previous *Breaking Amish* or Discovery Channel's *Amish Mafia*, not only will the "reality" show include heavy doses of fiction, it will also fabricate more myths about Amish life that deserve a good debunking."

52. Daniel Laikind, "Amish Diaries: Why Do You Care about the Amish?" See also Kraybill, Johnson-Weiner, and Nolt, *The Amish*, chapter 21, for a more in-depth look at such "virtual tourism."

10. The Future of New York's Amish

1. "Amish Population Grows, Thanks to Affordable Rural Farmland," July 17, 2011, http://www.syracuse.com/news/index.ssf/2011/07/amish_population_in_new_york_g.html. More recent statistics published on the Amish Studies website from the

Young Center for Anabaptist and Pietist Studies at Elizabethtown College, Elizabethtown, Pennsylvania, show New York's Amish population climbing: "Amish Population by State (2014)," Young Center for Anabaptist and Pietist Studies, Elizabethtown College, http://www2.etown.edu/amishstudies/Population_by_State_2014.asp.

2. "Amish Population Change 2010–2015, Summary," Young Center for Anabaptist and Pietist Studies, Elizabethtown College, https://groups.etown.edu/amishstudies/files/2015/08/Population_Change_2010-2015.pdf.

3. Edsel Burdge Jr. (Young Center for Anabaptist and Pietist Studies), Personal communication, March 16, 2016.

4. Question posted on Trip Advisor, November, 2015, https://www.tripadvisor.com/ShowTopic-g47428-i34492-k8990825-Amish_trail-Cattaraugus_New_York.html.

5. "Buffalo-area Amish youth Ticketed for Having Beer in Horse-drawn Buggy." Associated Press, May 12, 2009, http://www.syracuse.com/news/index.ssf/2009/05/buffaloarea_amish_youth_ticket.html. See also "Police Ticket Amish Teen for Having Beer in His Horse-drawn Buggy," May 13, 2009, http://www.topix.com/forum/city/leon-ny/TC7R56LG3R7979B7P.

6. "Norfolk Man Accused of Endangering Welfare of Child, Unlawful Use of Vehicle," *Watertown Daily Times*, February 12, 2016, https://www.watertowndailytimes.com/news05/norfolk-man-accused-of-endangering-welfare-of-child-unlawful-use-of-vehicle-20160212.

7. Lowville, NY, *Die Botschaft*, February 5, 2016.

8. Fort Plain, NY, East, *Die Botschaft*, February 19, 2016, 41.

9. Brian Amaral, "NY to Amish: Power Up," *Watertown Daily Times*, June 26, 2011, http://www.watertowndailytimes.com/article/20110626/NEWS03/306269928.

10. Senator Patty Ritchie represents New York's Forty-Eighth District, which spreads from Massena to the outskirts of Syracuse and includes a number of different Amish settlements. According to a representative of her office, the senator is close to many Amish families and so hears about difficulties they may be having. As the representative put it, "Since no one else seemed interested (after all, the Amish don't vote), she decided she would be their advocate."

11. Holland Patent, NY, *Diary*, January 2016.

12. See "Local Laws and Agricultural Districts: Guidance for Local Governments and Farmers," http://www.agriculture.ny.gov/AP/agservices/new305/guidance.pdf.

13. As quoted in "Citing Religious Beliefs, Amish Balk at Pa. Outhouse Regulations," First Amendment Center, Thursday, May 29, 2008, http://www.firstamendmentcenter.org/citing-religious-beliefs-amish-balk-at-pa-outhouse-regulations.

14. Interview, February 10, 2016.

15. One good example of this approach is the involvement of Senator Ritchie's office in bringing St. Lawrence County legislators together with Swartzentruber Amish bishops in St. Lawrence County to discuss proposed legislation mandating use of the orange SMV triangle, use of which is forbidden by Swartzentruber Ordnungs. See "Amish Bishops Meet With County Officials About Safety Triangles On Buggies," WWNY-TV7, http://www.wwnytv.com/news/local/Amish-Bishops-Meet-With-County-Officials-About-Safety-Triangles-On-Buggies-304610761.html.

16. Betsy Hodge, personal correspondence, March 31, 2016.

17. For more on SPARX, see "United Helpers Opening For-Profit Business in Canton," *North Country Now* (2012), http://northcountrynow.com/news/united-helpers-opening-profit-business-canton-060582.

18. Stephen Knight, personal correspondence, March 29, 2016.

19. Interview, February 1, 2016.

20. Interview, February 4, 2016.

21. Conewango Valley, NY, *Diary*, February 2016.

22. Quoted by Brian Amaral, "NY to Amish: Power Up," *Watertown Daily Times*, June 26, 2011, http://www.watertowndailytimes.com/article/20110626/NEWS03/306269928.

Bibliography

Anderson, B. E. 1998. "The U.S. Department of Labor Wants to Protect All Children." *Washington Times*, December 5.

Anderson, C. 2012. *The Amish Mennonites of North America: A Portrait of Our People.* Medina, NY: Ridgeway.

——. 2014. "Horse and Buggy Crash Study II: Overstretching the Slow-Moving Vehicle Emblem's Abilities: Lessons from the Swartzentruber Amish." *Journal of Amish and Plain Anabaptist Studies* 2 (1): 100–115.

Anonymous. 1982. *History of the Amish Colony in Conewango Valley, New York.* Pamphlet in the archives of the Heritage Historical Library, Aylmer, Ontario.

Archard, D. W. 2016. "Children's Rights," *The Stanford Encyclopedia of Philosophy,* Summer 2016 edition, edited by Edward N. Zalta, http://plato.stanford.edu/archives/sum2016/entries/rights-children/.

Argetsinger, A. 1997. "Amish Market Cultivates an Eager Clientele." *Washington Post,* March 16.

Barrionuevo, A. 2005. "Amish May Be Good Neighbors, but Not Their Horses." *New York Times,* October 18, 2005. http://www.nytimes.com/2005/10/18/us/amish-may-be-good-neighbors-but-not-their-horses.html?_r=0.

Bender, A. Z. n.d. *A History of the Mennonites in Croghan and Lowville (Lewis County) New York: Stories and Sketches as Told by Others; Genealogies of Deacons, Ministers, and Bishops from Beginning of Church until Present Day; Introducing the Mennonites.* Booklet in archives of the Owen D. Young Library, St. Lawrence University, Canton, NY.

——. 1953. "From Alsace to Adirondacks." *Mennonite Community* (October): 18–19.

Bender, H. S. 1938. "Conrad Grebel, the Founder of Swiss Anabaptism." *Church History* 7 (2): 157–178.

——. 1944. "The Anabaptist Vision." *Church History* 13 (1): 3–24.

——. 1953. "Amish Mennonites." *Global Anabaptist Mennonite Encyclopedia Online.* http://www.gameo.org/encyclopedia/contents/A4594ME.html.

Bender, S. 1989. *Plain and Simple: A Woman's Journey to the Amish.* New York: Harper-Collins.

Blank, B. S. 2001. *The Amazing Story of the Ausbund.* Sugar Creek, OH: Carlisle Printing.

Bobseine, K. R. 2006. *Working with Amish Communities in New York State: Tips for Health Professionals.* Albany, NY: SUNY School of Public Health.

Bone, J. 2000. "Amish Fight to Keep Child Labour: U.S. Law Prevents Apprentice-ships." *Ottawa Citizen*, December 5.

Braght, Thieleman J. van, comp. *The Bloody Theater or Martyrs Mirror of the Defenseless Christians, Who Baptized Only upon Confession of Faith, and Who Suffered and Died for the Testimony of Jesus, Their Savior, From the Time of Christ to the Year A.D. 1660.* 2nd English ed., 24th printing. Scottdale, PA: Herald Press, 2002.

Bronner, S. J., and J. R. Brown. 2017. *Pennsylvania German Encyclopedia*. Baltimore, MD: Johns Hopkins University Press.

Buck, R. C. 1978. "Boundary Maintenance Revisited: Tourist Experience in an Old Order Amish Community." *Rural Sociology* 43 (2): 221–234.

———. 1979. "Bloodless Theatre: Images of the Old Order Amish in Tourism Literature." *Pennsylvania Mennonite Heritage* 2 (3): 2–11.

Burns, E. 1996. "Cultural Identity and Ethnic Boundary Maintenance: The Old Order Amish." MA thesis, Kent State University.

Byler, D. T. 2004. *The Geography of Difference: Constructing Identity in the Holmes County, Ohio, Amish Community.* http://www.mcusa-archives.org/jhorsch/jhorsch2004/byler_essay.htm.

Cates, J. 2014. *Serving the Amish. A Cultural Guide for Professionals.* Baltimore, MD: Johns Hopkins University Press.

Cheng, D. G. 2010. "*Wisconsin v. Yoder*: Respecting Children's Rights and Why Yoder Would Soon Be Overturned." July 7, 2010. http://papers.ssrn.com/sol3/papers.cfm?abstract_id=1636503.

Child, H., ed. 1872. *Gazetteer and Business Directory of Lewis County, NY for 1872–73.* http://www.rootsweb.com/~nylewis/1872-3busdirect/1872busindex.html.

Cleveland Clinic. 2015. *Treating the Amish and Addressing their Health Care Concerns: A Practical Guide for Health Care Providers.* http://www.health-share.org/health-info/docs/1700/1783.asp?index=3971.

Conners, M. A. 1961. "The Hook and Eye People of Northern New York." *New York Folklore Quarterly* 17: 63–69.

Corcoran, J. 2015. "Amish vs. Auburn over Horse Manure." WKU Public Radio, June 16, 2015. http://wkyufm.org/post/amish-vs-auburn-over-horse-manure#stream/0.

Cronk, S. 1981. "Gelassenheit: The Rites of the Redemptive Process in Old Order Amish and Old Order Mennonite Communities." *Mennonite Quarterly Review* 55: 5–44.

Crowley, W. K. 1978. "Old Order Amish Settlement: Diffusion and Growth." *Annals of the Association of American Geographers* 68 (2): 249–264.

Davis, Dena S. 1997. "The Child's Right to an Open Future: Yoder and Beyond." *26 Capital University Law Review* 93: 93–105. http://engagedscholarship.csuohio.edu/cgi/viewcontent.cgi?article=1397&context=fac_articles.

Dean, D. 1974. "North Amish Community Expands to Five Families." *Watertown Daily Times,* May 4.

Dewalt, M. W. 2006. *Amish Education in the United States and Canada.* Lanham, MD: Rowan and Littlefield Education.

Donnermeyer, J., and E. Cooksey. 1984. "The Demographic Foundations of Amish Society." Paper Presented at the Annual Meeting of the Rural Sociological Society, Sacramento, California, August 11–15.

Donnermeyer, J., and D. Luthy. 2013. "Amish Settlements across America." *Journal of Amish and Plain Anabaptist Studies* 1 (2): 107–129.

Ellen, M. 1980. "DePeyster Townsfolk See Amish as Reason for Population Surge." *Watertown Daily Times,* July 25.

———. 2007. "Defender Wants Charges against Amish Dropped. Building Codes: Religious Freedom Violation Is Alleged in Papers Filed in Morristown Court." *Watertown Daily Times,* December 8.

———. 2012. "Horse Diaper Law Rejected." *Watertown Daily Times,* February 10.

Enninger, W. 1987. "On the Organization of Sign-Processes in an Old Order Amish (OOA) Parochial School." *Research on Language and Social Interaction* 21: 143–170.

Ericksen, E. P., J. A. Ericksen, and J. A. Hostetler. 1980. "The Cultivation of the Soil as a Moral Directive: Population Growth, Family Ties, and the Maintenance of Community among the Old Order Amish." *Rural Sociology* 45: 49–68.

Esh, J. F. 1965. *The Amish Moving to Maryland, 1940.* Gordonville, PA: A. S. Kinsinger.

Farmanfarmaian, R. 1991. "Autumn in Amish Country." *New Choice* (September): 24–27.

Feinberg, J. 1980. "A Child's Right to an Open Future." In *Whose Child? Parental Rights, Parental Authority and State Power,* edited by W. Aiken and H. LaFollette, 124–153. Totowa, NJ: Littlefield, Adams.

Fisher, W. L. 1996. *The Amish in Court.* New York: Vantage Press.

Foderaro, L. W. 2003. "No Wiggle Room in This Window War: Amish in Upstate New York Are Resisting a Change in the Building Code." *New York Times,* November 15. http://query.nytimes.com/gst/fullpage.html?res=9E03E0DB1238F936A25752C1 A9659C8B63&sec=&spon=&pagewanted=all.

Foster, T. W. 1984. "Separation and Survival in Amish Society." *Sociological Focus* 17 (1): 1–15.

Friedmann, R. 1953. "Ernsthafte Christenpflicht." *Global Anabaptist Mennonite Encyclopedia Online.* http://www.gameo.org/encyclopedia/contents/E7565ME.html.

Galet, S. 1990. "Stepping Back: Amish Community in New York State Welcomes Visitors in a Noncommercial Way, but They Expect Visitors to Respect Such Wishes as Not Taking Photos of Them." *Toronto Globe and Mail,* July 7.

Gatehouse Ohio Group. 2009. "Amish Family Dead after an Apparent Murder-Suicide near Millersburg." CantonRep.com. February 25. http://www.can tonrep.com/news/x349783424/Amish-family-dead-after-apparent-murder-suicide-near-Millersburg.

Gingerich, J. N. 1986. "Ordinance or Ordering: Ordnung and Amish Ministers Meetings, 1862–1878." *Mennonite Quarterly Review* 60: 180–199.

Gingerich, M. 1959. "Reformed Amish Christian Church (Berne, Indiana, USA)." *Global Anabaptist Mennonite Encyclopedia Online.* http://www.gameo.org/encyclopedia/ contents/reformed_amish_christian_church_berne_indiana_usa.

Goth, G. 1988. "Old Order Finds New Life Upstate." *Poughkeepsie Journal,* April 10.

Graber, O. A. 1988. "Gleanings from Yesterday." *Die Botschaft,* April 6.

Gratz, D. L. 1953. *Bernese Anabaptists and Their American Descendants: Being Mainly the History of Those Who Migrated to America in the Beginning of the Nineteenth Century.* Scottsdale, PA: Herald Press.

———. 1993. "L'emigration anabaptiste de l'ancienne republique de Berne." In *L'emigration: Une réponse universelle à une situation de crise. Un colloque international au coeur d'une dynamique étonnante.* Bulletin no. 3. Sembrancher, Switzerland: Centre Regional d'Études des Populations Alpines.

Greenhouse, S. 2003. "Foes of Idle Hands, Amish Seek an Exemption from a Child Labor Law." *New York Times*, October 18.

Haas, J.C. 1992. *Readings from Mennonite Writings, New and Old*. Intercourse, PA: Good Books.

Hall, E.T. 1976. *Beyond Culture*. New York: Anchor Books.

Halloran, A. 2013. "Milk Cooperative Joins with Amish to Open New Markets," *Lancaster Farming*, June 15, 2013, http://www.lancasterfarming.com/Milk-Cooperative-Joins-With-Amish-to-Open-New-Markets.

Harris, G. 2005. "5 Cases of Polio in Amish Group Raise New Fears." *New York Times*, November 8.

Hewner, S.J. 1998. "Fertility, Migration, and Mortality in an Old Order Amish Community." *American Journal of Human Biology* 10: 619–628.

Hostetler, B. 1992. "The Formation of the Old Orders." *Mennonite Quarterly Review* 66 (January): 5–25.

Hostetler, J.A. 1949. "Amish Problems at the Diener-Versammlungen." *Mennonite Life* 4 (October): 34–39.

———. 1993. *Amish Society*. 4th ed. Baltimore, MD: Johns Hopkins University Press.

Hough, F.B. 1860. *A History of Lewis County, in the State of New York, from the Beginnings of Its Settlement to the Present Time*. Albany, NY: Munsell and Rowland.

Houpert, J. 1985. *Les Lorrains en Amérique du Nord*. Sherbrooke, Quebec: Éditions Naaman.

Huntington, G.E. 1994. "Persistence and Change in Amish Education." In *The Amish Struggle with Modernity*, edited by D.B. Kraybill and M.A. Olshan, 77–96. Hanover, NH: University Press of New England.

Hurst, C.E., and D.L. McConnell. 2010. *An Amish Paradox. Diversity and Change in the World's Largest Amish Community*. Baltimore, MD: Johns Hopkins University Press.

Hutterian Brethren. 1986. *The Chronicle of the Hutterian Brethren*. Walden, NY: Plough.

Johnson-Weiner, K.M. 1989. "Keeping Dutch: Linguistic Heterogeneity and the Maintenance of Pennsylvania German in Two Old Order Amish Communities." In *Studies on the Verbal Behavior of the Pennsylvania Germans*, edited by W. Enninger, J. Raith, and K.-H. Wandt, 95–101. Stuttgart: Franz Steiner Verlag Wiesbaden.

———. 1992. "Group Identity and Language Maintenance: The Survival of Pennsylvania German in Old Order Communities." In *Diachronic Studies on the Languages of the Anabaptists*, edited by K. Burridge and W. Enninger, 26–42. Bochum, Germany: Universitätsverlag Dr. N. Brockmeyer.

———. 1998. "Community Identity and Language Change in North American Anabaptist Communities." *Journal of Sociolinguistics* 2 (3): 375–394.

———. 2001. "The Role of Women in Old Order Amish, Beachy Amish, and Fellowship Churches." *Mennonite Quarterly Review* 75 (April): 231–256.

———. 2006. *Train Up a Child: Old Order Amish and Mennonite Schools*. Baltimore, MD: Johns Hopkins University Press.

———. 2008. "The Weaverland Mennonite Schools and the Negotiation of an Old Order Identity." *Mennonite Quarterly Review* 82 (April): 249–279.

———. 2014. "Technological Diversity and Cultural Change among Contemporary Amish Groups." *Mennonite Quarterly Review* 88 (January): 5–22.

——— 2015. "Old Order Amish Education: The Yoder Decision in the 21st Century." *Journal of Amish and Plain Anabaptist Studies* 3 (spring 2015): 25–44.

Kaiser, G.H. 1986. *Dr. Frau: A Woman Doctor among the Amish*. Intercourse, PA: Good Books.

Keim, A. N. 1975. *Compulsory Education and the Amish: The Right Not to Be Modern.* Boston: Beacon Press.

Kephart, W. 1987. *Extraordinary Groups: An Examination of Unconventional Lifestyles.* New York: St. Martin's Press.

Kinney, J. 1996. *The Amish of Holmes County.* Orrville, OH: Spectrum.

Kinsinger, A. S. 1997. *A Little History of Our Parochial Schools and Steering Committee from 1956–1994.* Compiled by S. A. Kinsinger. Gordonville, PA: Gordonville Print Shop.

Kinsinger, S. A. 1988. *Family and History of Lydia Beachy's Descendants 1889–1989.* Gordonville, PA: Gordonville Print Shop.

Klaassen, W. 1977. "The Anabaptist Understanding of the Separation of the Church." *Church History* 46 (4): 421–436.

Klimuska, E. 2001. "N.Y. Farmer Seeks Amish 'Home Run.'" *Lancaster* (PA) *New Era,* February 24.

Kollmorgen, W. M. 1942. *Culture of a Contemporary Rural Community: The Old Order Amish of Lancaster County, Pennsylvania.* Washington, DC: U.S. Department of Agriculture.

——. 1943. "The Agricultural Stability of the Old Order Amish and the Old Order Mennonites of Lancaster County, Pennsylvania." *American Journal of Sociology* 49: 233–241.

Kraybill, D. B., ed. 1993. *The Amish and the State.* Baltimore, MD: Johns Hopkins University Press.

——. 1994. "Plotting Social Change across Four Affiliations." In *The Amish Struggle with Modernity,* edited by D. B. Kraybill and M. A. Olshan, 52–74. Hanover, NH: University Press of New England.

——. 1998. "Plain Reservations: Amish and Mennonite Views of Media and Computers." *Journal of Mass Media Ethics* 3 (2): 99–110.

——. 2001. *The Riddle of Amish Culture.* Rev. ed. Baltimore, MD: Johns Hopkins University Press.

——. 2013. "Fake Amish and the Real Ones." *Huffington Post Blog.* http://www.huffingtonpost.com/donald-kraybill/fake-amish-and-the-real-o_b_3617736.html.

Kraybill, D. B., and C. F. Bowman. 2001. *On the Backroad to Heaven: Old Order Hutterites, Mennonites, Amish, and Brethren.* Baltimore, MD: Johns Hopkins University Press.

Kraybill, D. B., K. M. Johnson-Weiner, and S. M. Nolt. 2013. *The Amish.* Baltimore, MD: Johns Hopkins University Press.

Kraybill, D. B., S. M. Nolt, and D. L. Weaver-Zercher. 2007. *Amish Grace: How Forgiveness Transcended Tragedy.* San Francisco: John Wiley and Sons.

Kraybill, D. B., and M. A. Olshan. 1994. *The Amish Struggle with Modernity.* Hanover, NH: University Press of New England.

Kremer, R. 2015. "New Waiver Exempts Wisconsin Amish from Some Building Code Requirements." Wisconsin Public Radio, August 27, http://www.wpr.org/new-waiver-exempts-wisconsin-amish-some-building-code-requirements.

Laikind, D. 2012. "Amish Diaries: Why Do You Care about the Amish?" *Faster Times,* May 15, www.thefastertimes.com/tv/2012/05/15/the-amish-diaries-why-do-you-care-about-the-amish/.

Lamme, A. J. III. 1983. "Amish Farmers 'Redeveloping' Marginal Land in Rural U.S." *Lancaster* (PA) *Intelligencer Journal,* September 21.

Lamme, A. J. III, and D. B. McDonald. 1984. "Recent Amish Settlement in the North Country." *Material Culture* 16 (2): 77–91.

——. 1993. "The 'North Country' Amish Homeland." *Journal of Cultural Geography* 13 (2): 107–118.

Landing, J. 1975. "The Old Order Amish: Problem Solving through Migration." *Bulletin of the Illinois Geographical Society* 17 (2): 36–48.

Lapp, C. 1991. *Pennsylvania School History 1690–1990*. Gordonville, PA: Christ S. Lapp.

Lapp, H. B. 1997. "Labor Department vs. Amish Ways." *Wall Street Journal*, April 10.

Lewis County Comprehensive Economic Development Strategy Committee and the Lewis County Planning Department. 2006. "Lewis County Comprehensive Economic Development Strategy." Adopted by Lewis County Comprehensive Economic Development Strategy Committee, August 22, 2006, and endorsed by Lewis County Board of Legislators, September 5, 2006. http://www.lewiscountyny.org/content/Departments/View/2:field=documents;/content/Documents/File/263.pdf.

Lindholm, W. C. 1993. "The National Committee for Amish Religious Freedom." In *The Amish and the State*, edited by D. B. Kraybill, 108–123. Baltimore, MD: Johns Hopkins University Press.

Louden, M. 1991. "The Image of the Old Order Amish: General and Sociolinguistic Stereotypes." *National Journal of Sociology* 5 (2): 111–142.

——. 2016. *Pennsylvania Dutch: The Story of an American Language*. Baltimore, MD: Johns Hopkins University Press.

Lowry, S., and A. G. Noble. 2000. "The Changing Occupational Structure of the Amish of the Holmes County, Ohio, Settlement." *Great Lakes Geographer* 7 (1): 26–37.

Luthy, D. 1985. *Amish Settlements across America*. Aylmer, ON: Pathway.

——. 1986. *The Amish in America: Settlements That Failed, 1840–1960*. Aylmer, ON: Pathway.

——. 1997; rev. 2003. *Why Some Amish Communities Fail: Extinct Settlements, 1961–2003*. Aylmer, ON: Pathway.

——. 1998. "The Origin and Growth of the Swartzentruber Amish." *Family Life* (August/September): 19–22.

——. 2003. "Amish Settlements across America: 2003." *Family Life* (October): 17–23.

Lyndaker, R. J. 2004. *Beginnings: The History and Genealogy of an Amish-Mennonite Family from New York*. Geneva, NY: Roland John Lyndaker.

Lyons, R. D. 1981. "Conservative Sects Find Home in New York." *New York Times*, October 3. Reprinted as "New York a Magnet for Religious Groups" in *Terre Haute* (IN) *Tribune-Star*, October 4, 1981.

Martin, J. H. 2012. Groffdale Old Order Mennonite Conference. *Global Anabaptist Mennonite Encyclopedia Online*. http://gameo.org/index.php?title=Groffdale_Old_Order_Mennonite_Conference&oldid=123674.

Mathiot, C., and R. Boigeol. 1969. *Recherches historiques sur les Anabaptistes de l'ancienne principauté de Montbeliard, d'Alsace et du Territoire de Belfort*. Flavon, Belgium: Le Phare.

McKinley, J. 2014. "Casino Plan Frays Ties Between Amish and Neighbors." *New York Times*, October 4, 2014. http://www.nytimes.com/2014/10/06/nyregion/upstate-new-york-casino-plan-divides-amish-and-neighbors.html?_r=0.

Mende, S. 2014. "Amish Father: Compassion." *Watertown Daily Times*, August 18, A1, A9.

Mennonite Confession of Faith. 2nd printing. 1966. Crockett, KY: Rod and Staff Publishers.

Meyers, T. 1994. "Lunch Pails and Factories." In *The Amish Struggle with Modernity*, edited by D. B. Kraybill and M. A. Olshan, 164–181. Hanover, NH: University Press of New England.

Meyers, T. 1994. "The Old Order Amish: To Remain in the Faith or to Leave." *Mennonite Quarterly Review* 68 (July): 308–321.

Miller, J. V. 2002. *Both Sides of the Ocean: Amish-Mennonites from Switzerland to America.* Morgantown, PA: Masthof Press.

Morse, D. 2006. "Still Called by Faith to the Booth; As Pay Phones Vanish, Amish and Mennonites Build Their Own." *Washington Post,* September 3.

Mortimer, D. 2015. "Why Are We Evicting the Amish?" Submitted to various Wisconsin newspapers on March 11, 2015.

Mulder, J. T. 1980. "The Non-Conformists." *Empire Magazine*, supplement to *Syracuse Herald American*, June 20.

Nafziger, C. M. 1933. "A Brief Historical Sketch of the Amish Mennonite Church in Lewis County, New York." *Herold der Wahrheit:* 537–538.

Neff, C., and E. H. Correll. 1955. "Alsace (France)." *Global Anabaptist Mennonite Encyclopedia Online.* http://www.gameo.org/encyclopedia/contents/A4526.html.

Neff, C., and N. van der Zijpp. 1957. "Napoleon I, Emperor of France (1769–1821)." *Global Anabaptist Mennonite Encyclopedia Online.* http://www.gameo.org/ency clopedia/contents/N363.html.

Nittler, J., and G. Cotterill. 2014. "Lawyer Expects Amish-Mennonite Exodus if Casino Comes to Town of Tyre," http://fingerlakesdailynews.com/news/details. cfm?id=120910#.Vx1XC9Lmpjo.

Nolt, S. 2015. *A History of the Amish.* 3rd ed. Intercourse, PA: Good Books.

Nolt, S., and T. Meyers. 2007. *Plain Diversity: Amish Cultures and Identities.* Baltimore, MD: Johns Hopkins University Press.

Ochs, E., and B. B. Schieffelin. 2001. "Language Acquisition and Socialization: Three Developmental Stories and Their Implications." In *Linguistic Anthropology: A Reader,* edited by A. Duranti, 263–301. Malden, MA: Blackwell.

Office of Public Affairs, U.S. Treasury Department. 2003. "Treasury and Federal Financial Regulators Issue Final Patriot Act Regulations on Customer Identification." http://www.treas.gov/press/releases/js335.htm.

Ohio Old Order Amish Ministers. n.d. *Events That Took Place in the Old Order Amish Churches of Holmes and Wayne County, Ohio: From 1938 to 1958.* Trans. by Bishop P. Yoder, 1973. Heritage Historical Library, Aylmer, Ontario.

Olshan, M. 1979; rev. 1981. *The Old Order Amish in New York State.* Cornell Rural Sociology Bulletin Series, 94. Ithaca, NY: Cornell University.

——. 1990. "Affinities and Antipathies: The Old Order Amish in New York State." Paper presented at the American Anthropological Association Meetings, New Orleans, LA.

——. 1993. "The National Amish Steering Committee." In *The Amish and the State,* edited by D. B. Kraybill, 66–84. Baltimore: Johns Hopkins University Press.

——. 1994. "Amish Cottage Industries as Trojan Horse." In *The Amish Struggle with Modernity,* edited by D. B. Kraybill and M. A. Olshan, 133–146. Hanover, NH: University Press of New England.

1001 Questions and Answers on the Christian Life. 1992. Aylmer, ON: Pathway.

Pedley, M. 1990. "Land Company Mapping in North America: Fiefdom in the New Republic." *Imago Mundi* 42: 106–113.

Peters, S. F. 2003. *The Yoder Case: Religious Freedom, Education, and Parental Rights.* Lawrence: University Press of Kansas.

Rhodes, R. 2002. "No Longer Living Off the Land: Fewer Amish Are Farming, Bringing Change to Their Lives." *Mennonite Weekly Review* (October 21): 1, 7.

Robinson, J.H., ed. 1906. *Readings in European History.* Hanover Historical Texts Project. Boston: Ginn. http://history.hanover.edu/texts/luthad.html.

Robinson, L. 2014. "Amish Horse Manure Causing Stink in Village of Heuvelton." *Journal* (Ogdensburg, NY), August 14, 2014. http://www.ogd.com/article/20140814/OGD/140819374.

Roth, J.D., trans. and ed. 1993. *Letters of the Amish Division: A Sourcebook.* Goshen, IN: Mennonite Historical Society.

Rupp, E.E., and S. Nussbaum. 1987. "Evangelical Mennonite Church (United States)." *Global Anabaptist Mennonite Encyclopedia Online.* http://www.gameo.org/encyclopedia/contents/E936.html.

Ruth, J.L. 2007. *Forgiveness: A Legacy of the West Nickel Mines Amish School.* Scottdale, PA: Herald Press.

Schrock, F.J. 2001. *The Amish Christian Church: Its History and Legacy.* Monterey, TN: Fredrick J. Schrock.

Schwieder, E., and D. Schwieder. 1975. *A Peculiar People: Iowa's Old Order Amish.* Ames, IA: Iowa State University Press.

Scott, S. 1997. *Why Do They Dress That Way?* Rev. ed. Intercourse, PA: Good Books.

Scott, S. 1996. *An Introduction to Old Order and Conservative Mennonite Groups.* Intercourse, PA: Good Books.

Shepard, J. 1990. "Amish Resurrect a County." *Albany Times-Union,* July 29.

Shipler, D.K. 1972a. "A Family of Plain People Seeking Still Plainer Life." *New York Times,* November 17.

——. 1972b. "Onlookers Greet Amish Travelers." *New York Times,* November 18.

Shirk, E.M. 1939. "Report of Committee of Plain People Making Pleas for Leniency from Depressive School Laws." Ephrata, PA.

Skolnick, D. 1990. "Amish Complain of Rising Taxes." *Watertown Daily Times,* May 20.

Smyczynski, C.A. 2006. "Exploring Western New York's Amish Community." *Buffalo News,* October 19. http://explorewny.home.att.net/wnyamish.html.

Snyder, C.A., and L.A. Huebert Hecht. 1996. *Profiles of Anabaptist Women: Sixteenth-Century Reforming Pioneers.* Waterloo, ON: Wilfrid Laurier University Press.

Sorensen, A. 2013. "Alleged Amish Discrimination on Madison County Lakes." *YNN-Time Warner Cable News,* August 24. http://www.twcnews.com/archives/nys/central-ny/2013/08/24/alleged-amish-discrimination-on-madison-county-lakes-NY_686050.old.html.

Stevick, R.A. 2014. *Growing Up Amish: The Rumspringa Years.* 2nd ed. Baltimore, MD: Johns Hopkins University Press.

Stoll, E. n.d. "The Nature of the Church." Unpublished essay in author's possession.

Stoll, J., ed. 1967. *The Challenge of the Child: Selections from "The Blackboard Bulletin," 1957–1966.* Aylmer, ON: Pathway.

Stoltzfus, G.M. 1969. *Mennonites of the Ohio and Eastern Conference from the Colonial Period in Pennsylvania to 1968.* Scottdale, PA: Herald Press.

Stoltzfus, V. 1973. "Amish Agriculture: Adaptive Strategies for Economic Survival of Community Life." *Rural Sociology* 38: 196–206.

Tobin, D. 2007. "No Serenity in Summerhill: How Far Should Rules Be Bent to Accommodate Amish?" *Syracuse Post-Standard,* November 25.

——. 2008. "Subdued Victory for Religious Freedom." *Syracuse Post-Standard,* January 12. http://www.syracuse.com/poststandard/stories/index.ssf?/base/news-13/1200131765307610.xml&coll=1.

Umble, J. S. 1939. "The Old Order Amish, Their Hymns and Hymn Tunes." *Journal of American Folklore* 52 (203): 82–95.

——. 1948. "Memoirs of an Amish Bishop." *Mennonite Quarterly Review* 22: 94–115.

Usborne, D. 2003. "Amish Fight for the Right to Put Their Children to Work." *London Independent*, October 23.

Virkler, S. 2002. "Amish to Be Topic of Seminar: Cooperative Extension Hosts Expert on Group." *Watertown Daily Times*, October 19.

——. 2011. "Lowville Supervisor Retiring After 20 Years." *Watertown Daily Times*, Monday, February 11. http://www.watertowndailytimes.com/article/20110228/NEWS04/302289982.

Vogt, B. 1919. "A Pioneer Mennonite Settlement in Northern New York." *Ecclesiastical Review*. Reprinted in A. Yousey, *Strangers and Pilgrims: A History of the Lewis County Mennonites*, 399–409. Croghan, NY: Lewis County Conservative Mennonite Churches, 1987.

Von Dobeneck, M. 2001. "Neighbors to North Cast Lure for Amish: Otsego County, N.Y. Seeks to Battle Sprawl, Offers Cheap Farmland." *Harrisburg* (PA) *Patriot News*, February 21.

Wagler, D. 1963. Education: "A Grave Responsibility." Reprinted in *The Challenge of the Child, Selections from "The Blackboard Bulletin" 1957–1966*, edited by J. Stoll, 65–67. Aylmer, ON: Pathway, 1967.

Weaver, R. M. 1995. "An Account of a Church Division in Holmes Co. in 1922." *Heritage Review* 5: 4–5.

——. 2002. "Amish Ministers' Meetings of 1865 and 1917." *Heritage Review* 11: 9–13.

——. 2007. "Glimpses of the Amish Church in Holmes County, Ohio, 1917–1922, and Report of a Ministers' Meeting in 1922." *Heritage Review* 16: 9–13.

Weaver-Zercher, D. 2001. *The Amish in the American Imagination*. Baltimore, MD: Johns Hopkins University Press.

Weaver-Zercher, V. 2013. *Thrill of the Chaste: The Allure of Amish Romance Novels*. Baltimore, MD: Johns Hopkins University Press.

Wengerd, R. 2003. "The Move We Made." *Plain Interests*, November, 8.

Yoder, P. 1991. *Tradition and Transition: Amish Mennonites and Old Order Amish, 1800–1900*. Scottdale, PA: Herald Press.

——. 1993. "The Amish View of the State." In *The Amish and the State*, edited by D. B. Kraybill, 22–40. Baltimore, MD: Johns Hopkins University Press.

Yousey, A. 1987. *Strangers and Pilgrims: A History of the Lewis County Mennonites*. Croghan, NY: Lewis County Conservative Mennonite Churches.

Zimmerman Umble, D. 1996. *Holding the Line: The Telephone in Old Order Mennonite and Amish Life*. Baltimore, MD: Johns Hopkins University Press.

Zimmerman Umble, D., and D. Weaver-Zercher, eds. 2008. *The Amish and the Media*. Baltimore, MD: Johns Hopkins University Press.

Zook, N., and S. L. Yoder. 1988. "Berne, Indiana, Old Order Amish Settlement." *Global Anabaptist Mennonite Encyclopedia Online*. http://www.gameo.org/encyclopedia/contents/B4762.html.

Zuck, L. H. 1957. "Anabaptism: Abortive Counter-revolt within the Reformation." *Church History* 26 (3): 211–226.

Index